OXFORD DATA PROTECTION AND PRIVACY LAW

Series Editors

CHRISTOPHER KUNER

Affiliated Professor of Law, University of Copenhagen

GRAHAM GREENLEAF

Professor of Law and Information Systems, University of New South Wales

Data Protection Law and Emotion

OXFORD DATA PROTECTION AND PRIVACY LAW

The aim of this series is to publish important and original books on legal issues of data protection and privacy. This includes many different areas of law, including comparative law, EU law, human rights law, international law, privacy on the Internet, and others.

Prospective authors are welcome to submit proposals for the series, as outlined on the series website: https://global.oup.com/academic/content/series/o/oxford-data-protection-and-privacy-law-odppl/?cc=au&lang=en&

Data Protection Law and Emotion

DAMIAN CLIFFORD
ANU College of Law

OXFORD
UNIVERSITY PRESS

OXFORD
UNIVERSITY PRESS

Great Clarendon Street, Oxford, OX2 6DP,
United Kingdom

Oxford University Press is a department of the University of Oxford.
It furthers the University's objective of excellence in research, scholarship,
and education by publishing worldwide. Oxford is a registered trade mark of
Oxford University Press in the UK and in certain other countries

Published in the United States of America by Oxford University Press
198 Madison Avenue, New York, NY 10016, United States of America

British Library Cataloguing in Publication Data

Data available

Library of Congress Control Number: 2023951145

ISBN 978–0–19–284586–3

DOI: 10.1093/oso/9780192845863.001.0001

Printed and bound by
CPI Group (UK) Ltd, Croydon, CR0 4YY

Acknowledgements

I started researching the topic of this book when I was writing the proposal for my PhD. If I had been told then that it would take about ten years for me to publish the manuscript, I am not sure I would have had the strength to continue. The funding I received from the Research Foundation—Flanders (FWO Aspirant Fellowship) and the Australian Research Council (LP210200818: Socially Responsible Insurance in the Age of Artificial Intelligence)—allowed me the time to research the topic and develop my argument.

Writing the book was also very challenging. It would not have been possible without the help of many very kind people. A lot has changed in the time since my PhD proposal and the book only vaguely resembles the thesis as I presented it at the public defence of my PhD in 2019. The help I have received, however, has been the constant support I needed to finalize the manuscript. I am particularly indebted to my PhD supervisors Peggy Valcke and Eleni Kosta: I hope this book has made both your efforts seem worthwhile and I am grateful for your continued kindness and support. During the preparation of my PhD, I also benefited from the feedback of my supervisory committee, Orla Lynskey, Evelyne Terryn, and Patrick Van Eecke and, at the end, the other members of my jury, Jacques Herbots and Elise Muir. Special thanks go to Orla in particular who was kind enough to also give me feedback on a chapter of the book.

In addition to my supervisors, panel, and jury members, I drew significant inspiration from conversations with a number of brilliant people during my PhD. Special thanks in particular go to Valerie Verdoodt, Jef Ausloos, and Inge Graef, with whom I collaborated on several projects and benefited enormously from being around, and not just intellectually. Valerie and Jef also generously gave further feedback on chapters of this book. During the PhD, I benefited greatly from the suggestions of Edina Harbinja, Andy McStay, Gianclaudio Malgieri, Yann Lorans, and Amandine Leonard, who kindly acted as my discussants at my doctoral seminars, and Lorenzo Dalla Corte, Nóra Ní Loideáin, and Beth Shiner who also gave me important feedback. Gianclaudio was kind enough to give me comments on a chapter of the book as well. I would also like to thank my former office mate at the KU Leuven, Natalie Bertels, who contributed significantly to the way in which I think about the issues discussed in this book from the start. I was very lucky and happy at the KU Leuven and the atmosphere was the product of really nice people. Special thanks in particular go to Shuki Tang, Edith Appelmans, and Ivo Emanuilov for their kindness and brilliant sense of humour which made things so much more fun.

My transition to academia in Australia and my development as a researcher owe a lot to the people that I have worked with since my arrival. Megan Richardson in particular was kind enough to get me started with a research stay at Melbourne Law School and this opportunity paved the way for my position at the ANU College of Law. I joined the ANU in 2020 and during the time since my arrival I have worked with brilliant people. Sally Wheeler provided invaluable mentorship at various points and special thanks go to Heather Roberts for her feedback on a chapter of this book. There are also several people who deserve thanks for listening to me during my many meltdowns regarding its structure, including Jo Ford, Clement Chen, Wenting Cheng, Faith Gordon, and Andrew Ray. I had excellent research assistance from Niamh Brazil when I was first reframing the book from the thesis and I benefited hugely from the comments of the anonymous reviewers. My thanks also go to Alex Flach and Kezia Johnson at OUP and Shenbagarajan at Newgen for their help throughout the production process as well as Caroline Valia-Kollery for her work on the final copy-edit.

I have benefited (and continue to benefit) from collaborating with Megan Richardson in particular but also the people to whom she has introduced me since we first met. More specifically, I have been lucky to collaborate with Jeannie Paterson, Normann Witzleb, Lee Bygrave, and Rachelle Bosua on different projects. Megan, Jeannie, Normann, Lee, and Rachelle also offered me comments on draft chapters of this book and gave me the confidence to work through my uncertainties. Jeannie in particular gave me the push I needed during a chat over coffee at the ANU and inspired the motivation and enthusiasm necessary to prioritize the book.

I would like to say that I left my writing problems at the office but that would be a lie. My partner, Sarah, has really put up with a lot so that I could finish this book. I think she has heard enough about data protection law to fill a lifetime. At the end of the writing, I was in a race to see if I could finish the book before my son Tadhg was born, Tadhg won or, as Sarah suggested, he was so sick of hearing about the book he tried to escape by being born prematurely. My parents, siblings, and broader family have also supported me hugely—you don't write a book overnight. The moral and financial support of my parents in particular was really important. I was given the best possible start and continue to be lucky to have such a great family in Ireland and Australia.

Damian Clifford
Canberra, 22 January 2024

Contents

List of Abbreviations

ACCC	Australian Competition and Consumer Commission
APEC	Asia-Pacific Economic Cooperation
APP	Australian Privacy Principles
ATT	App Tracking Transparency
CNIL	Commission nationale de l'informatique et des libertés
DP/PIA	data protection/privacy impact assessment
DPA	data protection authority
DPIA	data protection impact assessment
E-AI	Emotional Artificial Intelligence
ECHR	European Convention on Human Rights
EDPB	European Data Protection Board
EDPS	European Data Protection Supervisor
EU	European Union
FACS	Facial Action Coding
FIPPs	Fair Information Practice Principles
FTC	Federal Trade Commission
GDPR	General Data Protection Regulation
ICCPR	International Covenant on Civil and Political Rights
ICO	Information Commissioner's Office
IEEE	Institute of Electrical and Electronic Engineers
IT	information technology
ML	machine learning
OECD	Organisation for Economic Co-operation and Development
PDPA	Singaporean Personal Data Protection Act 2012
UI	user interface
UK	United Kingdom
UN	United Nations
US	United States
UX	user experience

1
Introduction

A. Datafication, Data Protection, and Emotion

We are living in a world mediated by technology. The advancement in technological capacity has led to the 'datafication' of our everyday lives.[1] From browsing habits, to sleep patterns, hormonal cycles, and emotion analytics, we are living in what Zuboff has referred to as 'the age of surveillance capitalism'.[2] This is a concern for many but, as Zuboff's title would suggest, is understood as an opportunity by others. Gandy describes the complex technologies used to control our access to goods and services, and the collection, processing, and sharing of the information we generate on a daily basis, as a 'system of power' that he names the 'panoptic sort'.[3] Despite twenty-five years between their publications, Zuboff's surveillance capitalism and Gandy's panoptic sort share a common theme—the threat posed by surveillance technologies and the impact of power imbalances.

The tangible and intangible, objective and subjective, harms associated with surveillance unsurprisingly also pepper the data protection and privacy law literature. In recent years, concerns have given rise to an intense debate regarding the need for law reform in many jurisdictions.[4] Data protection law and its reform have been centre-stage in these debates. As will be described in this book, however, data protection law is not a recent phenomenon. People have been writing about the role, strengths, and weaknesses of data protection (or data or informational privacy as it is otherwise known) for some time. The European Union (EU) and European scholarship has been particularly influential in this

[1] Viktor Mayer-Schonberger and Kenneth Cukier, *Big Data: A Revolution That Will Transform How We Live, Work and Think* (Houghton Mifflin Harcourt 2013); José van Dijck, 'Datafication, Dataism and Dataveillance: Big Data between Scientific Paradigm and Ideology' (2014) 12(2) Big Data Surveillance 197.

[2] Shoshana Zuboff, *The Age of Surveillance Capitalism: The Fight for a Human Future at the New Frontier of Power* (1st edn, PublicAffairs 2019).

[3] Oscar H Gandy, *The Panoptic Sort: A Political Economy of Personal Information* (Westview 1993).

[4] For a discussion of the emergence of data protection law frameworks in different jurisdictions, see Graham Greenleaf, 'Global Data Privacy 2023: DPA Networks Almost Everywhere' (28 February 2023) <https://papers.ssrn.com/abstract=4461729> accessed 12 June 2023.

Data Protection Law and Emotion. Damian Clifford, Oxford University Press. © Damian Clifford 2024.
DOI: 10.1093/oso/9780192845863.003.0001

regard. The EU's General Data Protection Regulation (GDPR),[5] which was adopted in 2016 and entered into force in 2018, was introduced in response to the challenges posed by intensive personal data processing. The Regulation is seen by many as a significant response to fears of the risks posed by technological development and has exerted a significant influence in the development and/or reform of similar laws in many other jurisdictions.[6]

However, the GDPR was neither the first move towards the protection of personal data (in the EU, its Member States, or indeed elsewhere) nor the first instrument to exert a global influence on the development of data protection law. As Chapter 2 explores, data protection law emerged in an era of socio-economic and technological change at the national level in the 1960s and 1970s, with strong influence from European countries but also from the United States (US). This influence then manifested itself at the international level in the form of the Organisation for Economic Co-operation and Development (OECD) Guidelines and the Council of Europe Convention 108[7] in the early 1980s, and later, for instance, in the predecessor to the GDPR, the Data Protection Directive 95/46/EC.[8] Despite data protection law's established nature in many jurisdictions however, the GDPR still caused policymaking ripple effects across the globe. Data protection reforms are seen as a means of curtailing the 'negative' impacts of the emergence of the digital economy; repeated data breaches, the use of facial recognition technology, and psychometric profiling for micro-targeted political advertising are just some of the areas that brought have data protection and privacy law reform debates to the fore again.[9]

Data protection law is thus often positioned as 'the'—or at least 'a'—regulatory solution to the challenges posed by technological change. The importance of data protection law is logical given its focus on the protection of personal data, the application of notions such as informed data subject consent, and data subject rights. By protecting the personal data of individuals, the control rights

[5] Regulation (EU) 2016/679 of the European Parliament and of the Council of 27 April 2016 on the protection of natural persons with regard to the processing of personal data and on the free movement of such data, and repealing Directive 95/46/EC (General Data Protection Regulation) [2016] OJ L119/1–88.

[6] See Anu Bradford, 'The Brussels Effect' (2012) 107 Northwestern University Law Review 1.

[7] Guidelines on the Protection of Privacy and Transborder Flows of Personal Data (OECD) 1980.

[8] Directive 95/46/EC of the European Parliament and of the Council of 24 October 1995 on the protection of individuals with regard to the processing of personal data and on the free movement of such data [1995] OJ L281/31–50.

[9] See eg 'The Cambridge Analytica Files' *The Guardian* <www.theguardian.com/news/series/cambridge-analytica-files> accessed 4 October 2023; Agustín Rossi, 'How the Snowden Revelations Saved the EU General Data Protection Regulation' (2018) 53 The International Spectator 95; Sarah Hanselaer, 'Facial Recognition in School Renders Sweden's First GDPR Fine' (*European Data Protection Board*, 22 August 2019) <https://edpb.europa.eu/news/national-news/2019/facial-recognition-school-renders-swedens-first-gdpr-fine_en> accessed 1 July 2020.

and the obligations provided for in data protection law impose responsibilities on those processing personal data and give choice to the identified or identifiable natural persons to whom the data relate. Through these control rights, as strengthened by, inter alia, key principles (often referred to as the fair information practice principles, or FIPPS, eg data minimization, purpose limitation, accuracy, and security), a risk-based approach, and accountability mechanisms such as impact assessments, data subjects are positioned as the key actors 'empowered' to determine the fate of their personal data.[10] On paper, therefore, data protection law seems to be the perfect legislative response.

However, criticisms of data protection law's capacity to regulate personal data processing effectively are also widely expressed in the literature.[11] Indeed, notwithstanding the seemingly simple division between rights and responsibilities in data protection law, there has been a continuous undercurrent of criticism regarding the framework's capacity to respond to the challenges posed by digital technologies. These have not been displaced by the changes introduced by legislation such the EU's GDPR or, for example, the California Consumer Privacy Act[12] or similar state-level Acts in the US,[13] and the moves towards data subject empowerment through control rights. Even prior to the adoption and entry into force of these high-profile exemplars, data protection law's capacity to deal with the challenges posed by technological development had been repeatedly questioned.[14] This literature's robust critical scrutiny often centres on the instrumental role played by the notion of control, which manifests itself in the form of specific data subject rights. This scholarship is particularly evident in the work of US scholars and, this book is in part a work inspired by, and in response to, their insights.

Despite the intellectual depth evident in this critical literature, I believe that there has been little account of what Stark refers to as the 'lived nuances and messy complexities of how ordinary people engage with their own feelings

[10] For a discussion of this instrumental role, see Christophe Lazaro and Daniel Le Métayer, 'Control over Personal Data: True Remedy or Fairy Tale?' (2015) 12 SCRIPTed 3.

[11] See eg Ari Waldman, 'Privacy's Rights Trap' [2022] Northwestern University Law Review Online <https://scholarlycommons.law.northwestern.edu/nulr_online/327> accessed 4 October 2023; Daniel Solove, 'The Limitations of Privacy Rights' (2023) 98 Notre Dame Law Review 975; Julie E Cohen, 'How (Not) to Write a Privacy Law' (2021) 21 Knight First Amendment Institute <https://knightcolumbia.org/content/how-not-to-write-a-privacy-law> accessed 4 October 2023.

[12] California Consumer Privacy Act of 2018.

[13] See Virginia Consumer Data Protection Act (2021), Utah Consumer Privacy Act (2022), Texas Data Privacy and Security Act (2023), Tennessee Information Protection Act (2023), Montana Consumer Data Privacy Act (2023), Iowa Consumer Data Protection Act (2023), Indiana Consumer Data Protection Act (2023), Connecticut Data Privacy Act (2022), and Colorado Privacy Act (2021).

[14] See Bert-Jaap Koops, 'The Trouble with European Data Protection Law' (2014) 4 International Data Privacy Law 250.

about informational privacy'.[15] Underpinning this point is the fact that plotting the role of emotion and its effects has been only a fringe topic in the law more generally, and data protection law in particular. At first pass, this may seem like a bizarre statement. It is obvious that the law has always involved emotion—or, in Bandes' words, '[e]motion pervades the law'.[16] In criminal law, for instance, we can consider the role of disgust (and remorse) in judicial decisions regarding sentencing of particularly heinous crimes.[17] In private law, damages for pain and suffering have a long history in common law torts, and, more generally, the need to provide emotional satisfaction through the award of remedies such as damages in common law contract and torts for certain types of non-pecuniary loss is part of the rationale of *restitutio in integrum* and general damages.[18] Emotion, therefore, undoubtedly plays a significant role in the law.

More to the point, in data protection law, the fear of invasions of our privacy and anger and/or embarrassment when such invasions occur are inherent to the existence, and indeed operation, of the protections and remedies provided for respectively. As will be analysed in Chapter 2, certain fears have played an important role in the development of data protection law, and these include not only the public's fears of the risks posed by technology but also the fears of the legislator (and economic actors) that consumer/citizen trust will be impacted by those fears. Moreover, their adoption has caused anxiety amongst those tasked with compliance, and since their adoption there has been frustration with their impact (or lack thereof). Despite the important and obvious intersection between the law and emotion (and, more specifically, between data protection law and emotion), the relationship is in fact far more complicated, this complication being linked to the way in which the law seemingly fails to account for the role played by emotion in decision-making.

Our rational capacity to make choices has been criticized by a range of legal theorists. Behavioural law and economics has been at the forefront of these debates, but law and emotion research has also emerged as a means of challenging notions of rationality in the law.[19] In data protection law, behavioural law and economics research has gained widespread popularity, in particular in discussions regarding the legitimacy of individual consent to the processing of

[15] Luke Stark, 'The Emotional Context of Information Privacy' (2016) 32 The Information Society 14, 16.
[16] Susan Bandes, *The Passions of Law* (New York University Press 2001) 1.
[17] See eg Dan M Kahan, '"The Anatomy of Disgust" in Criminal Law' (1998) 96 Michigan Law Review 1621.
[18] See eg *Baltic Shipping Co v Dillon* (1993) 176 CLR 344.
[19] Kathryn Abrams and Hila Keren, 'Who's Afraid of Law and the Emotions' (2009) 94 Minnesota Law Review 1997, 1999.

personal data.[20] However, in contrast, there has been little attention paid to law and emotion scholarship.[21]

B. Aims, Themes, and the E-AI Case Study

This book will explore the relationship between data protection law and law and emotion in detail. It aims (1) to highlight the importance of a more accurate understanding of the role of emotion in decision-making in the analysis and reform of data protection law, but also (2) to demonstrate the potential conceptual value played by the notion of control as manifested instrumentally through control rights and thus the ongoing significance of data protection law despite the criticisms levied against it.

Law and emotion scholars challenge the traditional conceptualizations of the law by exploring how emotions are infused in decision-making and analysing how decision-making is enriched by emotion.[22] The scholarship builds on interdisciplinary analysis which explains that there is no such thing as an emotionless, cold, deliberative state in order to question what this might mean for the key positioning of individuals in the law. Law and emotion scholars rely on a range of interdisciplinary research that demonstrates that emotions are the 'dominant driver of most meaningful decisions in life'[23] and aim to reflect this reality in legal analysis. As emotion has been a strong driver in the development of data protection law and, for instance, data subjects play a key role in making choices regarding the processing of their personal data, the insights that a law and emotion analysis might provide data protection are significant. This book thus aims to bring the law and emotion and data protection law literatures together through the lens of the critiques of control found in the data protection and privacy law literature.

Data subject control rights such as the right of access, the right to object, and, arguably more generally, the right to information (which links to the operation

[20] For some early examples, see Shmuel I Becher and Uri Benoliel, 'Law in Books and Law in Action: The Readability of Privacy Policies and the GDPR' in Klaus Mathis and Avishalom Tor (eds), *Consumer Law and Economics* (Springer International 2021).

[21] For some exceptions, Damian Clifford, 'Citizen-Consumers in a Personalised Galaxy: Emotion Influenced Decision-Making, A True Path to the Dark Side?' in Lilian Edwards, Burkhard Schafer, and Edina Harbinja (eds), *Emerging Technology, Regulation and Ethics* (1st edn, Edinburgh University Press 2020); Andrew McStay and Lachlan Urquhart, '"This Time with Feeling?" Assessing EU Data Governance Implications of out of Home Appraisal Based Emotional AI' (2019) 24(10) First Monday <https://journals.uic.edu/ojs/index.php/fm/article/view/9457> accessed 25 January 2023.

[22] Abrams and Keren (n 19) 1999.

[23] Jennifer S Lerner and others, 'Emotion and Decision Making' (2015) 66 Annual Review of Psychology 799, 801.

of these rights but also, for instance, individual consent), play an instrumental role in data protection law, providing individuals with the capacity to make subjective choices. As alluded to in the previous section, this instrumental role of control has been severely criticized in the data protection literature, partly through insights from behavioural law and economics research.[24] Law and emotion research is distinct from theories such as behavioural law and economics, however, as it aims to account more accurately for the role of emotion in decision-making.[25] This separation between emotion as a bias or goal of decision-making in behavioural law and economics literature versus emotion as something operating in conjunction with rationality reflects the separation in the philosophical accounts of emotion as discussed in the law and emotion literature.

Law and emotion literature often relies on the conceptual starting point that emotions are typically based on a belief or judgement.[26] This literature is thus influential in law and emotion scholarship and will therefore form the basis of the critique in this book. Although intuitively we understand what emotions are, they are notoriously difficult to define. It is therefore unsurprising that researchers have categorized a wide variety of mental states as emotional, analysing the effects of emotions on judgements and decision-making.[27] Pinning down what is meant by emotion is thus difficult, and accurately understanding and classifying the relationship between the various mental states is of key importance in this regard. That being said, there has been long-standing agreement that certain experiences can be grouped together as emotions and that these are distinct from 'from bodily appetites such as hunger and thirst, and also from objectless moods, such as irritation or endogenous depression'.[28]

As noted by Phelps and colleagues, 'the term emotion refers to a discrete reaction to an internal or external event that can yield a range of synchronized responses, including physiological responses (e.g., flight or fight), facial and/or bodily expressions, subjective feelings, and action tendencies, such as

[24] See eg Waldman (n 11); Solove (n 11); Cohen (n 11).

[25] Abrams and Keren (n 19); Jeremy A Blumenthal, 'Emotional Paternalism' (2007) 35 Florida State University Law Review 1.

[26] See eg Martha C Nussbaum, *Upheavals of Thought: The Intelligence of Emotions* (CUP 2003); Jon Elster, *Alchemies of the Mind: Rationality and the Emotions* (Digital printing, CUP 2003); Martha C Nussbaum, '"Secret Sewers of Vice": Disgust, Bodies, and the Law' in Susan Bandes (ed), *The Passions of Law.* (New York University Press 2001); Dan M Kahan and Martha C Nussbaum, 'Two Conceptions of Emotion in Criminal Law' (1996) 96 Columbia Law Review 269.

[27] Jennifer S Lerner and others, 'Emotion and Decision Making—Supplementary Text' (2015) 66 Annual Review of Psychology 1.

[28] Kahan and Nussbaum (n 26) 276.

approach or avoid.'[29] This classification of emotion creates a clear distinction between emotions and feelings. Indeed, according to the authors an emotion can give rise to subjective feelings rather than their being viewed as synonymous. Hence, this appears to reflect the conventional distinction between emotions and feelings as recognized by researchers such as Damasio, who have illustrated that feelings emerge when individuals become aware of their emotions, thereby facilitating, but also building upon, conscious attention and reflection on emotions.[30] Emotions must also be clearly delineated from mood, which according to the prevalent opinion in the psychology and neuroscience literature is characterized by subjective feelings that persist in duration without necessarily being linked to a specific triggering event.[31]

As such, it is important to mention that across both the psychology and neuroscience literature the term 'affect' is generally used as the superordinate umbrella term for a collection of component processes which include emotions, moods, and subjective feelings.[32] It is therefore 'affect' that concerns us here (whether that be emotions, moods, and/or subjective feelings) and its impact on decision-making, even if the word emotion is used in this book to better align to the law and emotion scholarship. As will be explored, emotion plays a role in all decision-making—good, bad, or indifferent—both in the analysis of risks posed and the need for legislative responses, but also in the choices available to individual data subjects to operate their subjective rights, or not. I believe that the failure to account for this role of emotion undermines the protections provided. This book therefore aims to better account for the role of emotion and to explore how data protection law can be interpreted, supplemented, and/or altered to overcome the challenges identified. Although the analysis calls for a more accurate understanding of emotion in decision-making in data protection law, I appreciate that emotion is only part of the picture for alternative theoretical accounts and, in particular, behavioural law and economics.

More specifically, many of the cognitive biases established by behavioural law and economics focus on non-affective cognitive biases that cause a departure from rationality with emotions seemingly positioned as an irrational

[29] Elizabeth A Phelps, Karolina M Lempert, and Peter Sokol-Hessner, 'Emotion and Decision Making: Multiple Modulatory Neural Circuits' (2014) 37 Annual Review of Neuroscience 263, 266.

[30] As described by Mireille Hildebrandt, *Smart Technologies and the End(s) of Law: Novel Entanglements of Law and Technology* (Edward Elgar 2015).

[31] Although differentiating between these categories is interesting it is outside the scope of this particular research and also unnecessary, given that our aim here is to study the effect of such mental states on decision-making more generally.

[32] See generally Lerner and others, 'Emotion and Decision Making' (n 23); Phelps, Lempert, and Sokol-Hessner (n 29).

bias.[33] In a data protection law context, we can refer here to the discussion in the literature exploring the role played by default settings, cognitive or information overload, and biases such as confirmation bias which can lead individuals to seek the information that reinforces their decision and to not engage with unfavourable information (see Chapter 4). The book's focus, therefore, is not to develop a competing account for how to understand the reasons behind 'irrational' decision-making but instead to account for a more accurate understanding of emotion in the discussions of the limitations of the instrumental role played by control rights and to build on this literature.[34] The analysis challenges the traditional separation between reason and emotion in data protection law and thus the underlying objective rationalist approach by representing the role of emotion more accurately.

Indeed, given the key positioning of the rational and autonomous data subject in data protection law, one must wonder whether the interdisciplinary insights on the role of emotion as the key driver in decision-making effectively undermine the protections afforded in data protection law in various jurisdictions. Ultimately, therefore, I will examine whether accounting for the role of emotion will enhance the effectiveness of the legal protections. In her taxonomy of the law and emotion field, Maroney suggests a number of ways to account for how 'the law reflects or furthers conceptions' of humans as 'emotional creatures'.[35] These include, for example, the legal actor approach (where those who participate in the law are analysed), theories of law (such as behavioural law and economics), and the more normative question of how emotion should be reflected or incorporated in the law and legal doctrine.[36] This book explores key actors in data protection law but also the role of the legislator and regulators in the adoption and enforcement of these laws, in order to assess how failing to account for emotion impacts the protections provided and, accordingly, should shape reform. To a certain degree, then, the book aims to straddle a number of the sub-fields of the law and emotion literature identified by Maroney.

The first key theme of the book is the exploration of the incorporation of law and emotion insights in data protection law and the associated practical and

[33] Abrams and Keren (n 19) 2018–27.

[34] In fact, Martha Nussbaum, for instance, who has championed an approach where emotions are understood as cognitive/rational, has also explored how heuristics discussed in behavioural economics may affect emotional responses, in particular individual and collective fear. Martha C Nussbaum, *The Monarchy of Fear: A Philosopher Looks at Our Political Crisis* (Simon & Schuster 2018).

[35] Terry A Maroney, 'Law and Emotion: A Proposed Taxonomy of an Emerging Field.' (2006) 30 Law and Human Behavior 119.

[36] ibid.

theoretical struggles. More specifically, the book explores the challenges for the effective operation of data protection law and the control-rights-orientated approach more specifically, presented by US critical scholars in particular, with reference to three important challenges to data protection law's effectiveness. First, how the 'categories' approach to data protection (ie personal data, and, where relevant, sensitive personal data categories) arguably results in emotional disengagement from the dangers associated with intensive data processing. This reflects the capacity to make sensitive inferences from seemingly innocuous personal data (Chapter 3). Secondly, how a more realistic understanding of the role of emotion in decision-making may contextualize the role played by individual choice in the exercising of the individual control rights while also explaining the instrumental role of control in facilitating the operation of subjective rights (Chapter 4). And finally, in their practical application, how accountability mechanisms arguably fail to consider the subjective intentions/aspirations of data subjects by affording those processing personal data significant scope and failing to recognize how compliance in process and not in substance (ie through outsourced objectified methods) impacts the application of the law and the exercise of the subjective control rights (Chapter 5).

Chapters 3–5 demonstrate data protection law's weaknesses and the challenges associated with operationalizing the instrumental role of control rights. In these three chapters, the book thus aims to add value by (1) illuminating the affective features of problems through a law and emotion exploration of data protection law's core aspects, (2) investigating these features through interdisciplinary analysis, and exploring the limits of the challenge presented, before (3) integrating that understanding into practical, normative proposals, which are then discussed in Chapter 6. This approach relies on Abrams and Keren's categorization of the three dimensions in which law and emotion scholarship can inform the law in order to form the methodology and structure in these chapters.[37]

The book will contextualize the investigation of the features of the challenge in each chapter. This will focus on the protections afforded in the EU's GDPR in particular, but these deep-dives will be framed by more general and comparative research with references to jurisdictions such as the US, Singapore, and Australia in order to demonstrate the significance of the challenge for data protection law more broadly and the limits of the critique from a law and emotion perspective. The analysis is, hence, not a complete comparative examination of data protection law but instead a more targeted one, reflecting (1) the sheer

[37] See Abrams and Keren (n 19).

number of jurisdictions that now have data protection law frameworks, rendering a complete analysis impossible in this book,[38] but also (2) the specific focus of the book on the role of control, its critique, and thus how a law and emotion analysis contributes to its understanding.

The analysis focuses specifically on the GDPR for the deep-dives in the middle section of each of these chapters, both because it is widely regarded as the high-water mark globally in terms of the protections it affords, and also because it has had a significant influence on law reform in several jurisdictions. At the time of writing, the EU GDPR is also part of United Kingdom law (UK GDPR) despite Brexit and reform discussions.[39] Moreover, as the critique of control rights in data protection law is most obvious in the US scholarship, specific reference will also be made the ongoing debate regarding the legitimacy of data protection law as a regulatory response in this literature. In fact, the dominant criticisms of these scholars will be tested through an analysis of the most protective version of data protection frameworks that they criticize: the EU's GDPR.

As mentioned above, to ground the analysis of the GDPR the Regulation's provisions will be explored through the lens of a particularly apt case study—the emergence of Emotional Artificial Intelligence (E-AI). Developments in affective computing, or E-AI as it is often now referred to—ie technologies that are *supposedly* capable of detecting, classifying, and responding appropriately to users' emotional lives, thereby appearing to understand their audience[40]—are playing a role in shaping the technology we engage with on a daily basis. The term 'affective computing' was coined by Rosalind Picard and defined by her as 'computing that relates to, arises from, or deliberately influences emotions'.[41] Inherent in the development of affective computing is the objective of making people care about machines.[42] Since the birth of the E-AI sub-discipline, research in this area has expanded dramatically and, in addition to exploring the role of emotions in computing, this research has also encompassed emotion detection.[43] E-AI was originally broadly defined in terms of enhancing the

[38] See Graham Greenleaf, 'Global Data Privacy Laws 2023: International Standards Stall, but UK Disrupts' (2023) 183 Privacy Laws & Business International Report 8; Graham Greenleaf, 'Global Data Privacy Laws 2023: 162 National Laws and 20 Bills' (2023) 181 Privacy Laws and Business International Report 2.

[39] See Catherine Fairbairn and others, 'Research Briefing: The Data Protection and Digital Information Bill 2022–23' (UK House of Commons Library 2023) 9606 <https://commonslibrary.parliament.uk/research-briefings/cbp-9606/> accessed 28 June 2023.

[40] Andrew McStay, *Emotional AI: The Rise of Empathic Media* (1st edn, SAGE Publications 2018) 3.

[41] Rosalind W Picard, *Affective Computing* (MIT Press 1997) 1.

[42] McStay, *Emotional AI* (n 40) 18.

[43] Sylvie Delacroix and Michael Veale, 'Smart Technologies and Our Sense of Self: Going Beyond Epistemic Counter-Profiling' in Mireille Hildebrandt and Kieron O'Hara (eds), *Life and the Law in the Era of Data-Driven Agency* (Edward Elgar 2019).

understanding of human emotion and computer functionality. Developments were focused in particular on 'computer-assisted learning, perceptual information retrieval, arts and entertainment, human health and interaction'.[44] These technologies arguably facilitate the opening of new commercial opportunities in areas such as the healthcare and/or 'wellness' sectors,[45] thereby reflecting Rosalind Picard's work in particular in the development of devices designed to help children with autism.[46] Picard's vision was defined in terms of E-AI offering a means of enhancing our daily lives with a rather limited exploration of the associated dangers. Although she acknowledged the potential for advertisers to exploit emotions, the possibility of intrusive employee monitoring, and the dystopian prospect of the malevolent use of affective computing to control the emotions of populations, she believed that safeguards could be developed to mitigate these risks. Recent history tells us, however, that this optimism may have been misplaced, given the significant role played by the advertising and marketing industries in particular in the uptake of the technology.[47]

The reasons for this industry's interest are obvious—advertising and emotions go hand and in hand, and a technology which seemingly promises to provide insights into a person's emotional state brings clear commercial benefits.[48] However, the purported applications of E-AI extend well beyond advertising and marketing. Consumer safety in vehicles, public security in airports, attention monitoring in meetings and classrooms, and even the facilitation of engagement with government services are all examples of technological deployments that have incorporated some aspect of E-AI. Buzzwords like security, safety, and engagement are often linked to deployments of these innovations and from the classroom and the office to commercial and public

[44] Picard (n 41) 1.

[45] Andrew McStay, 'Empathic Media: The Rise of Emotion in AI' <www.researchgate.net/publication/317616480_EMPATHIC_MEDIA_THE_RISE_OF_EMOTION_AI> accessed 4 October 2023.

[46] See generally Picard (n 41) 1.

[47] See Zuboff (n 2) 285–90.

[48] For instance, in the context of advertising and marketing, commercial entities induce emotional responses in order to create awareness and positive brand association, and, as a consequence, evoke an emotional desire for a product or service. Campaigns aim to induce a 'positive' or 'negative' appeal to elicit an emotional response. Positive appeals promise positive emotions through the use or purchase of the advertised product or service. In contrast, negative appeals suggest negative consequences for those who ignore the commercial message. Karolien Poels and Siegfried Dewitte, 'How to Capture the Heart? Reviewing 20 Years of Emotion Measurement in Advertising' (2006) 46 Journal of Advertising Research 18; Larry Percy and John R Rossiter, 'A Model of Brand Awareness and Brand Attitude Advertising Strategies' (1992) 9 Psychology & Marketing 263. This is significant as the use of emotional appeal is not restricted to the content of commercial communications, and research has also shown the potential for a positive emotional impact of advertising formats, branding, product design, and indeed virtually all aspects of consumer-facing interactions. Blumenthal observes that the use of emotion biases could also extend to the development of manipulative and arguably unconscionable contract terms, see Blumenthal (n 25) 47–48.

spaces, E-AI is increasingly interacting with us in our roles as student, employee, consumer, and citizen. This is despite significant concerns related to, amongst other things, the accuracy of this technology (Chapter 5).

Reliance on E-AI in each setting certainly raises issues and, although there are broad similarities across each domain, context matters. Data protection laws such as the GDPR often apply to both public and private sector uses of personal data and rely on a principles-based approach (ie the FIPPs) to determine the legitimacy of the personal data processing depending on the context. By focusing on E-AI and its deployment in different contexts through hypothetical examples, the objective of the analysis is to tease out the challenges to the data protection law framework posed by a law and emotion analysis. There is therefore an added incentive for relying on the GDPR for the deep-dive analysis, since it is often presented as the standard-setter; but there is also a practical motivation, given that it also has the most comprehensive list of subjective control rights in legislation of its kind.[49] The book focuses on E-AI in particular because (1) there is a synergy with the book's more fundamental focus as the development of such technology could actually further undermine existing legal protections designed for rational unemotional decision-makers, and (2) E-AI presents problems that provide an excellent illustration of the challenges faced by data protection law.

Emotions are certainly perceived to be sensitive, but E-AI raises a number of interesting points of analysis regarding the blurring boundaries between the personal and sensitive personal data categories (Chapter 3). It also seems obvious that the emergence of E-AI technologies may further challenge the rationality paradigm inherent in areas of law such as consumer protection for instance, given that emotions are key drivers in the decision-making processes. This could be an issue in relation to both the further gathering of personal data but also, and more specifically, the harnessing of such insights for commercial gain. For example, building on the granular insights provided by big data, the technological developments allow commercial entities to move beyond the mere targeting of behaviour in advertisements to the personalization of services, interfaces, and the other consumer-facing interactions, based on personal preferences and biases gleaned from the tracking of online activity and profiling.[50] Indeed, as alluded to above, the rapid development of E-AI in recent

[49] See Solove (n 11).

[50] See Ryan Calo, 'Digital Market Manipulation' (2014) 82 George Washington Law Review 995; Jon D Hanson and Douglas A Kysar, 'Taking Behavioralism Seriously: The Problem of Market Manipulation' (1999) 74 New York University Law Review 630; Jon D Hanson and Douglas A Kysar, 'Taking Behavioralism Seriously: Some Evidence of Market Manipulation' (1999) 112 Harvard Law

years largely stems from the interest of the advertising and marketing industries, and therefore it is interesting to consider the potentially manipulative effects of these technologies (Chapter 4). This focus on the private sector is also of interest as criticisms of data protection law often focus on private sector uses of personal data. Indeed, the US scholarship criticizing control in particular is heavily weighted towards the critiques of private sector data processing.

However, one must also recognize that there has been widespread criticism of the accuracy of E-AI, raising important concerns regarding the potential for harm. E-AI is extremely controversial, with many authors questioning the legitimacy of such technologies and labelling them as pseudoscientific.[51] In the EU, these concerns have fuelled moves towards banning the use of the technology in certain contexts (see Chapter 5). Despite these concerns, E-AI is still being implemented in a range of applications in many jurisdictions such as the future smart home (adjusting of lighting or music depending on mood), health- or *pseudo*-health care (the tracking of mood for the purposes of improving mental well-being), and automobile safety (counteracting the potential effects of road rage and drink driving[52]). This is indicative of the move towards what McStay has referred to as empathic media or 'technologies that track bodies and react to emotions and intentions'.[53] But as E-AI would seem to necessitate the processing of personal data, is data protection law not capable of providing the necessary safeguards? Is the GDPR, as the high-water mark example of such laws, in fact the proper place to have these discussions, given that any harmful impact resulting from the use of E-AI may have relied on data subject consent in the first place?

In essence, therefore, data protection law will be explored as the regulatory 'solution' to the risks associated with E-AI (which themselves will be explored in Chapter 3 (sensitivity), Chapter 4 (choice), and Chapter 5 (inaccuracy)). To clarify, as E-AI would seem to necessitate the processing of personal data, it seems logical to view data protection law as the solution. As will be demonstrated, however, E-AI presents interesting challenges for data protection law, both in terms of how to classify E-AI deployments within the personal and

Review 1420; Jon D Hanson and Douglas A Kysar, 'Taking Behavioralism Seriously: A Response to Market Manipulation' (2000) 6 Roger Williams University Law Review 259.

[51] See Kate Crawford, *The Atlas of AI: Power, Politics, and the Planetary Costs of Artificial Intelligence* (1st edn, Yale University Press 2021).

[52] Jasper Jolly, 'Volvo to Install Cameras in New Cars to Reduce Road Deaths' *The Guardian* (20 March 2019) <www.theguardian.com/business/2019/mar/20/volvo-to-install-cameras-in-new-cars-to-reduce-road-deaths> accessed 24 March 2019.

[53] McStay, 'Empathic Media' (n 45).

sensitive personal data definitions and thus the categorical division evident in data protection law (Chapter 3) and in relation to the mechanisms for individual empowerment in these frameworks(Chapters 4 and 5). The E-AI case study is thus an excellent way in which to demonstrate the critique of the instrumental role of control and the insights provided through a law and emotion analysis, and the double focus on emotion reinforces the importance of interdisciplinary insights.

The challenges discussed in Chapters 3–5 focusing on the risks associated with E-AI will be explored as potential shortcomings in regulatory design; implementation, in terms of (design) choices; and enforcement of data protection, as they represent the key characteristics of the instrumental role of control. Although the analysis will expose systemic weaknesses through its aim of integrating law and emotion scholarly insights into the discussion of control rights' instrumental role, it also aims to defend the legitimacy of data protection law's policy objectives, again with reference to the law and emotion scholarship, and to explore the potential conceptual value of control. The capacity to make subjective choices through control rights is of significant importance. There is thus a potential conceptual value to control distinct from its instrumental role.

The second key theme of this book then reflects on how the delineation of the instrumental role and the potential conceptual value of control underlying data protection law changes how instrumentalist criticisms of data protection law are understood. My argument is that instrumentalist critiques often fail to account for the conceptual values underpinning data protection laws and that more research is required to distil what these are—and indeed should be—going forward. Without an understanding of data protection's underlying conceptual values, the more critical literature may be making assumptions when judging the success or failure of these laws.[54] As will be explored in Chapter 6, I believe the control-rights-orientated approach and the potential conceptual value of control aims to safeguard the subjective interests of data subjects and, hence, the liberal foundations of the law. We create data protection laws to protect our capacity to safeguard our subjective interests for a reason, and this point reflects the key conclusion of this book. Data protection law should better account for how people actually feel about the protection of their personal data, but such protections may need to be provided by other areas of law. E-AI is again an excellent illustration of this point (Chapters 3–5). Substitutes

[54] This argument builds on a point made by Cane and colleagues in an administrative law context, see Peter Cane and others, *Principles of Administrative Law* (3rd edn, OUP 2018) 346–64.

for data protection law, however, are likely to be one-size-fits-all, top-down approaches that further objectify the subjective interests of data subjects. It is arguable, therefore, that such an approach would further undermine the interests of individuals. Further reforms should instead be understood as supplementary to the goals of data protection law and not as alternatives.

Control rights in data protection law certainly need to be supplemented both in data protection law through accountability mechanisms and outside it through a more transversal analysis of the challenges posed by technological developments like E-AI. I believe, however, that data protection law is an important piece in the regulatory jigsaw. Data protection law is not the last regulatory intervention that will be necessary nor is it a block on future regulation. Instead it must be seen as a necessary component in the governance of computational systems and the risks of harm they pose.

C. How this Book is Organized

The book is divided into seven chapters, this introduction being Chapter 1. Chapter 2 introduces the fundamentals of data protection law with specific reference to how the US and European countries (and the EU in particular) have shaped the development of data protection law. I have focused the analysis in this way given the clear and significant influence of these jurisdictions on the development of data protection law, but also because the GDPR represents the high-water mark example of a data protection law, and US scholars have been particularly critical of what they perceive to be the limitations of these frameworks. The chapter introduces data protection law's fundamentals features by analysing the motivations surrounding the adoption of legislative interventions and the fears associated with data processing that have shaped the substance and form of data protection law. Chapter 2 also introduces the core features of data protection law to set the scene for the later chapters and to demonstrate how data protection law's complexity has given rise to significant anxiety in those tasked with compliance. Finally, the chapter also explores the frustrations with data protection law's application and enforcement (or lack thereof) in order to situate the more specific analysis which follows in Chapters 3–5 on the challenges posed by law and emotion scholarship for the framework.

There are some core features of data protection law that are challenged by technological developments and the realities of human behaviour. In Chapter 3, I describe our emotional disengagement from the risks of harm associated with personal data processing due to the blurring boundaries between the personal data and sensitive personal data categories protected in data protection law. In Chapter 4, I analyse the emotional disconnect between how data subjects behave and the risks of harm associated with personal data processing. Then, in Chapter 5, I examine how the failure to reach the hearts of those regulated has led to compliance in process but not in substance, thereby undermining the effectiveness of frameworks such as the GDPR and exposing individuals to risks of harm. The analysis also reveals that although data protection law has limitations, the reality is far more complex than the sweeping criticisms might suggest.

Despite the criticisms presented in Chapters 3–5, therefore, Chapter 6 aims to defend the legitimate aims of data protection law and risks of harm it aims to address. The chapter argues that in order to assess the effectiveness of data protection law we need a better understanding of its underlying values. More specifically, Chapter 6 examines how control, as a conceptual value, points to the significance of the capacity to make subjective choices given its instrumental link to the subjective control rights evident in data protection law. Building on this analysis, the chapter then analyses how, although data protection law affords us subjective rights so that we can make our own choices, it also assumes our objective rational capacity to make them and then fails to account for the role of our emotions in decision-making. This analysis is used to describe how the false dichotomy between rationality and emotions arguably undermines the instrumental role played by control. The chapter concludes by stressing the need to delineate between data protection law's limitations (ie its weaknesses) and its limits (ie where other regulatory frameworks step in) and highlighting the need to look to a more transversal analysis of the issues posed by intensive personal data processing.

Chapter 7 concludes the analysis by emphasizing the limits and limitations of data protection law in regulating the gaps identified in Chapters 2–6. It argues that data protection law benefits from a law and emotion analysis and questions how the insights may be useful beyond mere diagnostic purposes in light of the conceptual value of control and in safeguarding the decision-making capacity of individuals. The book concludes by conveying the challenge of integrating the practical and normative proposals described, calling for more research on the conceptual values underpinning data protection law, and outlining a future for data protection law and emotion research in the regulation of computational systems.

2

The Fundamentals of Data Protection Law

A. Introduction

Data protection law is designed to mitigate the power and information asymmetries between those processing personal data and individuals, ie data subjects. It offers data subjects tools to bolster their position that aim to rebalance the existing asymmetries.[1] Data protection law attributes rights to data subjects and imposes obligations on those doing the processing and is seen as an important response to the risks posed by technology. As will be described in Section B, there are several catalysts for the development of data protection laws, but fear has played an important role in their adoption and in the shaping of their contents. The fear of the risks posed by intensive personal data processing but also the fear of failing to regulate and provide an environment that data subjects trust have arguably contributed to the proliferation of data protection laws across the globe.[2]

The adoption of these frameworks, however, has also led to significant anxiety due to their complexity and perceived uncertainty. To a certain extent this uncertainty is unavoidable. Data protection law is clearly a response to legitimate concerns but it also raises difficulties associated with compliance. However, as will be demonstrated, its core features are not new and scholars have questioned its utility in tackling the challenges raised by technological developments for some time. The aim of this chapter, then, is to set the scene for the later chapters of the book by exploring the fundamentals of these laws in terms of how they developed, their defining features, and what scholars have considered to be their key limitations.

Section B introduces data protection law as a response to fears regarding pervasive personal data processing and its effects through a more historical analysis. Section C introduces what constitutes a data protection law with reference to the key international instruments historically: the Organisation

[1] Orla Lynskey, 'Deconstructing Data Protection: The "Added-Value" of a Right to Data Protection in the EU Legal Order' (2014) 63 International & Comparative Law Quarterly 569.

[2] See Graham Greenleaf, 'Global Data Privacy 2023: DPA Networks Almost Everywhere' (28 February 2023) <https://papers.ssrn.com/abstract=4461729> accessed 12 June 2023.

Data Protection Law and Emotion. Damian Clifford, Oxford University Press. © Damian Clifford 2024.
DOI: 10.1093/oso/9780192845863.003.0002

for Economic Co-operation and Development (OECD) Guidelines and the Council of Europe Convention 108, but also the modernized Convention 108 +, the General Data Protection Regulation (GDPR), and some national laws. The focus of the analysis will reflect the focus of the book and will therefore aim to demonstrate the contrasts between the United States (US) and the European Union (EU) (and its Member States in particular). This analysis will be used to frame the discussion surrounding the complexity of some of the key aspects of these laws in order to emphasize how uncertainty in terms of its application has led to anxiety amongst those required to comply. Finally, Section D maps scholarly frustrations with data protection law. It refers (somewhat crudely, perhaps) to those who are pessimistic about data protection law's capacity to regulate personal data processing risks and those who are more optimistic about its ongoing role before then briefly setting the scene for the chapters that follow.

B. Fear and Data Protection Law Reform

Data protection law developed in an era of socio-economic change and can be categorized as part of the complex reforms (and hence the move towards a post-industrial economy) that were taking place during the second half of the twentieth century. The introduction of computers into daily administration increased public awareness, leading to concerns that technology could alter the citizen–state relationship.[3] There were a number of catalysts for this development. These included the development of centralized and computerized population databanks; the closely related introduction or extended use of citizen personal identification numbers; the scheduled population censuses (both in terms of the questions asked and the automation of the process); and, finally, the publication of a large volume of 'alarmist' material during the 1960s and 1970s.[4] In his analysis of these motivations and, in particular, the 'alarmist' material published, Bennett emphasizes that, although the significance of the 'foreboding language' in such material should not be overstated, the volume of such works indicates that they played some part in the societal shift which

[3] Frits W Hondius, *Emerging Data Protection in Europe* (Amsterdam North-Holland 1975) 3–4; Colin J Bennett, *Regulating Privacy: Data Protection and Public Policy in Europe and the United States* (Cornell University Press 1992) ix.

[4] Bennett (n 3) 46–53. See also Viktor Mayer-Schönberger, 'Generational Development of Data Protection in Europe' in Philip E Agre and Marc Rotenberg (eds), *Technology and Privacy: The New Landscape* (MIT Press 1998) 222–23; Lee A Bygrave, *Data Protection Law: Approaching Its Rationale, Logic and Limits* (Kluwer Law International 2002) 94.

pushed these issues 'from the systemic to [the] institutional agenda'.[5] This arguably reflects the standard political argument used to explain the global variations in the steps taken to regulate data protection from the 1970s onwards: the impact of the authoritarian or fascist legacies in Europe.[6]

Although scholars have disputed the extent to which European history influenced the initial development and form of legislative developments,[7] the need to protect civil liberties, and the risk to privacy (and more generally dignity[8]), certainly played a role in ensuring that such concerns were very much in the public's consciousness. Bygrave notes that it would be wrong, however, to see the developments mentioned as the sole catalysts for the emergence of data protection laws and also points to the importance of other forces driving their development.[9] These include modern organizations' appetite for data, their desire for efficiency, emotional factors such as our innate fascination with gadgetry, and also the fact that all of these factors contributed to the development of systems of mass surveillance and the connected capacity to exert social control or influence over the subjects of that surveillance.[10] He also points to deficiencies in the quality of data held by organizations and, hence, how poor thinking and the resulting scandals played a role in the development of data protection laws.[11] There appear therefore to have been a range of interrelated catalysts for the development of these frameworks. However, irrespective of the specific relative importance of any of these catalysts, it was the public's expressions of fear in relation to the disempowerment of individuals; their loss of control over technology, given its complexity; and the potential dehumanization of societal processes that helped them develop into issues of concern for legislatures.[12]

1. The emergence of data protection law

Data protection frameworks began to surface at the sub-national and national levels[13] before then emerging at the international level (ie the OECD Guidelines

[5] Bennett (n 3) 53.

[6] For a discussion, see Abraham L Newman, *Protectors of Privacy: Regulating Personal Data in the Global Economy* (Ill edn, Cornell University Press 2008) 52–54.

[7] See ibid.

[8] See James Q Whitman, 'The Two Western Cultures of Privacy: Dignity versus Liberty' (2004) 113 Yale Law Journal 96.

[9] Bygrave, *Data Protection Law* (n 4) 93–105.

[10] ibid.

[11] ibid 105–06.

[12] ibid 107–16.

[13] The first data protection law was adopted at a sub-national level, namely in the Hessian Act of 7 October 1970. The first national law was adopted by Sweden in 1973, followed by Germany, France,

on the Protection of Privacy and Transborder Flows of Personal Data, the Council of Europe Convention for the Protection of Individuals with Regard to the Processing of Personal Data, and the United Nations (UN) Guidelines for the regulation of computerized personal data files).[14] Early progress was concentrated on the public sector, but legislative developments soon began to include processing by the private sector.[15] Due to the international developments, a raft of further national data protection legislation emerged.[16] Several of these national-level legislative developments took place in Europe in particular.[17] Due to the disparity created by these national initiatives, by the mid-1980s it was perceived by what was then the European Community that harmonization was required and, in 1990, the European Commission published its first draft of the harmonizing legislation of what would eventually become Data Protection Directive 95/46/EC.[18] The inclusion of the private sector in this data protection legislation reflected the concern regarding increasing business use of data processing. It was also indicative of the general move towards the acknowledgement of the need for consumer and employee protections during the post-World War II period and the internal market-making objectives and legislative competence of the European Community. This market-making aspect points to another set of fears that acted as catalysts, namely economic concerns that were shared largely by governments and businesses.[19] These are explained well through the examples of the OECD Guidelines and the adoption of the old EU Data Protection Directive 95/46/EC.

First, the adoption of the OECD Guidelines was the first, and perhaps most obvious, example of economic fears shaping the early development of rules at the international level. Indeed, as noted by Kirby, the chairman of the OECD expert group that developed the Guidelines, the focus of the working group

Denmark, Norway, and Austria in 1978. A total of seven European countries had enacted general data protection laws by the end of 1970s. Brendan Van Alsenoy, *Data Protection Law in the EU: Roles, Responsibilities and Liability* (Intersentia 2019) 155–206.

[14] Guidelines on the Protection of Privacy and Transborder Flows of Personal Data (OECD) 1980; Convention for the Protection of Individuals with regard to Automatic Processing of Personal Data (Council of Europe) 1981 (Convention 108).

[15] Hondius (n 3) 20.

[16] For an overview, see Bennett (n 3) 57.

[17] For a discussion, see Gloria González Fuster, *The Emergence of Personal Data Protection as a Fundamental Right of the EU* (1st edn, Springer 2014) 55–73.

[18] See Directive 95/46/EC of the European Parliament and of the Council of 24 October 1995 on the protection of individuals with regard to the processing of personal data and on the free movement of such data [1995] OJ L281/31–50.

[19] See Bygrave, *Data Protection Law* (n 4) 112–15; Lee A Bygrave, *Data Privacy Law: An International Perspective* (OUP 2014) 10–11.

established to develop the Guidelines is revealed through its initial title: 'Transborder data *barriers* and the protection of privacy'.[20] Kirby further reflects that the development of the Guidelines (and, indeed, the choice of guidelines as opposed to a treaty) was inherently shaped by the OECD's fears of European countries responding to the challenges of transboundary data flows by erecting barriers through national statutes, built strongly around the need to protect privacy, that were blind to the economic costs (and that were perceived by some as protectionist).[21] On the other side of the Atlantic, there was strong support to leave data flows unimpeded by regulation.[22] An important point to note here is that, even to this day, apart from some sectoral laws at the federal level, in the US data protection law and the Fair Information Practice Principles (the FIPPs) have been implemented only in soft law form. These principles were developed by the US Department of Health & Human Services in 1973, seemingly to avoid the economic effects of overregulation. However, although the principles made it into hard law in the Federal Privacy Act 1974, which establishes safeguards for the personal data held by the federal government, there is no equivalent Act regulating the private sector at the federal level in the US.[23] The principles largely mirror those which were developed in European countries around the same time and, as will be described in Chapter 5, have been extremely influential in the adoption of other such laws, despite the uncertainty as to first point of origin.[24] The version of these principles in the OECD Guidelines in particular has been influential in the adoption of a range of national data protection regimes.[25]

Secondly, the EU legislator aimed to improve the functioning of the internal market by introducing a harmonized legal environment through the adoption of the Data Protection Directive 95/46/EC. More specifically, from a policy perspective, the Directive aimed to eliminate disparities by creating a shared framework of protection, thereby removing obstacles to free movement. There

[20] Michael Kirby, 'The History, Achievement and Future of the 1980 OECD Guidelines on Privacy' (2011) 1 International Data Privacy Law 6, 8 (emphasis added).

[21] ibid 8–9.

[22] ibid.

[23] As will be noted at various points in this book, there are however various laws regulating the private sector that have been adopted at the state level. See Virginia Consumer Data Protection Act (2021), Utah Consumer Privacy Act (2022), Texas Data Privacy and Security Act (2023), Tennessee Information Protection Act (2023), Montana Consumer Data Privacy Act (2023), Iowa Consumer Data Protection Act (2023), Indiana Consumer Data Protection Act (2023), Connecticut Data Privacy Act (2022), Colorado Privacy Act (2021), and California Consumer Privacy Act of 2018.

[24] See Robert Gellman, 'Fair Information Practices: A Basic History—Version 2.22' (6 April 2022) <https://papers.ssrn.com/abstract=2415020> accessed 1 June 2023.

[25] eg both the New Zealand and Australian statutes, in particular, were heavily influenced by the Guidelines. See Michael Kirby, 'Privacy Protection, a New Beginning: OECD Principles 20 Years On' (1999) 6 Privacy Law and Policy Reporter 125.

was a fear that, without the adoption of the Directive, transnational data flows would be interrupted or at least hindered by differing national regimes. There was thus an important market-making aspect to the old Directive. This market-making focus was also used to push for strong harmonized protections at the European level as a failure to adopt them could have resulted in barriers being erected between the Member States. Indeed, scholars have also highlighted the significant role played by national data protection authorities (DPAs) in particular countries as political actors, calling for reforms and highlighting the risks associated with fragmentation for the internal market if data transfers between countries were blocked.[26] Accordingly, although the European countries and the US diverge in terms of their apparent legislative appetite for strong data protection (at least historically), there are overlaps in terms of economic concerns. The weighting of the concerns for individual rights and how it is presented, however, differ. Concerns for individual rights in certain of the data protection laws appear to be more closely linked to how the public's fear can affect economic players and, hence, to preventing restrictions on data flow as opposed to there being a distinct concern about rights more generally. This is evident in both the OECD Guidelines and the US approach, but also in the 'predominance of economic concerns' in the Asia-Pacific Economic Cooperation (APEC) Privacy Framework for example[27] that were strongly influenced by the OECD Guidelines.[28]

The difference in approach between the EU and the US can be explained in part by significant disparities in the conceptual underpinnings of their approaches. As alluded to already, informational privacy in the US has historically been dealt with by a patchwork of sector-specific statutes and in soft law. Although there have been significant developments in the adoption of statutory consumer privacy protections at the state level, this has yet to manifest itself in federal legislation or in the form of a federal constitutional right to data privacy/protection.[29] In contrast, as Lynskey notes, independent of the EU's internal market objective, Data Protection Directive 95/46/EC also constituted

[26] See Newman (n 6) 74–98.

[27] 'Asia-Pacific Economic Cooperation (APEC) Privacy Framework' <www.apec.org/docs/default-source/Publications/2017/8/APEC-Privacy-Framework-(2015)/217_ECSG_2015-APEC-Privacy-Framework.pdf> accessed 4 October 2023, 3.

[28] Bygrave, *Data Privacy Law* (n 19) 75–76.

[29] For a discussion, see eg Margot Kaminski, 'The Case for Data Privacy Rights (Or "Please, a Little Optimism")' (2022) 97 Notre Dame Law Review Reflection 385; Ari Waldman, 'Privacy's Rights Trap' [2022] Northwestern University Law Review Online <https://scholarlycommons.law.northwestern.edu/nulr_online/327> accessed 4 October 2023.

a measure for the protection of fundamental rights, as from the early 1970s onwards the European Parliament had expressed its commitment to their protection.[30] Reference can be made here to the influence of the adoption of Council of Europe Convention 108, with its direct link to the need for the protection of the right to respect for private life in Article 8 of the European Convention on Human Rights (ECHR). This adds further shape to the significance of rights protection-based arguments in the adoption of legislation such as the Data Protection Directive 95/46/EC. A similar focus on human rights-based concerns was evident in the adoption of the UN Guidelines, where the commercial fears regarding the restrictions on transborder data flow seemingly took a back seat.[31] Indeed, in its General Comment 16 of 1988, the UN Human Rights Committee recognized that personal data processing needed to be undertaken in accordance with basic data protection principles, albeit in an arguably truncated form compared to Convention 108.[32]

It would be incorrect to say, however, that the need to protect the right to privacy has necessarily been the key driver for legislatures to develop rules in hard law in every jurisdiction (as the US example demonstrates). For instance, in Australia there is also no constitutional right to privacy recognized at the federal level, but data protection legislation was still adopted in the form of the Privacy Act 1988 (Cth), with only a preambular reference to the right protected in Article 17 of the International Covenant on Civil and Political Rights (ICCPR). Thus, although the desire to protect the right cannot be wholly discounted, there were clearly other motivating factors driving the development of these laws. Nevertheless, the absence of a constitutional right or indeed even a common law tort, in Australian law, for instance, arguably affects the protections provided as there is no regime for the protection of privacy more generally. This has led scholars such as Lindsay to note, for example, that there has been a failure to enunciate clearly the conceptual underpinnings of Australia's information privacy laws[33] and Richardson to reflect on the impact of Australia's colonial past in this regard.[34]

[30] Orla Lynskey, *The Foundations of EU Data Protection Law* (1st edn, OUP 2016) 50–51.

[31] See Bygrave, *Data Privacy Law* (n 19) 51–53.

[32] ibid 83–86.

[33] David Lindsay, 'An Exploration of the Conceptual Basis of Privacy and the Implications for the Future of Australian Privacy Law' (2005) 29 Melbourne University Law Review 131, 133.

[34] Megan Richardson, 'From Lenah Game Meats to Farm Transparency: Cultures of Privacy and Surveillance in Australia', Current Legal Issues Seminar Series (Brisbane, November 2023) <https://law.uq.edu.au/files/100082/australian-cultures-of-privacy-and-surveillance-uq_law-cli.pdf> accessed 20 December 2023.

However, even where the conceptual underpinnings of data protection law appear clearer, such as in the EU, the apparent tension between the market-making and privacy protecting objectives of these laws still causes conceptual problems. Indeed, Lynskey suggests that the EU Court of Justice was hesitant to fully embrace the fundamental rights objective of the old Data Protection Directive in its early jurisprudence.[35] Despite any such reluctance, the jurisprudence of the Court has considered fundamental rights, and thus data protection more specifically, to be of clear importance since the adoption of the Lisbon Treaty and the designation of binding status on the Charter of the Fundamental Rights of the European Union (the Charter) in 2009.[36] However, the Charter has also brought its own conceptual challenges. Of particular importance here is Article 8 of the Charter, which recognizes the right to data protection as a fundamental right distinct from the right to respect for private and family life in Article 7. The development of the fundamental right to data protection as a separate right is an interesting historical progression, having been preceded by the Data Protection Directive 95/46/EC.[37] Indeed, in the Explanations to the Charter it is apparent that Article 8 of the Charter was adopted on the basis of a series of other instruments, in particular the Data Protection Directive 95/46/EC, the Council of Europe Convention 108,[38] and Article 8 ECHR.[39] Consequently, the boundaries between the rights to privacy

[35] As noted by Lynskey, the Court's hesitancy and lack of confidence in terms of the fundamental rights at the root of the Directive even brought the market integration objective into question in subsequent judgments. In assessing the balancing of data protection and privacy with other rights in cases such as Case C–73/07 *Tietosuojavaltuutettu v Satakunnan Markkinapörssi Oy and Satamedia Oy*, ECLI:EU:C:2008:727 and Case C–275/06 *Productores de Música de España (Promusicae) v Telefónica de España*, ECLI:EU:C:2008:54, the Court awarded a large degree of discretion to Member States in the application of this balancing exercise thereby endangering the market integration goal which had been key in the earlier case law. See Lynskey, The Foundations of EU Data Protection Law (n 30) 55–58.

[36] In particular, see eg Joined Cases C–92/09 and 93/09 *Volker und Markus Schecke GbR and Hartmut Eifert v Land Hessen*, ECLI:EU:C:2010:662. And other subsequent rulings, such as Case C–28/08 *Commission v The Bavarian Lager Co Ltd*, ECLI:EU:C:2010:378; Case C–131/12 *Google Spain SL and Google Inc v Agencia Española de Protección de Datos (AEPD) and Mario Costeja González*, ECLI:EU:C:2014:317; Joined Cases C–293/12 and 594/12 *Digital Rights Ireland Ltd v Minister for Communications, Marine and Natural Resources and Kärntner Landesregierung. Requests for a preliminary ruling from the High Court (Ireland) and the Verfassungsgerichtshof*, ECLI:EU:C:2014:238.

[37] Directive 95/46/EC (n 18).

[38] Guidelines on the Protection of Privacy and Transborder Flows (n 14); Convention 108 (n 14).

[39] Interestingly, the explanations also indicate that Directive 95/46/EC contains 'conditions and limitations for the exercise of the right to the protection of personal data'. As noted by González Fuster, this assertion is somewhat puzzling given the fact that Directive 95/46/EC was 'drafted in the pre-Charter era, when EU personal data protection was typically framed as serving in general the fundamental rights and freedoms of individuals (among which the right to personal data protection had yet to be identified), and in particular their right to privacy with respect to the processing of personal data'. Gloria González Fuster, 'Curtailing a Right in Flux: Restrictions of the Right to Personal Data Protection' in Artemi Rallo Lombarte and Rosario García Mahamut (eds), *Hacia un nuevo derecho europeo de protección de datos = Towards a New European Data Protection Regime* (Tirant lo Blanch 2015) 519.

and data protection are often blurred, reflecting constitutional traditions and the debate surrounding the development of data protection as a distinct right in the EU legal order (see Chapters 5 and 6).

Leaving these conceptual uncertainties to one side for now, put simply, the introduction of the Lisbon Treaty was a watershed moment for the protection of the fundamental right to data protection in the EU. Through the adoption of the Lisbon Treaty, the Charter was given binding force and, as a result, the right to data protection contained in Article 8 was recognized as a distinct, fully fledged right for the first time. The Treaty of Lisbon also includes Article 16 of the Treaty of the Functioning of the European Union, which provides a distinct basis for the adoption of legislation designed to provide protection to individuals with regard to the processing of their personal data, thereby providing a specific legislative basis for the adoption of the GDPR. The adoption of the GDPR has had a significant impact on the development of data protection globally. This impact has been direct, in terms of its transborder application, but also more indirect, as an influence on the reform of the law in other jurisdictions. It is therefore important to consider in detail its development as the high-water mark example of modernized data protection law.

2. The emergence of modernized data protection law

The GDPR aims to protect the right to data protection in particular but also rights and freedoms more generally where personal data are processed (Article 1(2) GDPR) reflecting the functionality of the Regulation in enabling fundamental rights protection.[40] The Regulation was therefore adopted with the Charter in mind and not merely the right to data protection, in that it aims to safeguard fundamental rights where personal data are processed. The GDPR, however, is also clearly designed to facilitate the functioning of the internal market. This internal market functioning objective, which was also evident in the old Data Protection Directive 95/46/EC, is therefore also a core objective of the GDPR. Indeed, in the explanatory memorandum to the European Commission's initial proposal, it was argued that although

[40] See Damian Clifford and Jef Ausloos, 'Data Protection and the Role of Fairness' [2018] Yearbook of European Law 1, 20–21. and the discussion by Manon Oostveen and Kristina Irion, 'The Golden Age of Personal Data: How to Regulate an Enabling Fundamental Right?' in Bakhoum and others (eds), *Personal Data in Competition, Consumer Protection and IP Law—Towards a Holistic Approach?* (Springer 2017) <https://papers.ssrn.com/abstract=2885701> accessed 20 January 2017.

the core features of Data Protection Directive 95/46/EC were sound, there were a number of practical issues affecting its effectiveness. In particular, the Commission highlighted how fragmentation in the implementation of the Directive was creating uncertainty for economic operators and public authorities and how the public's perception of the privacy risks associated with online activity were affecting trust and thus economic development. In the proposal's impact assessment, individuals' perceived lack of control was further referenced as a motivating factor behind the proposal.[41] Alleviating public fears about the potential misuse of personal data was therefore a key motivating factor behind the proposal and eventual adoption of the GDPR. The fears pointed out in the impact assessment hark back to those discussed above in Subsection B.1, in that they also clearly have an economic aspect: public fears lead to a lack of trust, the lack of trust leads to the failure to adopt new technologies, which in turn reduces economic growth and raises the concerns of businesses and government.[42]

Another important part of these developments was issue salience.[43] The timing of events certainly shaped the Regulation that would ultimately be adopted, with several authors pointing to the pivotal role played by the Snowden revelations during June 2013 in the adoption of more robust protections.[44] These leaks brought the GDPR to the public's attention in a way that the reform of the data protection framework might otherwise not have done.[45]

[41] eg it was noted that '[i]ndividuals limit their use of new technologies, particularly the internet and online services, because of lack of trust in the digital environment and fears about possible misuse of their personal data. Those not benefitting from ICT because of fears over data protection lose out in terms of price benefits online and in time taken to access goods and services.' European Commission, 'Commission Staff Working Paper Impact Assessment Accompanying the Document Regulation of the European Parliament and of the Council on the Protection of Individuals with Regard to the Processing of Personal Data and on the Free Movement of Such Data (General Data Protection Regulation) and Directive of the European Parliament and of the Council on the Prosecution of Criminal Offences or the Execution of Criminal Penalties, and the Free Movement of Such Data, SEC(2012)72' 29 <https://ec.europa.eu/transparency/documents-register/detail?ref=COM(2012)11&lang=en> accessed 4 October 2023.

[42] See ibid.

[43] See generally George Christou and Imir Rashid, 'Interest Group Lobbying in the European Union: Privacy, Data Protection and the Right to Be Forgotten' (2021) 19 Comparative European Politics 380.

[44] See Agustín Rossi, 'How the Snowden Revelations Saved the EU General Data Protection Regulation' (2018) 53 The International Spectator 95; Moritz Laurer and Timo Seidl, 'Regulating the European Data-Driven Economy: A Case Study on the General Data Protection Regulation' (2021) 13 Policy & Internet 257.

[45] For a discussion, see generally 'Analysis | Today, a New E.U. Law Transforms Privacy Rights for Everyone. Without Edward Snowden, It Might Never Have Happened' *Washington Post* (7 December 2021) <www.washingtonpost.com/news/monkey-cage/wp/2018/05/25/today-a-new-eu-law-transforms-privacy-rights-for-everyone-without-edward-snowden-it-might-never-have-happened/> accessed 18 June 2023.

Empirical research[46] and discourse network analysis-based research,[47] for instance, have both been relied on to suggest that there was a marked point of departure in policymakers' positions following the Snowden revelations, due to issue salience and thus the prominence given to the scandal in the mainstream media. Similar to when the first data protection laws emerged, therefore the publication of alarmist material was also an important catalyst in the development of the Regulation. This altered the political debate and the balance of power between stakeholders, as civil society activists were essentially given the tools to counter the lobbying interests and, crucially, Member States such as Germany and France were in the pro-GDPR camp, driven by public pressure in the respective countries.[48] Timing, therefore, appears to have been significant in the shaping of EU policymakers' attitudes to the reform process. These developments, and in particular the Snowden revelations, have also fundamentally changed the way international data transfers are perceived in the EU.

The zeitgeist of this period was captured well by the judgment of Hogan J in the Irish High Court in his ruling in the original case brought by Max Schrems against the Irish Data Protection Commission. In that case, Schrems argued that the Commissioner should have exercised his powers to prevent Facebook from transferring his personal data to Facebook's parent company in the US, with Hogan J describing the Snowden revelations which formed the backdrop for the complaint as having 'caused a sensation'.[49] We are still experiencing the effects of this sensation. There is a seemingly never-ending back-and-forth between EU and US diplomats (and the EU Court of Justice) regarding the legitimacy of such data transfers due to the perceived inadequacy of protections in the US and the broad-scale national security powers that exist, allowing for the accessing of the transferred personal data. These ongoing problems, and the adoption of the GDPR as a specific example, have led some scholars to again question whether the EU is being steered by economic protectionist motivations as opposed to concerns regarding data protection and/or privacy.[50] Certainly, the EU requires adherence to their rules to access its market, and the GDPR has been seen by many as a global standard. Indeed, in this respect, reference can be made to the literature exploring the so-called 'Brussels effect' and hence the influence of the GDPR as an EU legislative mechanism on the laws of

[46] See Rossi (n 44).
[47] See Laurer and Seidl (n 44).
[48] See ibid.
[49] Case C-362/14 *Maximillian Schrems v Data Protection Commissioner*, ECLI:EU:C:2015:650, para 1.
[50] See Bygrave, *Data Protection Law* (n 4) 112–15.

other jurisdictions.[51] Other scholars have questioned the economic impact of these protections, but again this is not a new argument.[52]

Even since the adoption of the GDPR, however, there has been a swell of news reports, blogs, documentaries, and works of fiction in cinema and literature that have raised the challenges posed for our society by the emergence of digital technologies. This material has been fuelled by our increasing reliance on technology but also by various scandals. Reference here can be made to examples such as the now infamous Facebook 'emotional contagion' experiment, which involved the manipulation of users' newsfeeds to assess whether Facebook posts with emotional content were more engaging and whether changes in emotional state could be transferred indirectly between individuals.[53] More specifically, amongst other things, the researchers showed users fewer positive posts in order to see whether there would be a corresponding increase in user expressions of sadness. The study sparked a fierce debate in the mainstream media coverage, largely framed in terms of research ethics and the blurring lines separating the realms of academic and commercial research.[54]

The emotional contagion example stoked people's fears and there are many other examples we can draw upon. Indeed, even if we only take the examples of where developments in Emotional Artificial Intelligence (E-AI)—which will be used in Chapters 3–5 as a case study—entered the public consciousness, we get a good sense of the anxiety raised by technology and the role of regulation as a response. Reference here can be made to the leaked Facebook document reported in *The Australian* regarding the gathering of psychological insights and the targeting of insecure youths with 'vulnerable' moods in Australia and New Zealand,[55] but also the Facebook-Cambridge Analytica

[51] Anu Bradford, *The Brussels Effect: How the European Union Rules the World* (OUP 2020) 131–69.

[52] For a review of GDPR related literature, see Garrett Johnson, 'Economic Research on Privacy Regulation: Lessons from the GDPR and Beyond' (15 June 2023) <https://papers.ssrn.com/abstract=4290849> accessed 19 June 2023.

[53] See eg Adam DI Kramer, Jamie E Guillory, and Jeffrey T Hancock, 'Experimental Evidence of Massive-Scale Emotional Contagion through Social Networks' (2014) 111 Proceedings of the National Academy of Sciences 8788.

[54] Kashmir Hill, 'Facebook Manipulated 689,003 Users' Emotions For Science' *Forbes* (28 June 2014) <www.forbes.com/sites/kashmirhill/2014/06/28/facebook-manipulated-689003-users-emotions-for-science/> accessed 28 September 2023.

[55] Sam Levin, 'Facebook Told Advertisers It Can Identify Teens Feeling "Insecure" and "Worthless"' *The Guardian* (1 May 2017) <www.theguardian.com/technology/2017/may/01/facebook-advertising-data-insecure-teens> accessed 29 August 2017; Olivia Solon, '"This Oversteps a Boundary": Teenagers Perturbed by Facebook Surveillance' *The Guardian* (2 May 2017) <www.theguardian.com/technology/2017/may/02/facebook-surveillance-tech-ethics> accessed 29 August 2017;'Facebook Research Targeted Insecure Youth, Leaked Documents Show' *The Independent* (1 May 2017) <www.independent.co.uk/news/media/facebook-leaked-documents-research-targeted-insecure-youth-teenagers-vulnerable-moods-advertising-a7711551.html> accessed 29 August 2017.

scandal,[56] where data analytics was used to gauge the personalities of voters and nudge them towards certain viewpoints. Examples such as these have fed into the policy debates not only in Europe but also in other jurisdictions. Reference can be made, for instance, to the developments in certain states in the US, where consumer data protection legislation has been adopted in the absence of similar laws at the federal level. More specifically, the preamble to the California Consumer Privacy Act, for instance, refers explicitly to the Cambridge Analytica scandal and how it highlighted the desire for privacy and control over personal information.[57] Such examples further underline that it is our sense that we have lost control of our personal data that plays a significant part in the adoption of data protection laws.[58]

C. Anxiety and Data Protection's Complexity

Data protection can therefore be understood, at least partly, as a response to the fears examined in the previous section. People are concerned about the intensive data processing taking place, and data protection law or its reform is often presented as the solution to these problems. Although concern regarding intensive data processing fuelled the moves towards the adoption of frameworks, their adoption has also led to significant industry anxiety, given their perceived complexity. This is despite the fact that the basic structure of data protection law has remained the same since its beginnings.[59] As such, although the GDPR, for example, certainly introduced some updates, the essence of the data protection edifice has remained constant for decades and, at least on paper, straightforward in terms of its division of rights and responsibilities.[60] The novelty of frameworks such as the GDPR is therefore perhaps somewhat overstated at times. It would however be misleading to suggest that nothing has changed in practice.

Although the division of rights and responsibilities in such frameworks may seem simple, data protection law is certainly complex. This complexity

[56] Here one can refer in particular to *The Guardian*'s coverage of this story, see 'The Cambridge Analytica Files' *The Guardian* <www.theguardian.com/news/series/cambridge-analytica-files> accessed 4 October 2023.

[57] See California Consumer Privacy Act of 2018.

[58] See Kaminski (n 29).

[59] Paul De Hert and Vagelis Papakonstantinou, 'The Proposed Data Protection Regulation Replacing Directive 95/46/EC: A Sound System for the Protection of Individuals' (2012) 28 Computer Law & Security Review 130.

[60] ibid 130–42.

has caused a certain degree of anxiety for those tasked with compliance with the GDPR, and the lead-up to its entry into force, a clear example in this regard. As I will explain in this section, complexity has always been, and indeed will always be, intrinsic to data protection law. Nevertheless, the moves towards strong (or at least stronger) enforcement and the significant criticisms of data protection law as anachronistic and a relic incapable of appropriately regulating modern technological developments must also be considered. The purpose of this section is to explore data protection law's complexity with reference to what constitutes a data protection law, in terms of core definitions, principles, and rights, by demonstrating the similarities across the key exemplars internationally in order to establish a common understanding while also showing variations. The analysis will highlight (1) the room for complexity and comparative variation, and (2) the gradual adoption of increasingly robust data protection laws.

1. Definitions, principles, and rights

Data subjects are provided with certain rights while those processing personal data are obliged to comply with rules and apply principles. Although there is considerable variation, data protection laws often refer to at least two entities: the controller or the one processing the personal data, and the data subject, the identified or identifiable natural person to whom the data relate. It is therefore important to (a) understand these categories in order to better understand (b) the nature of principles, rules and rights provided for in data protection law.

(a) Controllers and data subjects

In both Convention 108 and the OECD Guidelines, for example, those responsible for compliance are defined as 'controllers'—'controller of the file' in the Convention[61] and 'data controller' in the Guidelines.[62] Although the definitions vary in terms of the precise language used, both refer to those entities which have the power to decide on the purposes/uses of the personal data but also the means relied upon. The key difference between the definitions relates to the fact that the OECD Guidelines leave it to national law to decide which

[61] Convention 108 (n 14) art 2(d).
[62] Guidelines on the Protection of Privacy and Transborder Flows, para 1(a).

entities can come within the scope of the definition whereas the Convention states that the definition includes 'natural or legal persons, public authorities, agencies or any other bodies competent according to national law'.[63]

A controller is defined in Article 4(7) of the GDPR as the natural or legal person 'which, alone or jointly with others, determines the purposes and means of the processing of personal data' and a processor, per Article 4(8) of the GDPR, refers to any natural or legal person 'which processes personal data on behalf of the controller'. In simple terms, processors always act on behalf of the controller and must only process personal data when and if they receive instructions from the controller. Hence, the controller is the key entity in the framework who must comply with the substantial provisions of the Regulation. The definition of a controller in the GDPR comprises three main elements. First, it states that a controller can be acting alone or together with some other person(s), thereby indicating the potential for co-controllers.[64] Secondly, the GDPR refers to the fact that the controller is the one who 'determines' and is therefore the decision-maker.[65] Thirdly, and building on the previous point, the controller's determination relates to the 'means and purpose(s)' of the processing and, therefore, the why and how personal data are processed. There is a certain degree of flexibility in this element, however, in that the controller may for instance delegate the technical and organizational means to a processor. Interestingly, in the updating of Convention 108, Convention 108 + has replaced 'controller of the file' with 'data controller' and has also added a definition of a processor that mirrors the one in the GDPR.

The existence of a processor therefore depends on whether the controller decides to entrust some aspect (whether very specific or comprehensive) of the processing activities to an external entity.[66] Importantly, however, processors always act on behalf of the controller and thus the processor must only process personal data when and if it receives instructions from the controller. Because of its secondary role, the processor's responsibility will be lower—the controller remains the principal responsible entity. If a processor goes beyond what it has agreed to with the controller it will acquire a relevant role in determining the

[63] Convention 108 (n 14) art 2(d).

[64] Joint controllers then share the subsequent responsibility and reference can also be made to art 24, which states that where there are two or more controllers jointly determining the purposes and means they are to be considered joint controllers.

[65] Article 29 Working Party, 'Opinion 1/2010 on the concepts of "controller" and "processor" ' (2010) WP 169 13 <https://ec.europa.eu/justice/article-29/documentation/opinion-recommendation/files/2010/wp169_en.pdf> accessed 20 December 2023.

[66] ibid 1.

purposes and means of the processing.[67] In such circumstances, the processor will then become a controller in its own right and will therefore be required to comply with the more stringent requirements for controllers. The boundary between a controller and a processor is therefore a porous one that refers to the particular context to determine what obligations apply (ie those of a controller or of a processor).

In contrast to the European instruments, the Australian Privacy Act 1988 (Cth) for instance, which was heavily influenced by the OECD Guidelines, applies to 'APP entities'. The definition of APP (Australian Privacy Principles) entities includes both the public and private sectors—albeit with certain exemptions for, inter alia, small businesses. However, there is a proposal to divide APP entities into APP entity controllers and APP entity processors.[68] In contrast, the Singaporean Personal Data Protection Act 2012 (PDPA) applies to 'organizations' which is defined only in terms of the private sector.[69] And another alternative is evident in the state consumer data protection laws in the US, where the California Consumer Privacy Act, for example, applies to a 'business that controls the collection' either for its own purposes or as a third party.[70] There is also a qualified exclusion for small businesses and, of course, the Californian Act only applies to the private sector.[71] The other US State consumer privacy laws that have been adopted refer to the notion of a controller specifically but also contain similar exclusions for small businesses and only apply to the private sector.[72]

These controllers (or APP entities, businesses, etc) then owe their obligations to data subjects, the natural persons to whom the personal data relate. For instance, both the OECD Guidelines and Convention 108 define personal data as 'any information relating to an identified or identifiable individual ("data subject")' and this reflects the dominant focus of data protection laws generally.[73] However, it should be noted that in certain jurisdictions alternatives are used, such as in the state consumer data protection laws adopted in the US, which rely on the term 'consumer' reflecting the narrower focus of this

[67] ibid 25.

[68] See proposal 22.1: 'Government Response to the Privacy Act Review Report' (Australian Government 2023) <www.ag.gov.au/rights-and-protections/publications/government-response-privacy-act-review-report> accessed 4 October 2023.

[69] See Personal Data Protection Act 2012, ss 2(1) and 4.

[70] California Consumer Privacy Act of 2018, s 1798.100.

[71] See California Consumer Privacy Act of 2018.

[72] See Virginia Consumer Data Protection Act (2021), Utah Consumer Privacy Act (2022), Texas Data Privacy and Security Act (2023), Tennessee Information Protection Act (2023), Montana Consumer Data Privacy Act (2023), Iowa Consumer Data Protection Act (2023), Indiana Consumer Data Protection Act (2023), Connecticut Data Privacy Act (2022), and Colorado Privacy Act (2021).

[73] See Bygrave, *Data Privacy Law* (n 19) 139–40.

legislation.[74] Although the data subject or consumer is a key actor in data protection law, they often remain undefined. It is generally assumed, however, that these individuals are natural persons presumed capable of being active market participants and thus acting rationally in their own self-interest.[75] As will be explored in detail in Chapter 4, this has been the focus of significant criticism, which questions data subjects' important role in protecting their own interests.

(b) Process and outcome

There are therefore certain similarities and these also manifest themselves in the principles, requirements, and rights provided in these laws. When processing personal data, controllers are required to comply with certain principles (ie the FIPPs) and data subjects are afforded certain rights. From the perspective of the data subject, for instance, in an *ex post* sense control rights are a particularly important example of data protection law's checks and balances. And, *ex ante*, the key accountability mechanisms that have developed in some jurisdictions, such as data protection/privacy by design and by default and impact assessments, are therefore seen as key to safeguarding the rights and interests of data subjects.[76] These aspects of data protection frameworks will be explored in detail in Chapters 4 and 5 but, generally, there is significant similarity and there has been a noticeable trend in moves towards the bolstering of these protections. This is reflected in particular in the expansion of the control rights provided to the data subject.[77]

The principles play an important role in anchoring the requirements and rights provided[78] and owe their origins to the development of the FIPPs at the national level and the adoption of variations of these in instruments such as the OECD Guidelines and the Council of Europe's Convention 108 in particular. Versions of the FIPPs have since proliferated. Although significant differences are evident

[74] See Virginia Consumer Data Protection Act (2021), Utah Consumer Privacy Act (2022), Texas Data Privacy and Security Act (2023), Tennessee Information Protection Act (2023), Montana Consumer Data Privacy Act (2023), Iowa Consumer Data Protection Act (2023), Indiana Consumer Data Protection Act (2023), Connecticut Data Privacy Act (2022), Colorado Privacy Act (2021), and California Consumer Privacy Act of 2018.

[75] For a discussion of who the data subject is and a proposal for a vulnerability-aware conceptualization of the data subject, see Gianclaudio Malgieri, *Vulnerability and Data Protection Law* (OUP 2023).

[76] See Damian Clifford, 'Citizen-Consumers in a Personalised Galaxy: Emotion Influenced Decision-Making, A True Path to the Dark Side?' in Lilian Edwards, Burkhard Schafer, and Edina Harbinja (eds), *Emerging Technology, Regulation and Ethics* (1st edn, Edinburgh University Press 2020).

[77] For a discussion, see Daniel Solove, 'The Limitations of Privacy Rights' (2023) 98 Notre Dame Law Review 975.

[78] Karen Yeung and Lee A Bygrave, 'Demystifying the Modernized European Data Protection Regime: Cross-Disciplinary Insights from Legal and Regulatory Governance Scholarship' (2022) 16 Regulation & Governance 137, 139.

across jurisdictions,[79] some of the key principles evident in major international instruments are substantively very similar. Some of these principles have been analysed extensively in the literature whereas others have remained more at the fringes. For instance, in particular, purpose limitation, which prohibits the processing of personal data in a way incompatible with the specified purposes, preventing the reuse of personal data for later defined purposes, and data minimization, which requires controllers to strictly limit the gathering of personal data to that necessary for the purpose pursued by the processing, have been subject to extensive critical analysis.[80] The data security principle common across these frameworks has also been extensively analysed, particularly in light of the significant challenges posed to security and the high-profile data breaches in recent years.[81] In contrast, the accuracy principle, which requires that personal data should be accurate and if necessary updated, has been largely ignored (at least in recent years), with only passing references in literature and guidance documents.[82]

In analysing the application of data protection principles, it must also be noted that they are rather unusual in nature. Indeed, as analysed by Yeung and Bygrave, the principles demonstrate aspects of being both outcome- and process-based in character.[83] Outcome-based principles offer flexibility by affording the regulated entity freedom to decide on how to comply with the legislative objective, whereas process-based principles focus more precisely on the steps taken. There are clearly restrictions on how personal data must be processed demonstrating the process-based focus (eg data minimization, purpose limitation, and accuracy) but also an outcome-based approach is indicated by other principles (eg data security). Data protection law is thus characterized by dynamic and open-textured notions with the application (and the impact of its rules) and principles being dependent on the circumstances.

Although it is widely accepted that data protection law is complex, there are a variety of aspects to this complexity that are often mixed together. I believe that

[79] eg the GDPR provides for a list of principles in Article 5, with these principles then playing an overarching role in the application of the framework and, essentially, in guiding the controller's but also the processor's interpretation of the rights and obligations contained in the Regulation's other provisions. In contrast, the Australian Privacy Act (Cth) 1988, for instance, provides the Australian Privacy Principles (APPs), but many of these more closely resemble rules or at least are an amalgam of provisions found in other parts of the GDPR for instance. Another alternative is evident in the California Consumer Privacy Act, where there is no explicit list of principles included but there is still evidence of them implicitly. The point, therefore, is that there is significant variation despite the commonalities.

[80] See Tal Z Zarsky, 'Incompatible: The GDPR in the Age of Big Data' (2017) 47 Seton Hall Law Review 2.

[81] See Daniel J Solove and Woodrow Hartzog, *Breached!: Why Data Security Law Fails and How to Improve It* (OUP 2022).

[82] See Dara Hallinan and Frederik Zuiderveen Borgesius, 'Opinions Can Be Incorrect (in Our Opinion)! On Data Protection Law's Accuracy Principle' (2020) 10 International Data Privacy Law 1.

[83] Yeung and Bygrave (n 78) 139–40.

complexity in data protection law manifests itself in terms of (1) the law's rules and standards, but also (2) its regulatory practices, in the sense that compliance is also informed by standards and best practices and characterized by a mix of regulatory techniques. These two points will now be analysed.

2. Complexity (and uncertainty)

To a certain extent data protection law will always be complex, reflecting the rather obvious point that it regulates a variety of interests, technologies, and structures. However, open-texture notions such as 'risk' in particular certainly add to its complexity. This reflects the controller's role in complying, and therefore mitigating, any risks through for instance an impact assessment where 'high-risk' processing is often used as a threshold standard. Although risk has always been important in data protection law, as will be described in Chapter 5, the GDPR, for instance, is an example of a risk-based legislative framework.[84] Risk, however, remains an open concept, the general absence of a comprehensive taxonomy of risks in data protection laws being justified by the fact that 'risk' is to be understood broadly to include societal effects and potential as well as actual harms.[85] The role of controllers in the assessment of risk, the question marks surrounding the capacity of risk-based approaches to cater for intangible harms, and also the extent to which the risk-based approach applies and has an impact across data protection law frameworks (in particular in relation to control rights),[86] means that reliance on the effective operation of accountability mechanisms is questionable.[87] Accordingly, such examples arguably increase the complexity of data protection law.

[84] Article 29 Working Party, 'Statement on the role of a risk-based approach in data protection legal frameworks' (2014) WP 218; Raphaël Gellert, 'Understanding the Notion of Risk in the General Data Protection Regulation' (2018) 34 Computer Law & Security Review 279; Claudia Quelle, 'The "Risk Revolution" in EU Data Protection Law: We Can't Have Our Cake and Eat It, Too' in Ronald Leenes and others (eds), *Data Protection and Privacy: The Age of Intelligent Machines* (1st edn, Hart 2017); Raphaël Gellert, *The Risk-Based Approach to Data Protection* (OUP 2020).

[85] Article 29 Working Party, 'Statement' (n 84) 4.

[86] On the GDPR specifically, see Quelle (n 84).

[87] Importantly, a risk-based approach needs to be distinguished from risk as a threshold for application. See Peter Hustinx, 'EU Data Protection Law: The Review of Directive 95/46 EC and the Proposed General Data Protection Regulation' (2014) 20, 38 <https://edps.europa.eu/data-protection/our-work/publications/speeches-articles/eu-data-protection-law-review-directive_en> accessed 4 October 2023. See also the WP29's observation that:

> It is important to note that—even with the adoption of a risk-based approach—there is no question of the rights of individuals being weakened in respect of their personal data. Those rights must be just as strong even if the processing in question is relatively 'low risk'. Rather, the scalability of legal obligations based on risk addresses compliance mechanisms. This

The highly interwoven dependencies between the different parts of data protection law add to the complexity. This complexity, however, is then compounded by the fact that, more broadly, there are also rather open-textured principles that are often positioned as key in the interpretation and thus the application of data protection law. For example, to use a complementary but different example, despite the key positioning of lawfulness, fairness, and transparency as principles in the GDPR, when viewing Article 5(1)(a) in isolation it is unclear whether this provision was intended as one principle (ie the 'lawfulness, fairness, and transparency' principle), or two (ie lawfulness and transparency to be viewed through the lens of an overarching notion of fairness) or indeed three distinct principles. Although from a detailed reading of the Regulation it appears uncontroversial to suggest that Article 5(1)(a) stipulates three distinct (albeit inherently interwoven) principles, this requires a detailed reading and understanding.[88] As will be explained in more detail in Chapter 5, there is certainly a strong overlap between the principles and I believe that this reflects the significance of fairness in particular as a rather open-textured principle that goes to the heart of the framework.

Fairness is a rather elusive notion in data protection law; it appears to have a rather process-orientated meaning in some jurisdictions and a far more substantive or outcome-driven meaning in others, seemingly connected with the desire to safeguard fundamental rights.[89] However, as will be explored in Chapter 5, the focus on this substantive notion of fairness also raises important questions regarding the legitimacy and coherence of the risk-based approach. This example is thus illustrative of how seemingly simple parts of data protection law demonstrate complexity under scrutiny and this reflects the fact that the operationalization of these principles is further complicated by the fact that data protection law often relies on different regulatory techniques. Modern

> means that a data controller whose processing is relatively low risk may not have to do as much to comply with its legal obligations as a data controller whose processing is high-risk.

Article 29 Working Party, 'Statement' (n 84) 2.

[88] eg Recital 60 states that '[t]he principles of fair and transparent processing require that the data subject be informed of the existence of the processing operation and its purposes', thus clearly referring to principles in the plural and thereby indicating that fairness, transparency, and (seemingly also) lawfulness are distinct.

[89] eg Kaminski describes the FIPPs in the US as providing for a kind of due process. See Kaminski (n 29) 386. This contrasts sharply with the more substantive aspect to the notion of fairness found in the GDPR and Convention 108 + for example. See Gianclaudio Malgieri, 'The Concept of Fairness in the GDPR: A Linguistic and Contextual Interpretation' ('FAT* 20: Proceedings of the 2020 Conference on Fairness, Accountability, and Transparency, January 2020) 154 <https://doi.org/10.1145/3351095.3372868>, accessed 1 December 2023.

data protection laws such as the GDPR are often characterized by a mix of command and control, design-based, and meta-regulatory techniques.[90] Indeed, although data protection laws are generally characterized by rules that must be complied with, there has been a steady move towards requiring privacy/data protection by design and obliging controllers to conduct impact assessments within these legislative frameworks. Privacy/data protection by design effectively requires controllers to embed the FIPPs and thus to 'hard wire' data protection norms into the development of information systems.[91] Impact assessments are an important part of this process and essentially require controllers to consider the impact of higher risk processing. These requirements demonstrate the potential role of the controller, in that active participation of the regulated entity is inherent to these requirements even if they are backed by legislative authority.[92] This reflects the outcome-based aspect to the FIPPs but also the meta-regulatory strategies employed whereby the legislation does not prescribe how controllers should comply but instead obliges them to develop their own compliance systems stemming from a duty to conduct an impact assessment, for example.[93] These accountability mechanisms will be explored in Chapter 5 but, generally, the point is that the complexity of data protection law is often compounded by the fact that controllers are left to decipher their context-dependent responsibilities, thereby demonstrating the law's complex regulatory practices.

To illustrate both aspects with an example, we can refer to the delineation between personal and non-personal data and, more specifically, the uncertainty surrounding the notion of anonymous data as a type of non-personal data in order to tease out the two different aspects of data protection law's complexity highlighted. Indeed, as will be explored in more detail in Chapter 3, delineating between personal and non-personal and/or anonymous data is a significant challenge in practice. To clarify, it is obvious but worth emphasizing that data protection laws regulate the processing/collection of *personal data* and not all forms of information. Personal data is generally defined in terms of the 'identifiability' of the data subject. There are therefore types of information such as geospatial or weather data that are clearly non-personal. Even leaving aside the differences across jurisdictions that will be analysed in Chapter 3, however, there are significant complexities associated with the practical implementation of the anonymization process. There is an extensive body of research

[90] Yeung and Bygrave (n 78) 141–42.
[91] ibid 141.
[92] ibid.
[93] ibid 142.

questioning the utility of designing laws for the protection of personal data.[94] As technology is constantly changing, data previously considered to have been anonymized may effectively become personal in the future due to developments, technological or otherwise.[95] This example illustrates the potential complexity of data protection law's rules and standards in that it is hard to determine what 'identifiability' means in practice. It also demonstrates the practical limitations of anonymization, a narrow definition of personal data, and thus the significant issues with implementation and establishing best practice.

The key role played by those processing the personal data further illustrates the complexity of the regulatory practices in that, since enforcement authorities are incapable of effectively monitoring these practices and instead appear only to intervene when an obvious violation comes to light, there are thus clear complexities in determining the regulatory impact of the requirements provided. In short, much depends on how controllers conduct their impact assessments (if required under the law of the relevant jurisdiction) and additionally, how the significant variation in the quality of the templates and standards used affects this process.[96] A critical point then is that in addition to data protection laws there is a complex web of standards and norms that shape the application of the law and best practice. There are also competing normative or conceptual values that have led to the development of data protection law in different jurisdictions, and these also shape its interpretation. It is the contestation between these values that leads to the variations in approach that will be outlined in the later chapters of this book and thus the differences evident in data protection laws and the standards and best practices that inform their application. Part of the challenge in analysing data protection law and making comparisons between different jurisdictions is that there are significant variations despite the obvious similarities. This challenge is compounded by the fact that the technologies, services, business models, and the entities being regulated by data protection laws etc are obviously complex and require context-dependent assessments and nuanced applications of a controller's various processing operations. What is also obvious (and as will become more so through the analysis in Chapters 3–5 in particular) is that it is debatable whether more (in the sense of more protections) and stricter (in the sense of preserving an individual's

[94] See Chris Culnane and Kobi Leins, 'Misconceptions in Privacy Protection and Regulation' (2019) 36 Law in Context. A Socio-legal Journal 49.

[95] This point is made more significant when one considers the fact that in the GDPR, for instance, a third party may hold the information that may render a natural person identifiable. See Case C–582/14 *Breyer*, ECLI: EU:C:2016:779.

[96] See Lorenzo Dalla Corte and Rosamunde Elise Van Brakel, *Data Protection Impact Assessment Methods for the Urban Environment* (Tilburg Institute for Law, Technology and Society 2022).

interest in their personal data) legislative frameworks are always better and, in this regard, it is important to highlight the significant criticisms of data protection law.

Certainly, there are question marks as to the ongoing suitability of the anonymous–personal data division as the basis for regulation,[97] this debate being fuelled by a number of successful re-identifications.[98] In addition, data gathering in the big data environment often appears to be almost inherently in contradiction with the data minimization and purpose limitation principles, given that data are often gathered in an unrestricted manner for unspecified purposes and then mined for useful commercial applications.[99] These suggested failings highlight the potential for function creep and the repurposing of personal data.[100] Data security is also gradually becoming more difficult due to the increasing number of sophisticated cyber-attacks and high-profile data breaches.

There are therefore obvious issues. Indeed, even the definitions of controller and processor, the key actors tasked with compliance in the GDPR and Convention 108 +, for example, have caused confusion. More specifically, and arguably, the simple dichotomy between the notions of 'controller' and 'processor' provided for in legislation and described in guidance fails to account for the complexity of the relationship, rendering the obligations unclear for those trying to comply, with the guidance literature actually then adding to the complexity rather than providing clarity with this being a particular point of contention in the EU specifically.[101] Indeed, the separation between these actors

[97] Paul Ohm, 'Broken Promises of Privacy: Responding to the Surprising Failure of Anonymization' [2010] UCLA Law Review 1701; Ira S Rubinstein and Woodrow Hartzog, 'Anonymization and Risk' (2016) 91 Washington Law Review 703.

[98] See eg Latanya Sweeney, 'Simple Demographics Often Identify People Uniquely' (2000) Carnegie Mellon University, Data Privacy Working Paper 34; Latanya Sweeney, Akua Abu, and Julia Winn, *Identifying Participants in the Personal Genome Project by Name* (White Paper, 2013) <http://datapri vacylab.org/projects/pgp/> accessed 4 October 2023; Yves-Alexandre de Montjoye and others, 'Unique in the Shopping Mall: On the Reidentifiability of Credit Card Metadata' (2015) 347 Science 536; Arvind Narayanan and Vitaly Shmatikov, 'Robust De-Anonymization of Large Sparse Datasets' (Proceedings of the 2008 IEEE Symposium on Security and Privacy) <https://doi.org/10.1109/SP.2008.33> accessed 22 November 2018.

[99] Valerie Verdoodt, Damian Clifford, and Eva Lievens, 'Toying with Children's Emotions, the New Game in Town? The Legality of Advergames in the EU' (2016) 32 Computer Law & Security Review 599.

[100] Michael Curry, David Phillips, and Priscilla Regan, 'Emergency Response Systems and the Creeping Legibility of People and Places' (2004) 20 Information Society 357, 362. Function creep relates to a situation 'when a system developed for a particular purpose comes to be used for, or to provide the underpinnings for other systems that are used for, different purposes'. Bert-Jaap Koops, 'On Decision Transparency, or How to Enhance Data Protection after the Computational Turn' in Mireille Hildebrandt and Katja de Vries (eds), *Privacy, Due Process and the Computational Turn: The Philosophy of Law Meets the Philosophy of Technology* (Routledge 2013) 198; Bert-Jaap Koops, 'The Concept of Function Creep' (2020) Social Science Research Network Scholarly Paper ID 3547903 <https://papers. ssrn.com/abstract=3547903> accessed 16 October 2020.

[101] See René Mahieu, Joris van Hoboken, and Hadi Asghari, 'Responsibility for Data Protection in a Networked World: On the Question of the Controller, "Effective and Complete Protection" and Its

has been a source of confusion and, therefore, anxiety[102] and a clear point of contention in the academic literature and case law.[103] And, as a final example, as indicated at various points already, there has been a seemingly consistent line of criticism critiquing the role of data subjects on the basis of their perceived incapacity to act in their own best interests and the significant importance attached to their active participation in the protections afforded by data protection law.

The uncertainties and complexities created by these issues have not only caused anxiety amongst those having to comply with the data protection law, but also frustration. There is frustration with the open-textured nature of some aspects of the law, its complexity, and thus the associated costs of compliance. In certain quarters there has also been frustration with data protection's failure to have the immediate impact that some had expected and also with its unanticipated effects. In the next section, I will leave the frustrations of those having to comply with data protection law to one side and turn instead to the frustrations associated with data protection law's effectiveness, or lack thereof, and what that might mean going forward in light of the critiques of data protection law.

D. Frustration and Data Protection's Limitations

An optimistic account of the role and significance of data protection law often still points to the need for greater enforcement. The importance of a properly funded DPA with the capacity to generate meaningful change is a constant

Application to Data Access Rights in Europe' (2019) 10 Journal of Intellectual Property, Information Technology and Electronic Commerce Law<www.jipitec.eu/issues/jipitec-10-1-2019/4879> accessed 4 October 2023.

[102] See eg Jessica Davies, 'WTF Is a Data Controller vs. Data Processor?' (*Digiday*, 22 July 2019) <https://digiday.com/media/ico-wants-to-shed-light-on-data-sharing-between-businesses-under-gdpr/> accessed 18 June 2023.

[103] eg the EU Court of Justice has repeatedly stated the need to interpret the definition of a controller broadly to ensure a high level of protection for data subjects. Consequently, there is a very low threshold to be considered a joint controller, but this has raised significant problems with scholarship highlighting scenarios where compliance is effectively impossible for a joint controller. This criticism is in part linked to the fact that the Court has effectively established that even when you do not have access to personal data or have a very limited capacity to determine the means of the processing (eg you simply make the decision to use a particular platform), you may still be considered a joint controller if you determine the purposes of the processing. Case C–2010/16 *Wirtschaftsakademie Schleswig-Holstein*, ECLI:EU:C:2018:388; Case C–25/17 *Jehovan todistajat*, ECLI:EU:C:2018:551; Case C–40/17 *Fashion ID*, ECLI:EU:C:2019:62. For a discussion, see Mahieu, van Hoboken, and Asghari (n 101); Michèle Finck, 'Cobwebs of Control: The Two Imaginations of the Data Controller in EU Law' (2021) 11 International Data Privacy Law 333.

discussion point in the effectiveness and reform of data protection laws. For example, the potential enforcement of the modernized data protection laws has caused significant anxiety amongst those processing personal data. The GDPR in particular has raised significant concerns for industry. Countless media reports have been published on the levels of the fines which may be imposed under the rules and the feared impact on data subject trust of a breach of the rules.[104] Principles and requirements that were long part of EU law under the former Data Protection Directive 95/46/EC (and indeed, data protection more broadly) were also suddenly being presented as important developments.

During the Regulation's two-year transition period, companies made significant changes to their business models, with multinational businesses reported as having made global changes in response to the Regulation rather than creating different systems.[105] Certain scholars have pointed to this as a potential overreach of these frameworks[106] but of course transborder data flows have been the focus of data protection frameworks for some time.[107] Despite the length of the transition period, there was a palpable sense of anxiety amongst businesses leading up to its taking effect, this being strongly linked to the perceived complexity of the framework. On the day that the GDPR entered into force, a series of complaints were made to the national DPAs.[108] In contrast to this anxiety amongst businesses, there was a clear sense of optimism amongst civil society actors and academics as to the Regulation's capacity to institutionalize change. An important part of this was the potential for high-level fines under the Regulation.[109] As time went by, and individuals were left waiting for

[104] See 'What GDPR Means for Businesses Outside Europe' (*Quartz*, 22 May 2018) <https://qz.com/1284895/what-gdpr-compliance-means-for-american-businesses> accessed 19 June 2023; Davies (n 102); Jill Petzinger, 'The Genius of GDPR Is That It Forces Companies to Police Each Other' (*Quartz*, 1 June 2018) <https://qz.com/1293402/the-genius-of-gdpr-is-that-it-forces-companies-to-police-each-other> accessed 19 June 2023.

[105] See eg Nitasha Tiku, 'How Europe's New Privacy Law Will Change the Web, and More' *Wired* (19 March 2018) <www.wired.com/story/europes-new-privacy-law-will-change-the-web-and-more/> accessed 19 June 2023.

[106] See Oskar Josef Gstrein and Andrej Janko Zwitter, 'Extraterritorial Application of the GDPR: Promoting European Values or Power?' (2021) 10 Internet Policy Review <https://policyreview.info/articles/analysis/extraterritorial-application-gdpr-promoting-european-values-or-power> accessed 26 June 2023.

[107] See Directive 95/46/EC (n 18); Council of Europe Additional Protocol to the Convention for the Protection of Individuals with regard to Automatic Processing of Personal Data regarding supervisory authorities and transborder data flows, Strasbourg, 8 November 2001.

[108] A notable example was the one launched by Max Schrems's NOYB alleging that Facebook (and its subsidiaries) and Google forced the consent of its users, in violation of the Regulation's requirements in art 7, in France (Google), Austria (Facebook), Belgium (Instagram), and Germany (WhatsApp).

[109] Art 83(5) of the GDPR states that administrative fines can be up to €20 million or 4% total annual worldwide turnover of the preceding financial year, whichever is higher, if certain provisions are infringed.

the resolution of their complaints, however, many began to question the capacity of the framework to effectuate meaningful change.

Frustration at the lack of appropriate funding for DPAs was reported in the media, with the perception that the GDPR had failed to live up to expectations.[110] At the centre of these issues were small Member States—Ireland and Luxembourg. This reflects the manner in which cross-border personal data processing affects the resolution of disputes. Generally, in the EU, DPAs have sole competence to resolve disputes occurring within their jurisdiction. Article 56(1) of the Regulation provides an exception to this general rule, however, when the personal data processing happens in more than one Member State. In essence, Article 56(1) establishes that in such circumstances the DPA of the country where the controller is established, or where they have their main establishment, is the lead DPA for enforcement purposes. Although Articles 56(1) and 60 establish that the lead DPA cannot act alone and that it must take into account the reasoned objections of concerned DPAs (Article 60(4)) with a dispute resolution mechanism provided for in Article 65 in circumstances where consensus cannot be reached, some have questioned the viability of this approach.[111]

Connected to this point is the fact that there have also been ongoing tensions regarding what some activists perceive as the Irish Data Protection Authority's soft-touch approach towards US corporations in particular.[112] However, Gentile and Lynskey argue, for instance, that the flaws of the procedure are not limited to the inadequacy of one national DPA but are instead systemic and far-reaching and evidence a failure to engender a truly cooperative EU culture where divergences in the approaches of the specific Member States are harmonized.[113] Indeed, one could argue that the dispute resolution mechanisms and the 'one-stop-shop' procedure, which places the lead DPA in charge, have slowed enforcement in the EU (arguably almost to a standstill), thereby de facto crippling the effectiveness of the substantive protections. This is a significant criticism. Indeed, although it remains outside the scope of this book,

[110] See 'Ireland's Data Law Enforcement Criticised as EU Becomes "Laughing Stock"' *The Irish Times* (24 November 2020) <www.irishtimes.com/business/economy/ireland-s-data-law-enforcement-criticised-as-eu-becomes-laughing-stock-1.4418279> accessed 18 June 2023.

[111] eg Gentile and Lynskey outline four deficiencies in the cooperation and consistency mechanisms provided for in the GDPR: (1) procedural ambiguities and divergences in the cooperation procedure; (2) the lack of equality between the national supervisory authorities; (3) insufficient guarantees for procedural fairness; and (4) how the national supervisory authorities' discretion impedes enforcement. See Giulia Gentile and Orla Lynskey, 'Deficit by Design? The Transnational Enforcement of the GDPR' (2022) 71 International & Comparative Law Quarterly 799.

[112] See 'Ireland's Data Law Enforcement Criticised' (n 110).

[113] See Gentile and Lynskey (n 111).

it is important to note the inherent link between trust and access to justice and therefore the availability, suitability, and efficacy of redress mechanisms.[114] Certainly, direct rights of action are of significant importance in this regard but so too is a strong and effective DPA, given that the mere breach of data protection law will not generally result in legally cognizable damage capable of triggering the right to compensation.[115]

For critics, therefore, there is much to be sceptical about but there are also those who think that the issues with data protection law run deeper. The core of this more pessimistic view of data protection law can be summarized as a belief that a focus on the enhancing of individual control over personal data is futile. At the root of these fundamental criticisms, therefore, are those who question the role of us, the data subjects in these frameworks. To explain, this line of literature suggests that data subjects are neither best placed nor capable of acting in their own interests as they cannot appreciate the risks of personal data processing due to complexities and asymmetries and that controllers take advantage of this to do what they want due to limited enforcement by regulators—or, in simple terms, individual control is a fallacy and one that damages the interests of individuals and society. Nuances may be added here, but this summarizes the more broadly pessimistic view of the role and effectiveness of data protection simply in the literature.

To contextualize the significance of control, data protection establishes a system of checks and balances that aim to regulate the processing of personal data and, in doing so, according to the non-binding Recital 7, the GDPR for example aims to empower data subjects to 'control their own personal data'. It has been argued that control goes to the core of EU data protection law[116] but this notion, or at least the word 'control', is peppered throughout data protection scholarship, law reform, and policy reports in various jurisdictions. Indeed, as will be analysed in Chapter 6, in particular, privacy as control over information is seen as the classic understanding of informational privacy in the US,[117] and in recent law reform discussions in Australia, for example, the desire to provide individuals with control of their personal data has also played a role.[118] This appears to reflect the significance of the individual participation principles in the

[114] See Damian Clifford and Yung Shin Van Der Sype, 'Online Dispute Resolution: Settling Data Protection Disputes in a Digital World of Customers' (2016) 32 Computer Law & Security Review 272.

[115] See eg Case C-300/21 *Österreichische Post*, ECLI:EU:C:2023:370.

[116] See Chapter 6.

[117] See Alan F Westin, *Privacy and Freedom* (Atheneum 1967).

[118] See 'Privacy Act Review: Discussion Paper' (Australian Government, Attorney-General's Department 2021) <https://consultations.ag.gov.au/rights-and-protections/privacy-act-review-discussion-paper/user_uploads/privacy-act-review-discussion-paper.pdf> accessed 4 October 2023. 'Government Response to the Privacy Act Review Report' (n 68) 17–20.

OECD Guidelines[119] but also the control rights and reliance on consent found across these laws more generally. The ongoing legitimacy of this approach, however, is arguably increasingly under strain in the data-driven world, as the practical application of these provisions remains challenging. Waldman positions the GDPR, for example, as a rights-and-compliance-based model of such frameworks and believes that it suffers from the same fundamental weakness.[120] Such criticisms are seemingly ubiquitous but have been particularly prevalent in the more recent US scholarship.

For example, in describing US data privacy scholarship Waldman observes that the modern debate 'pits scholars who support individual rights of control as good first steps against scholars who believe that individual rights will do additional harm to privacy without concurrent structural reform'.[121] In her criticism of the more compliance-orientated aspects of some of these data protection laws, Cohen suggests that [p]roponents of those tools, however, tend to engage in considerable over-claiming. To begin with, information businesses have little incentive to respect such restrictions and tend to use broad consent provisions systematically as a way of circumventing them.'[122] The evident asymmetries certainly diminish the legitimacy of user participation, present barriers to finding businesses accountable, and also clearly impact the data subject's bargaining power.[123] There is also evidence of this more critical view in the EU data protection law literature. For example, due to issues stemming from the evident asymmetry (eg social lock-in effects), Mantelero has noted that 'the self-determination of the single individual is inadequate and insufficient to create an effective and conscious market activity concerning personal data'.[124] As such, the focus on data subject empowerment remains questionable for some, which in turn undercuts the value of accountability given the data subject's role in operationalizing this principle.[125] This illustrates Koops' point that, in a practical sense, the involvement of data subjects has a limited effect

119 Guidelines on the Protection of Privacy and Transborder Flows (n 14) para 13.

120 Waldman (n 29) 104.

121 ibid 90.

122 Julie E Cohen, 'Turning Privacy Inside Out' (2019) 20 Theoretical Inquiries in Law 8–9.

123 Lynskey, 'Deconstructing Data Protection' (n 1).

124 Alessandro Mantelero, 'Competitive Value of Data Protection: The Impact of Data Protection Regulation on Online Behaviour' (2013) 3 International Data Privacy Law 229.

125 According to the EDPS, the notion of accountability could be made more effective. This would involve a shift in the attribution of responsibility from the consumers to policymakers, self-regulatory mechanisms, and/or businesses. European Data Protection Supervisor, 'Privacy and Competitiveness in the Age of Big Data: The Interplay between Data Protection, Competition Law and Consumer Protection in the Digital Economy' (European Data Protection Supervisor 2014) Preliminary Opinion of the European Data Protection Supervisor <https://secure.edps.europa.eu/EDPSWEB/webdav/site/mySite/shared/Documents/Consultation/Opinions/2014/14-03-26_competitition_law_big_data_EN.pdf> accessed 27 April 2019.

due to their ignorance regarding the extent of data gathering and processing operations.[126]

Several scholars, therefore, have exposed what they perceive as fundamental, if not (for some at least) fatal, weaknesses of data protection law. Although the criticisms were as relevant to the old frameworks as they are to frameworks such as the GDPR or, for instance, recent developments at the state level in the US, scholars have noted that the modern approaches seem to reinforce the existing issues as opposed to addressing them meaningfully.[127] In line with these criticisms, therefore, the perceived failure of data protection law to engender meaningful change is entirely in keeping with the failings associated with the core assumptions of the frameworks. In other words, data protection law is seen to have failed because it is structured in a manner that favours the interests of controllers by making the protection of personal data a matter for self-management. There is clearly a sense of frustration, therefore, in some parts of the literature.

Cohen, among other scholars, has been extremely critical of what she believes to be antiquated bottom-up approaches that rely on the assertion of individual rights and has argued against their adoption in the US.[128] Solove has declared that privacy self-management is incapable of providing the necessary protection even if it is a necessary component of these laws[129] and Hatzog similarly believes that such approaches are in fact harmful and contrary to good data practices.[130] Waldman in particular is a strong critic and has suggested that such approaches are in fact a 'privacy's rights trap' that will block more meaningful legislation through merely symbolic performances of regulation.[131] More specifically, he argues that legislative frameworks that prioritize data subject control rights fail to account for, amongst other things, the (1) social, (2) behavioural, and (3) practical realities of the information economy.[132] More specifically, he explains how decisions regarding the use of our personal data are never purely personal as they often implicate others and are thus social, thereby meaning that an individual rights-orientated approach will be ineffective in mitigating the social/collective harms.[133] Waldman's behavioural

[126] Koops, 'On Decision Transparency' (n 100).
[127] Waldman (n 29); Solove, 'The Limitations of Privacy Rights' (n 77).
[128] Julie E Cohen, 'How (Not) to Write a Privacy Law' (2021) 21 Knight First Amendment Institute <https://knightcolumbia.org/content/how-not-to-write-a-privacy-law> accessed 4 October 2023.
[129] Daniel J Solove, 'Introduction: Privacy Self-Management and the Consent Dilemma' (2013) 126 Harvard Law Review 1880.
[130] Woodrow Hartzog, 'Opinions—The Case Against Idealising Control' (2018) 4 European Data Protection Law Review 423.
[131] Waldman (n 29).
[132] ibid.
[133] ibid 93–94.

critique is one that is amply covered in the literature and essentially this speaks to our (in)ability as data subjects to act in our own best interests as actors in the information economy, hence the issues with relying on our rational capacity to make choices.[134] Practically, Waldman explains how concerns such as the costs of litigation (where there is a direct right of action) and the challenges of effective regulatory intervention, along with the difficulties of effectuating control rights also may reinforce the existing asymmetries between data subjects and those processing their personal data.[135]

These points echo the concerns of Koops, for instance, who, writing in an EU context but prior to the adoption of the GDPR, noted that self-determination over personal data is unenforceable,[136] or Finck who, writing after the introduction of the Regulation, suggests that self-determination is futile.[137] I believe that these points are all important—in fact this book aims in part to better categorize these challenges to the instrumental role played by control and/or their effects from a 'law and emotion' perspective while also describing their limits. The concerns have also filtered into law reform discussions in other jurisdictions as will be discussed in Chapter 6. In simple terms, then, these criticisms of data protection focus on the frameworks' centring of personal data, the role of choice (ie consent and data subject rights), and the reliance on the accountability of those who process the data. This pessimism and frustration have also fed into the public consciousness in jurisdictions with robust data protection legislation. For instance, empirical research conducted in the Netherlands has demonstrated that, although there are high levels of awareness of the GDPR, and its data subject rights in particular, there are significant doubts as to its effectiveness.[138] The same study has also demonstrated that there is widespread frustration regarding the impact of the Regulation on the work and personal lives of those living in the Netherlands.[139] However, although the legitimacy of some of the concerns raised by the public discussed in this research may be dismissed as misinterpretations of the GDPR (which is itself a concern), it is undoubtedly the case that scholars have questioned the fundamental parts of data protection law for years.

134 ibid 94–96.

135 ibid 96–98.

136 Bert-Jaap Koops, 'The Trouble with European Data Protection Law' (2014) 4 International Data Privacy Law 250, 251–53.

137 See Finck (n 103).

138 Joanna Strycharz, Jef Ausloos, and Natali Helberger, 'Data Protection or Data Frustration? Individual Perceptions and Attitudes Towards the GDPR' (2020) 6 European Data Protection Law Review 407.

139 ibid.

The concerns outlined are therefore far from new. In fact, the reforms introduced by the GDPR can be understood as being partly a response to these issues, which perhaps explains some of the frustrations about its impact, or lack thereof, depending on your perspective. The adoption of the GDPR as the high-water mark example of such frameworks, must therefore be understood in light of the well-documented criticisms and, for some, it (and more recent legislative developments such those as at the state level in the US) represented a doubling down on an obvious mistake in regulatory design. From a data protection purist's perspective, however, such criticisms more optimistically reflect the failure to enforce such frameworks as opposed to illustrating an underlying problem with their focus. The increase in high-profile and significant fines handed down more recently by the Irish DPA, for example, may therefore, from this perspective, indicate a change in the tide, at least in the EU.[140] Certainly, the enforcement of the GDPR has increased since its first adoption, with statistical analysis demonstrating that the number of enforcement actions has grown steadily since the Regulation entered into force.[141]

It could therefore be suggested that unqualified criticisms may be premature as such significant change and its enforcement take time.[142] The Regulation has also been influential in the debates regarding the need for more robust enforcement and remedies (and also a direct right of action).[143] For example, in Australia, in response to high-profile data breaches, the maximum civil penalty for serious and repeated interferences with privacy was increased and the Australian Information Commissioner was afforded broader regulatory powers through the expedited adoption of reforms in 2022.[144] The truth perhaps lies somewhere in between. Positioning data protection law as *the* solution arguably fails to consider the clear difficulties associated with its effective operation but, at the same time, dismissing it entirely ignores its effects and potential if enforced.

There are quite obviously many issues associated with both the enforcement and the complexities of data protection law. There is also the clear perception

140 See discussion in Chapters 4 and 5 where examples are given.

141 See 'GDPR Enforcement Tracker—List of GDPR Fines' <www.enforcementtracker.com> accessed 18 June 2023.

142 This is particularly the case in the EU, where there are complex divisions of competence in both primary and secondary EU law.

143 See Normann Witzleb, 'Private Enforcement of Data Rights through Direct Rights of Action: A Comparative Review' in Damian Clifford, Jeannie Marie Paterson, and Kwan Ho Lau (eds), *Data and Private Law* (Hart 2023).

144 See Privacy Legislation Amendment (Enforcement and Other Measures) Act 2022. This Act is part of an ongoing review into the Privacy Act (Cth) 1988 being conducted by Attorney-General's Department.

that such laws have the potential to disproportionately affect individuals and small businesses (when not exempt) as opposed to the real regulatory target—for example the big technology platforms.[145] Although these companies would certainly dispute this claim, there are reasons to be sceptical when even Mark Zuckerberg has called for a comprehensive globally harmonized data protection framework.[146] Even leaving aside the compliance costs for businesses (both big and small) and the precise motivations of big technology companies like Meta, however, the complexity has certainly added to the misunderstandings of data protection law's focus and real impact. A mythology surrounds the GDPR in particular and this relates not only to the failure to properly inform the public but also to the role of controllers (and processors) as the regulated entities and the public's interface with compliance efforts. As the sharing of personal data is an integral part of our everyday lives, it is unsurprising that rules that have been left in the hands of those benefiting from its processing have caused frustration and misunderstanding.

However, I also believe that in presenting their criticisms of control some scholars demonstrate an approach that identifies problems but proposes no real solutions, or at least no solutions beyond what has already been contemplated by scholars for some time as being consistent with data protection law. In fact, some of the reforms discussed in the literature are already in motion in certain jurisdictions, both in terms of the alignment of different policy agendas and also with regard to the collaboration between various regulators in certain jurisdictions (see Chapters 5 and 6). There has also been a failure to account for the importance of the subjective aspects of the protection of personal data. After all, is it not the fear of a loss of control and trust and the risks inherent in technological developments which have led to the development of these frameworks in the first place? As noted by Abrams, the mobilization of rights is 'informed and infused by varied forms of affect' and this extends to the legislator.[147] I believe that this demonstrates the subjective aspect of the need for protection of our personal data and its capacity to motivate legislative responses—that the protection of personal data, or rather illegitimate uses of our personal data, can feel deeply personal—but also explains the rather weak

[145] See generally, on the public's perceptions in the Netherlands, Strycharz, Ausloos, and Helberger (n 138).

[146] 'Opinion | Mark Zuckerberg: The Internet Needs New Rules. Let's Start in These Four Areas' *Washington Post* (1 April 2019) <www.washingtonpost.com/opinions/mark-zuckerberg-the-internet-needs-new-rules-lets-start-in-these-four-areas/2019/03/29/9e6f0504-521a-11e9-a3f7-78b7525a8d5f_story.html> accessed 6 March 2023.

[147] Kathryn Abrams, 'Emotions in the Mobilization of Rights' (2011) 46 Harvard Civil Rights-Civil Liberties Law Review 551, 570.

enforcement of the law. To properly account for the role and limitations of data protection law, I believe that we must be mindful of the role emotions play in the adoption but also the application of data protection law in light of the significant role played by data subjects. By accounting for the role of emotion in data protection law, we will know more about the challenges posed to control, and how to understand and contextualize them. I also believe, however, that we may gain a better understanding of the value of this notion more generally.

The next three chapters of this book will therefore focus on data protection law's centring of personal data, the role of choice (ie consent and data subject rights), and the reliance placed on those who process personal data to do so fairly through a 'law and emotion' lens in order to better contextualize the critique of control. In so doing, I will explore the instrumental role for control that is recognized in the GDPR in particular. To clarify, in examining control in EU data protection law, Lazaro and Le Métayer observe that this concept 'is strongly associated with the conventional figure of the "rational and autonomous agent", capable of deliberating about personal goals, controlling the course of the events and acting under the direction of such deliberation'.[148] The authors further note that this notion is both 'individualist', given the emphasis on individual sovereignty, and also 'active' in that it implies effective participation of the data subject and the liberty to alienate their personal data provided that such 'alienation' is 'informed and voluntary'.[149] Lazaro and Le Métayer further argue that in order to operationalize control and empower individuals, therefore, the framework also mobilizes protections or 'environmental variables' incorporating technological and organizational safeguards to ensure a secure personal data processing environment.[150] This understanding of the dual aspects of control seems to be well accepted in the analysis of the GDPR.[151] The data protection principles, the requirement to conduct data protection impact assessments, and data protection by default and by design are some important examples.

The operational mobilization of these protections and the risk-based approach enshrined in the GDPR are hence indicative of potentially a more collective view of control in that they aim to ensure the protection of data subjects (plural) in order to provide a secure personal data processing environment.

[148] See Christophe Lazaro and Daniel Le Métayer, 'Control over Personal Data: True Remedy or Fairy Tale?' (2015) 12 SCRIPTed 3.

[149] ibid 9.

[150] ibid 20.

[151] See eg Susanna Lindroos-Hovinheimo, *Private Selves: Legal Personhood in European Privacy Protection* (CUP 2021) 44–50.

Although it has been suggested that the dual approach to control which plays an instrumental role as the key means of individual empowerment in the Regulation is important for the proper operation of the data protection framework,[152] I will also reflect on data protection law's uncertain conceptual values and the value of control specifically. This analysis will therefore allow us to gain broader insights into why people act 'irrationally' and in non-privacy-preserving ways, and I believe that through a 'law and emotion' lens the critique of control will also highlight its value.

E. Conclusion

Data protection is, at least in part, a response to legitimate concerns associated with the proliferation of technology and the pervasive gathering of personal data. Despite this fact, data protection law's complexities have caused some to question its value, to fear the consequences of its introduction, and, following its implementation, to be frustrated about its impact or lack thereof, depending on your perspective. The analysis has highlighted that, although there are certainly complexities that cause headaches for those processing personal data, these are, at least in part, manifestations of the legislative desire for a high level of protection while also maintaining flexibility/adaptability in the framework.

The aim of the chapter was simply to introduce some core features of data protection law and its development. In the chapters that follow, I offer an account of how law and emotion theory helps to explain and contextualize criticisms of data protection law as manifested in three challenges. First, the 'information categories' approach in the Regulation; secondly, the role of individual choice; and thirdly, the controller's obligation to process personal data fairly. The analysis in these chapters will then form the basis for an examination of data protection's limits in Chapter 6. The analysis in this chapter has provided a primer for these more detailed considerations. The stage is now set for this deeper-level analysis.

[152] Lynskey, *The Foundations of EU Data Protection Law* (n 30) 258–62.

3

The Challenge to Information Categories

A. Introduction

Individuals often become attached emotionally to their devices and the connectivity and interactivity enabled by them in addition to the personal history they may represent.[1] People also grow attached, even romantically it seems, to tools like AI-powered chatbots,[2] despite the risks that they may pose.[3] We may be less attached, however, to the contents of the objects themselves and thus the data that is produced.[4] Although we may take steps to protect the privacy of our hardware, we may appear less concerned by the intangible information being processed on or through them. This is significant as data protection law restricts the processing of personal data to prevent harms arising from misuse and thus is focused on the protection of this intangible information by its very design.

My aim in this chapter is to explore the emotional disengagement between the risks posed by personal data processing and the objective categories of information protected. This requires an analysis of the limits of the definition of personal data. As described in the previous chapter, data protection laws generally define personal data broadly as information relating to an identified or identifiable natural person. However, there are significant differences across jurisdictions, and these relate both to the application and interpretation of the definition but also the exclusion of certain types of information from its scope. I believe that such exclusions create arbitrary lines disconnected from the risk of harm posed by personal data processing. Hence, I will explore whether uniform protections afforded to objective categories of information are too

[1] Luke Stark, 'The Emotional Context of Information Privacy' (2016) 32 The Information Society 14, 19.

[2] Chiara Wilkinson and Helen Frost, 'The People in Intimate Relationships with AI Chatbots' (*Vice*, 21 January 2022) <www.vice.com/en/article/93bqbp/can-you-be-in-relationship-with-replika> accessed 22 September 2023.

[3] See the enforcement action taken by the Italian Data Protection Authority against Replika, for example: 'Intelligenza artificiale, dal Garante privacy stop al chatbot "Replika". Troppi i rischi per i minori e le persone emotivamente fragili' <www.garanteprivacy.it:443/home/docweb/-/docweb-display/docweb/9852506> accessed 22 September 2023.

[4] Stark (n 1) 20.

Data Protection Law and Emotion. Damian Clifford, Oxford University Press. © Damian Clifford 2024.
DOI: 10.1093/oso/9780192845863.003.0003

simplistic to respond to the subjective and context-dependent nature of how individuals feel about the processing of their personal data.

The purpose of this chapter, therefore, is to explore this disconnect between how we feel about personal data and the risks posed through the lens of the categories-based approach in data protection laws. Section B explores the affective features of this problem by analysing, amongst other things, how the definition of personal data is engaged through the example of profiling. The chapter will then develop this problem through the lens of the Emotional Artificial Intelligence (E-AI) case study introduced in Chapter 1. Section C thus builds on this analysis by offering E-AI as a case study to demonstrate the practical challenges associated with applying sensitive data categories in practice. In this section, I will refer exclusively to the protections afforded in the General Data Protection Regulation (GDPR) as the high-water mark example of data protection law in order to demonstrate the challenge in detail. In doing so, I will first explore how emotion detection results in the processing of biometric data and I will then explore how uses of E-AI may also result in the processing of sensitive personal data such as data concerning health. Finally, Section D explores the limits of the challenge to the categories-based approach evident in data protection laws. In doing so, the section highlights the significant risks of harm that the framework aims to address and thus qualifies the critique presented accordingly.

B. Affective Features of the Challenge

Data protection law protects personal data. In some jurisdictions, however, certain information is excluded from the scope of the protections provided even if they might otherwise satisfy the definition, while further protections are often afforded to sensitive or special categories of personal data. As will be explored, these sensitive categories include information such as personal data revealing racial origin, political opinions, or religious or philosophical beliefs, as well as personal data concerning health or sexual life and biometric and genetic information. In the GDPR, for instance, the processing of sensitive personal data is prohibited, subject to a long list of exceptions.[5] In comparison,

[5] Indeed, to avoid the general prohibition contained in art 9(1) of the GDPR, a controller is required to satisfy one of the exceptions in art 9(2). This provision lists 10 potential exceptions, including the explicit consent of the data subject listed as an exception in art 9(2)(a). See Ludmila Georgieva and Christopher Kuner, 'Article 9. Processing of Special Categories of Personal Data' in Christopher Kuner and others (eds), *The EU General Data Protection Regulation (GDPR): A Commentary* (OUP 2020).

although not prohibited, some of the state consumer privacy laws in the United States (US), for example, require consent and an impact assessment[6] although there are other variations. For instance, the California Consumer Privacy Act merely affords consumers the right to object to the processing of their sensitive personal data.[7]

Despite the prevalence of these lists of sensitive personal data, the categories approach to data protection arguably exacerbates the emotional disengagement from the dangers associated with intensive data processing. Stark observes that the lack of a 'felt connection' to our data results in a 'data myopia' or an inability to appreciate the risks of data aggregation because our own experiences of data sharing do not feel risky.[8] I believe that this disengagement is linked to (1) the sheer extent of the personal data processing, (2) the capacity to make sensitive inferences from seemingly innocuous personal data, and, more fundamentally, (3) the fact that the objective categories of information recognized in data protection law fail to reflect the subjective and contextually dependent way we may feel about their processing. As will be demonstrated in this section, these points intertwine. However, before delving into the nuances it is first necessary to gain a better understanding of 'personal data'.

1. Personal data and the example of profiling

The definition of personal data is often broken down into four cumulative components, namely (1) information; (2) relating to; (3) identified or identifiable; and (4) an individual/natural person. The definition found in the Organisation for Economic Co-operation and Development (OECD) Guidelines and Convention 108 is mirrored in the updated Convention 108 + but also the GDPR, and EU Guidance documents suggest that these constitutive elements are cumulative and 'are closely intertwined and feed on each other'.[9]

The expression 'any information' demonstrates the breadth of the notion of personal data. Personal data, therefore, include not only our most intimate information but also any sort of information about a person, including economic and professional data. The definition is generally understood to cover

[6] See Virginia Consumer Data Protection Act (2021), s 580(4); Colorado Privacy Act (2021), s 1309(c).

[7] See California Consumer Privacy Act of 2018, s 1798.121(a).

[8] Stark (n 1) 21.

[9] Article 29 Working Party, 'Opinion 4/2007 on the concept of personal data' (2007) WP 136 6 <http://ec.europa.eu/justice/policies/privacy/docs/wpdocs/2007/wp136_en.pdf> accessed 9 December 2012.

both 'objective' information, such as occupation or income, and 'subjective' information, such as opinions or assessments irrespective of their accuracy as well as highly private or sensitive information.[10] Although there has been an ongoing academic discussion regarding the use of and differences between the words 'information' and 'data' in the definitions of personal data—in short highlighting that the definition requires some informational value—and in relation to whether the term 'information' includes, for instance, biological material, data protection laws generally fail to expressly deal with these issues.[11] Generally, the legislative intention is to leave the definition as broad as possible and it appears, therefore, that virtually anything can either *be* personal data or at least *contain* personal data (provided the other elements of the definition are met).

Information is considered to 'relate' to an individual when it is about that natural person and, in many circumstances, this relationship can be easily established. For instance, the personal data that we provide to register and purchase a service online (eg name, address, phone number, credit card number etc) are clearly 'related to' an identified individual. In other situations, however, it is not immediately possible to establish the relationship between the information and the individual, or at least in a manner that renders them identifiable. The definition does not require the knowledge of the person's name instead a natural person is considered to be 'identified' when they are distinguishable from all other members of a group and 'identifiable' as soon as it is possible to do so even if that has yet to occur. 'Identifiability' in the definition of personal data is thus a broad and dynamic notion.[12] For instance, although the term 'identifiable' was left undefined in Convention 108, guidance on its interpretation was provided through the adoption of a number of recommendations and resolutions.[13] More specifically, in the Explanatory Memorandum to recommendation R (97) 18 it is noted that:

[10] Case C-434/16 *Peter Nowak v Data Protection Commissioner*, ECLI:EU:C:2017:994, para 34: 'reflects the aim of the EU legislature to assign a wide scope to [the definition of personal data], which is not restricted to information that is sensitive or private, but potentially encompasses all kinds of information, not only objective but also subjective, in the form of opinions and assessments.'

[11] See Michèle Finck and Frank Pallas, 'They Who Must Not Be Identified—Distinguishing Personal from Non-Personal Data under the GDPR' (2020) 10 International Data Privacy Law 11; Lee A Bygrave, 'Information Concepts in Law: Generic Dreams and Definitional Daylight' (2015) 35 Oxford Journal of Legal Studies 91; Lee A Bygrave, *Data Privacy Law: An International Perspective* (OUP 2014) 126–39.

[12] W Kuan Hon, Christopher Millard, and Ian Walden, 'The Problem of "Personal Data" in Cloud Computing: What Information Is Regulated?—The Cloud of Unknowing' (2011) 1 International Data Privacy Law 211, 214.

[13] See eg Council of Europe—Committee of Ministers, Resolution (73) 22 on the Protection of the Privacy of Individuals vis-à-vis Electronic Data Banks in the Private Sector (26 September 1973); Council of Europe—Committee of Ministers, Resolution (74) 29 on the Protection of the Privacy of Individuals vis-à-vis Electronic Data Banks in the Public Sector (20 September 1974).

> Conditions for anonymity are relative, especially in relation to the technical means available for identifying data and taking away their anonymity. In this way, in view of the rapid progress in technological and methodological developments, the time and manpower required to identify a person, which would today be considered 'unreasonable', might no longer be so in the future. However, the present wording is sufficiently flexible to cover such developments.[14]

A critical element in the interpretation of the definition of personal data, therefore, is the constant development of computational power, and in the methods of data mining and the organization of information.[15]

Reasonableness as a standard for assessing whether a data subject is identifiable has gained significant traction. Interestingly, in the original explanatory memorandum to the OECD Guidelines it was noted that determining the point at which data would become 'identifiable' and no longer anonymous for the purposes of the definition would be challenging, but that this was a matter for national law.[16] The interpretative room in this definition means that even where substantively similar definitions are adopted, variations exist at the national level.

For example, in jurisdictions such as those states which recently adopted consumer privacy laws in the US, certain types of personal data are also specifically excluded from the scope of the protections, including publicly available information.[17] In this regard, a similar approach is also evident at the international level in the APEC Privacy Framework.[18] This contrasts sharply with the approach in the GDPR or the Singaporean Personal Data Protection Act (PDPA)'[19] for instance, where information in the public domain is still

[14] Council of Europe, Explanatory Memorandum to Recommendation No.R (97) 18 of the Committee of Ministers to Member States concerning the protection of personal data collected and processed for statistical purposes (30 Sepetember 1997), para 52(d).

[15] See Chris Culnane and Kobi Leins, 'Misconceptions in Privacy Protection and Regulation' (2019) 36 Law in Context. A Socio-legal Journal 49.

[16] Explanatory Memorandum to the Guidelines on the Protection of Privacy and Transborder Flows of Personal Data (OECD) 1980, 39, 52.

[17] See California Consumer Privacy Act of 2018, s 1798.140.(d); Virginia Consumer Data Protection Act (2021), s 59.1-576; Utah Consumer Privacy Act (2022), ss 13-61–102; Texas Data Privacy and Security Act (2023), s 541.003; Tennessee Information Protection Act (2023), ss 47-18–3202; Montana Consumer Data Privacy Act (2023), s 3; Iowa Consumer Data Protection Act (2023), s 715D.1.18; Indiana Consumer Data Protection Act (2023), s 1; Connecticut Data Privacy Act (2022), s 2; Colorado Privacy Act (2021), ss 6-1–1304.(1).

[18] Asia-Pacific Economic Cooperation (APEC) Privacy Framework <www.apec.org/docs/default-source/Publications/2017/8/APEC-Privacy-Framework-(2015)/217_ECSG_2015-APEC-Privacy-Framework.pdf> accessed 4 October 2023.

[19] Personal Data Protection Act 2012.

considered personal. Another example, which goes to the root of data protection law, relates to how these national laws treat 'de-identified' or anonymous information. In the Australian Privacy Act 1988 (Cth), for example, de-identified (ie anonymous and pseudonymous) data are excluded from the Act's scope of application.[20] In contrast, in the EU, although the GDPR excludes anonymous data from the scope of protection, the definition of pseudonymization in Article 4(11) makes it clear that pseudonymous data are considered personal under the Regulation, as such data can still be used to single out a data subject.[21]

This contrast highlights the significant issues and variation associated with the level of 'individuation' necessary to fall within the definition of personal data in different jurisdictions.[22] Importantly, although the EU approach arguably better reflects the risks posed (and, arguably, public expectation), this also presents issues of potential over-inclusiveness. More specifically, the EU Court of Justice's interpretation of 'relating to' and 'identified or identifiable' elements of the definition has led authors such as Purtova to question the ongoing utility of the definition, given what she perceives to be as the risk of the GDPR becoming the 'law of everything'.[23] An important qualification here is that the other elements of the definition must of course also be satisfied. Significantly, although information may relate to many individuals it must *identify a specific natural person* or at least render them identifiable for it to be considered personal data. Admittedly, however, although I believe that there are important boundaries to the definition of personal data and that Purtova somewhat overstates the issue,[24] it is unquestionably very broad, thereby creating a disconnect between the seemingly ubiquitous application of data protection law and the risks associated with the processing of personal data. We can tease out the boundaries of the definition of personal data more clearly with reference to the example of how the elements of the definition of personal data interact when it is processed during profiling.

[20] See Megan Richardson and others, 'The Internet of Things (IoT) and the Meaning of "Personal Data": A Case Study in Regulation for Rights' [2020] Revue européenne de droit de la consommation 503.

[21] To clarify, 'pseudonymisation' is defined in art 4(5) of the GDPR to mean 'the processing of personal data in such a manner that the personal data can no longer be attributed to a specific data subject without the use of additional information, provided that such additional information is kept separately and is subject to technical and organisational measures to ensure that the personal data are not attributed to an identified or identifiable natural person'.

[22] Bygrave, *Data Privacy Law* (n 11) 135.

[23] Nadezhda Purtova, 'The Law of Everything. Broad Concept of Personal Data and Future of EU Data Protection Law' (2018) 10 Law, Innovation and Technology 40.

[24] See Richardson and others (n 20).

According to Hildebrandt, profiling is 'the process of "discovering" correlations between data in databases that can be used to identify a human or non-human subject (individual or group) and/or the application of profiles (sets of correlated data) to individuate and represent a subject or to identify a subject as a member of a group or category'.[25] For group profiling, the subject of the profile is a group or category of persons, with any person who is considered a member being subject to the application of the profile, the profile becoming more sophisticated depending on the available data, thereby allowing for more subtle differentiation between members and non-members.[26] As defined by the entity gathering the data, these groups or categories do not (necessarily) fit within the traditional conceptualization of such a clustering. Instead, groups can also be defined in seemingly random ways, representing an apparent cross-section of society compared to the more traditionally accepted categories of individuals from a sociological perspective (eg the elderly, students, etc).[27] Indeed, it should be noted here that the majority of groups do not have distributive profiles, in that not all members of the group in question share all the attributes linked to the group's profile.[28] These groups are shaped by the data gatherers, with the members often being unaware of who the other members are or indeed the consequences of belonging to the group in question.[29] Hence, 'profiling' is widely used and does not necessarily rely on traditional categories of individuals.[30] Importantly, it is unclear how data protection law applies to group profiles as they are normally created via aggregate models and, through the categorical analytics methodology, an individual may not be 'identifiable' as understood in data protection law. The key point is that such profiles can be created using a synthetic data set or, alternatively, may be built with

[25] Mireille Hildebrandt, 'Defining Profiling: A New Type of Knowledge?' in Mireille Hildebrandt and Serge Gutwirth (eds), *Profiling the European Citizen: Cross-Disciplinary Perspectives* (Springer Netherlands 2008) 19.

[26] Wim Schreurs and others, 'Cogitas, Ergo Sum. The Role of Data Protection Law and Non-Discrimination Law in Group Profiling in the Private Sector' in Hildebrandt and Gutwirth (eds) (n 25) 241–42.

[27] See generally Lanah Kammourieh and others, 'Group Privacy in the Age of Big Data' in Linnet Taylor, Luciano Floridi, and Bart van der Sloot (eds), *Group Privacy: New Challenges of Data Technologies* (Springer International 2017).

[28] Hildebrandt (n 25) 21.

[29] Alessandro Mantelero, 'Personal Data for Decisional Purposes in the Age of Analytics: From an Individual to a Collective Dimension of Data Protection' (2016) 32 Computer Law & Security Review 238, 245.

[30] Here it is interesting to refer to Kammourieh and others, who outline four category types: (1) data analytics which help to discover new things about pre-identified groups; (2) the identification of non-apparent groups through pre-defined parameters; (3) the discovery of groups through analytical approaches without any pre-defined parameters; and (4) the potential for another group to remain unidentified even if they may be affected by analytical processes. See Kammourieh and others (n 27).

legitimately processed personal data thereby creating a model through which inferences are later applied to individuals.

Personal data may therefore be used (1), to train the model requiring that such processing complies with the law. This processing may involve both personal and sensitive personal data and may be a dynamic process. It may also involve the purchasing of certain data sets from data brokers, which raises a whole range of data protection law concerns.[31] Generally, however, once generated the model will not (necessarily) render any individual 'identifiable' as such, thereby excluding it from the material scope of the protections provided in data protection law.[32] Accordingly, such models are more commonly dealt with legally through intellectual property and trade secret rules as opposed to data protection law, given that they apply at an aggregate level.[33] In essence, therefore, although an individual's personal data may not have been used to develop a model, that model may still be used to affect that individual. However, it is important to clarify that for the profile to be applied to an individual, personal data may have to be processed and, further, when it is applied it may make inferences about the individual which then may also be classified as personal data. This points to two additional circumstances in which data protection law may apply, namely: (2) if personal data are used to query the model to activate the profile,[34] and (3) if inferences are then drawn when the model is applied, and these inferences fall within the definition of personal data. To understand these potential roles for data protection law better, Figure 3.1 illustrates in simplified form the three intersections described.

To understand point (2), it is important to note that the personal data used to query the model may include information inputted directly by the user, such as sign-up details and content shared (which may include sensitive personal data), but also behavioural tracking data. The application of data protection law to online tracking is an excellent illustration of how the personal data category

[31] See Katharine Kemp, 'Australia's Forgotten Privacy Principle: Why Common "Enrichment" of Customer Data for Profiling and Targeting Is Unlawful' (20 September 2022) <https://papers.ssrn.com/abstract=4224653> accessed 31 May 2023.

[32] Although Veale and colleagues have cautiously questioned the absolutist exclusion of such models from the definition of personal data on the basis of the potential for cybersecurity attacks which cause breaches of confidentiality, the authors note that such possibilities remain abstract and model-dependent, with the potential for such attacks in practice still somewhat hypothetical, potentially impossible depending on the model and difficult to prove in practice. More specifically, through their discussion of model inversion and membership inference attacks the authors described the potential of revealing insights relating to the training data used and convincingly illustrate how such techniques result in models being considered personal data. Michael Veale, Reuben Binns, and Lilian Edwards, 'Algorithms That Remember: Model Inversion Attacks and Data Protection Law' (2018) 376 Philosophical Transactions of the Royal Society A: Mathematical, Physical and Engineering Sciences 1.

[33] ibid.

[34] Schreurs and others (n 26) 248–49.

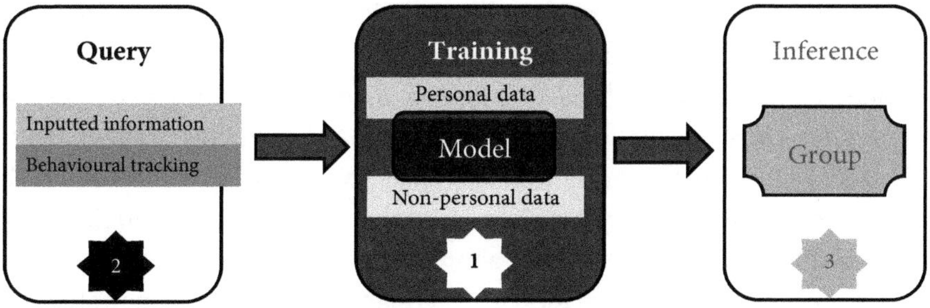

Figure 3.1 Personal data and profiling

may be challenged depending on the jurisdiction. More specifically, these issues have been at the forefront of legal debates in Australia for several years due to the apparent uncertainty as to whether machine-related information such as an IP address is 'about' a natural person and comes within the protections afforded in the Privacy Act 1988 (Cth).[35] However, it is often precisely these kinds of information that individuals are most concerned about when they are surveyed. For example, in the reporting of its survey of Australian consumer attitudes to behavioural advertising and tracking as part of its Digital Platforms Inquiry, the Australian Competition and Consumer Commission (ACCC) found that 77 per cent of digital platform users considered the tracking of behaviour to create profiles and target advertising to be a misuse of their personal data,[36] and there is currently a proposal to expand the definition provided in the Act to cover such device-related information, thus bringing it closer to the definition in the GDPR and other comparable jurisdictions.[37]

Indeed, in contrast to the narrower approach, it is broadly accepted that online identifiers such as cookies and/or cookie-like technologies used online to track individuals are personal data within the GDPR.[38] Although there are also *lex specialis* rules for the 'storing of information, or the gaining of access to information already stored, in the terminal equipment' of the user for

[35] For a more elaborate discussion of these issues, see Katharine Kemp, '"A Rose by Any Other Unique Identifier": Regulating Consumer Data Tracking and Anonymisation Claims' [2022] Competition Policy International TechREG Chronicle 21; Richardson and others (n 20).

[36] Australian Competition and Consumer Commission, *Digital Platforms Inquiry—Final Report* (June 2019) 389.

[37] See Proposal 4.1, 'Government Response to the Privacy Act Review Report' (Australian Government 2023) <www.ag.gov.au/rights-and-protections/publications/government-response-privacy-act-review-report> accessed 4 October 2023.

[38] For a discussion, see Damian Clifford, 'EU Data Protection Law and Targeted Advertising: Consent and the Cookie Monster—Tracking the Crumbs of Online User Behaviour' (2014) 5 Journal of Intellectual Property, Information Technology and Electronic Commerce Law 194.

non-functional purposes[39] provided in the ePrivacy Directive as this equipment is deemed part of their private sphere,[40] the 'information' is generally also considered personal data.[41] The fact that such device-related information can come within the scope of the definition of personal data in the European Union (EU) also reveals that information can 'relate to' a natural person even if the information in question is not strictly *about* them. To clarify, although cookies (or indeed IP addresses) are in fact about to the device in question in a literal sense, they may still be understood as 'relating to' a natural person for the purposes of the definition and they may still single out an individual in EU data protection law.[42]

Indeed, according to the case law of the Court of Justice, either the content (ie the substance in question refers to a natural person), purpose (the purpose is or incorporates the need to identify a natural person), or effect (ie irrespective of the content and purpose, the consequences are likely to have an impact on the rights and freedoms of a natural person) can mean that this component of the definition will be satisfied.[43] These three elements are considered as alternative conditions (ie they are not cumulative), so where one is satisfied there is no need to consider the others. The 'relating to' component of the definition of personal data in the GDPR is therefore very broad, meaning that the

[39] As described by the Article 29 Working Party, art 5(3) of the ePrivacy Directive allows for processing to be exempt from the requirement of consent if one of the following criteria is satisfied: (1) technical storage or access 'for the sole purpose of carrying out the transmission of a communication over an electronic communications network' or (2) technical storage or access which is 'strictly necessary in order for the provider of an information society service explicitly requested by the subscriber or user to provide the service'. See Article 29 Working Party, 'Opinion 04/2012 on cookie consent exemption' (2012) WP 194.

[40] As expressed in Recital 24 of the ePrivacy Directive, which provides that the 'terminal equipment of users [...] and any information stored on such equipment are part of the private sphere of these users requiring protection under the European Convention for the Protection of Human Rights and Fundamental Freedoms'. Consequently, it is information considered to be in the 'private sphere of the users' that triggers the application of art 5(3) of the ePrivacy Directive and hence, not if the information is classified as personal data.

[41] Indeed, as per the European Data Protection Board opinion on the relationship between the GDPR and the ePrivacy Directive where it is noted that it is only when the information for the purposes of art 5(3) ePrivacy in question also constitutes personal data that the GDPR also applies: European Data Protection Board, Opinion 5/2019 on the Interplay between the ePrivacy Directive and the GDPR, in Particular Regarding the Competence, Tasks and Powers of Data Protection Authorities (adopted on 12 March 2019) 13–14. See also generally Article 29 Working Party, 'Opinion 02/2010 on online behavioural advertising' (2010) WP 171 <http://ec.europa.eu/justice/policies/privacy/docs/wpdocs/2010/wp171_en.pdf> accessed 3 November 2012; Article 29 Working Party, 'Opinion 16/2011 on EASA/IAB best practice recommendation on online behavioural advertising' (2011) WP 188.

[42] Lorenzo Dalla Corte, 'Scoping Personal Data: Towards a Nuanced Interpretation of the Material Scope of EU Data Protection Law' (2019) 10 European Journal of Law and Technology.

[43] See *Peter Nowak v Data Protection Commissioner* (n 10); Joined Cases C–141/12 and 372/12, *YS v Minister voor Immigratie, Integratie en Asiel, and Minister voor Immigratie, Integratie en Asiel v M, S*, ECLI:EU:C:2014:2081. Dalla Corte (n 42). See also Article 29 Working Party, 'Opinion on personal data' (n 9) 11.

same piece of information may in fact relate to different individuals at the same time.[44] Importantly, however, this information must still render an individual 'identifiable'. The definition of personal data in the GDPR combined with that of pseudonymization in Article 4(5) (and indeed, the clarifications regarding their interaction provided in Recitals 26 and 28) indicate that any data capable of 'singling out' an individual is personal.[45] Similar approaches to the definition of personal data are common elsewhere, but there are variations. For instance, in the US several of the sector-specific federal statutes define personal data as 'information that identifies a person',[46] thereby seemingly excluding information that merely renders them identifiable. However, as Solove notes, these narrower approaches appear to be waning in the US with the various state consumer data protection laws adopting the approach in the GDPR.[47]

Information will, it seems, relate to an identifiable natural person when the controller aims to draw inferences through data processing, thereby also reflecting point (3) represented in Figure 3.1 above. It is the inference, as an output of a model that may also be personal. This information may be about a natural person—even if it is inaccurate. This may be simply expressed through an example. For instance, taking Figure 3.1 as a kind of flow chart for the different places in which personal data may be processed, imagine Sarah, a woman in her early 30s, who is signed up to Alphabet's services. She will input certain information such as sign-up data and may provide other information in a variety of ways (eg search queries). Her visits to various websites will also be tracked. All this personal data may then be used to profile Sarah, with her personal data potentially further used to train the model and personalize, to determine for example, that Sarah enjoys looking at shopping sites dedicated to products for newborn babies. This inference may then be used to target advertisements to Sarah. These inferences are therefore also generally considered personal data. Although this is often left implicit in data protection law, several of the state consumer privacy laws in the US explicitly include inferences as personal data, either within the definition of personal data in the case of the

[44] Article 29 Working Party, 'Opinion on personal data' (n 9) 11.

[45] See Frederik J Zuiderveen Borgesius, 'Singling out People without Knowing Their Names—Behavioural Targeting, Pseudonymous Data, and the New Data Protection Regulation' (2016) 32 Computer Law & Security Review 256 <www.sciencedirect.com/science/article/pii/S0267364915001788> accessed 1 March 2016.

[46] See eg Video Privacy Protection Act of 1988.

[47] Daniel J Solove, 'Data Is What Data Does: Regulating Based on Harm and Risk Instead of Sensitive Data' (11 January 2023) 7 <https://papers.ssrn.com/abstract=4322198> accessed 29 June 2023.

California Consumer Privacy Act[48] or, for instance, in the definition of 'targeted advertising'.[49]

2. Categories, complexity, and sensitive inferences

Through the processing of personal data, therefore, an individual can be profiled, and personal data may be used to (1) train and/or (2) query the model used to make correlations and identify a subject as a member of a group, thereby (3) drawing inferences about them. It is these three aspects that may have to comply with data protection law as they may involve some personal data processing. Importantly, however, it is also important to note more generally that, although the transparency requirements in the GDPR are designed to provide information on all three of these instances of personal data processing, the levels of individual understanding of them may also vary, and this may be due in part to regulatory design. To explain, for example we may be asked for login details or to accept the use of cookies repeatedly. In fact, consent, as defined under the *lex generalis* GDPR, to the use of non-functional cookies is required by the *lex specialis* obligations contained in Article 5(3) of the ePrivacy Directive mentioned above in Subsection B.1. In the EU, users are thus constantly reminded of the gathering of the information used to 'query' a model that may seem inconsequential given the routine nature of the requests, a point that will be analysed more extensively in Chapter 4. However, what is often less obvious to users is how these personal data may then be used through what Cohen has referred to as 'the invisible, predesigned webs of technical and economic arrangements under which their data travels among multiple parties'.[50] Through these arrangements, the participants in these webs can also draw inferences about individuals—even if the user would have opted out of the gathering of such data at the outset for use in the training data.[51] To further complicate matters, these inferences may be sensitive.

As I have explored with colleagues elsewhere, there are therefore question marks surrounding the ongoing viability of a categories-based approach.[52]

[48] ie due to the reforms introduced by the California Privacy Rights Act to the California Consumer Privacy Act. See California Consumer Privacy Act of 2018, s 1798.140.V.1.(k).

[49] See eg Colorado Privacy Act (2021), ss 6-1–1303.(25); Connecticut Data Privacy Act (2022), s 28; Montana Consumer Data Privacy Act (2023), s 2(25).

[50] Julie E Cohen, 'How (Not) to Write a Privacy Law' (2021) 21 Knight First Amendment Institute 5 <https://knightcolumbia.org/content/how-not-to-write-a-privacy-law> accessed 4 October 2023.

[51] ibid.

[52] Damian Clifford, Megan Richardson, and Normann Witzleb, 'Artificial Intelligence and Sensitive Inferences: New Challenges for Data Protection Laws' in Mark Findlay and others (eds), *Regulatory Insights on Artificial Intelligence: Research for Policy* (Edward Elgar 2022) 19.

Intensive personal data processing allows sensitive inferences to be drawn from seemingly innocuous data. Although the existing literature provides a valuable analysis of the problems posed by intensive personal data processing,[53] it does not fully account for how this may exacerbate the perceived emotional disconnect between personal data processing and its risks. Indeed, the varying emotional responses prompted by the processing of different types of personal data may not always be grounded in reality. We may be disconnected from the risk of harms associated with the processing of this 'ordinary' personal data even if we are aware that such risks exist.[54] I believe that this is significant and presents a key challenge to the effectiveness of data protection law. It is therefore somewhat counterintuitive for people to be less emotionally engaged with data such as machine-related information in practice, and it explains people's concerns with these practices more generally (ie despite the apparent 'paradox' between the feelings of unease and what happens in practice—see Chapter 4). Put simply, then, there is a disconnect between the perceived risks associated with the gathering of information such as cookie data and the actual risks associated with the extent to which it is shared and the inferences it can be used to generate, even if it is these concerns that are partly responsible for debates on reform.

It is with such considerations in mind that data protection law generally aims to protect against both tangible and intangible risks and harms and establish both proactive and reactive rights and obligations, including transparency requirements. That is not to say, however, that data protection law does not struggle. In part, this is due to difficulties associated with appropriately scoping the definition of personal data and the sensitive personal data categories often contained in data protection law. Once again, these points are connected in the sense that they both relate to the difficulty for objective categories of information to adequately reflect the subjective nature or experience of the protection of personal data. This will be explained further in Section C through the use of E-AI as a case study and the GDPR as the specific framework to be analysed.

[53] See Paul Quinn and Gianclaudio Malgieri, 'The Difficulty of Defining Sensitive Data—The Concept of Sensitive Data in the EU Data Protection Framework' (2021) 22 German Law Journal 1583; Sandra Wachter and Brent Mittelstadt, 'A Right to Reasonable Inferences: Re-Thinking Data Protection Law in the Age of Big Data and AI' [2019] Columbia Business Law Review 494; Solove, 'Data Is What Data Does' (n 47); Karen McCullagh, 'Data Sensitivity: Proposals for Resolving the Conundrum' (2007) 2 Journal of International Commercial Law and Technology 190; Clifford, Richardson, and Witzleb (n 52).

[54] Stark (n 1) 21.

C. Investigating the Features—Sensitivity and E-AI

E-AI provides an excellent case study to demonstrate the complexity in the interpretation of the personal data categories provided in the GDPR. The analysis in this section will expose how relying on objective categories of information as a blunt tool, aimed at accounting for sensitivity, creates problems at the fringes. E-AI often relies on biometric data. As we will see in this section, however, in the GDPR the protection of biometric data seems to be divided between (1) personal data that can be processed to reveal biometric data; (2) biometric data that is personal data; and (c) a subset of this data that is protected as sensitive personal data.[55] Determining whether sensitive personal data are processed thus depends on the interpretation of the differences between these categories.

Even leaving detection to one side, E-AI also demonstrates the challenge to the information categories approach in the GDPR, as deployments may rely on sensitive personal data in one context but not in another. This may depend on the purposes of the processing. More specifically, as will be explored, the use of E-AI for pseudo-healthcare or well-being purposes, for example, raises an important question regarding the precise boundaries of the 'data concerning health' category protected in Article 9(1). However, the use of E-AI may also arguably allow for sensitive inferences irrespective of the purposes of the processing. To examine this point, my analysis will explore how far the categories of sensitive personal data can be stretched to illustrate the blurring boundaries between the personal and sensitive personal data categories. I will first provide a detailed analysis of the GDPR provisions before then analysing how E-AI demonstrates the challenge identified and outlining the risks posed.

1. Detection and biometric data

Biometric data are defined in Article 4(14) of the GDPR as 'personal data resulting from specific technical processing relating to the physical, physiological or behavioural characteristics of a natural person, which allow or confirm the unique identification of that natural person, such as facial images or dactyloscopic data'. Given the breadth of this definition it would seem logical to conclude that E-AI will use these types of data to detect emotion. For

[55] On this categorization, see Els J Kindt, 'Having Yes, Using No? About the New Legal Regime for Biometric Data' (2017) 34(3) Computer Law & Security Review 523.

instance, outside of the detection of emotions through online browsing behaviour via text and or data mining, examples of methods of detection include the use of the Facial Action Coding System as first developed by Ekman and Friesen in the analysis of facial expressions (see Chapter 5),[56] the analysis of audio analysis to assess a person's speech through explicit (linguistic) and implicit (paralinguistic) messages, an examination of thermal signals to assess core body temperature, and also through technology reliant upon contact with the human body via bio-potential signals.[57] Before coming to this point, however, there are three elements within the definition of biometric data that require unpacking, namely (1) 'personal data [...] relating to the physical, physiological or behavioural characteristics of a natural person'; (2) 'specific technical processing'; and (3) 'allow or confirm the unique identification of that natural person'.

(a) The definitional components of biometric data

The first of the points listed seems obvious in that the biometric data covered by the Regulation are required to first satisfy the definition of personal data. Due to the wide interpretation attributed to the notion of personal data in the Regulation this does not present a high threshold, especially because of the nature of the information in question. The fact that biometric data constitute a specific category of personal data is then reflected in the fact that Article 4(14) specifies that the personal data in question must relate to the identified or identifiable natural person by virtue of the fact that they relate 'to the physical, physiological or behavioural characteristics' of that natural person. As noted by Jasserand, this aspect of the definition of biometric data serves as an acknowledgement of the fact that a broad range of measurable human characteristics can come within what is used for biometric recognition.[58] The author goes on to specify however, that the distinction between the terms physical and physiological (which is apparent from the fact that both terms are used) is unclear given that in the literature on biometric recognition they are seemingly used interchangeably.[59]

[56] See eg Paul Ekman and Wallace V Friesen, 'Measuring Facial Movement' (1976) 1 Environmental Psychology and Nonverbal Behavior 56.

[57] To further specify, these bio-potential signals refer in particular to galvanic skin response (skin's conductance, which increases with arousal or stress); electromyography (muscle activity or frequency of muscle tension); blood volume pulse (heart rate); skin temperature (skin surface temperature); electrocardiogram (measure of heart rate variability); and respiration rate (depth and speed of breathing). For a more comprehensive description, see Hatice Gunes and Maja Pantic, 'Automatic, Dimensional and Continuous Emotion Recognition' (2010) 1 International Journal of Synthetic Emotions 68.

[58] Catherine Jasserand, 'Legal Nature of Biometric Data: From "Generic" Personal Data to Sensitive Data' (2016) 2 European Data Protection Law Review 297, 304.

[59] ibid.

The second element in the definition is a curious clarification that, in essence, aims to differentiate 'personal data [...] relating to the physical, physiological or behavioural characteristics of a natural person', which relates to such characteristics but is not capable—or is merely potentially capable—of being used to extract biometric data (as opposed to that potential actually being realized), and those biometric data which have been extracted. Importantly, such an extraction of biometric data would amount to the 'processing' of personal data given (1) the first element, and (2) the fact that 'processing' amounts to pretty much any activity that can be performed on personal data (see Chapter 5).[60] However, it is important to highlight that processing for the purposes of Article 4(14) must be an example of 'specific technical processing' that allows or confirms 'the unique identification' of the natural person. This 'specific technical processing' would then appear to require, for instance, the breaking down of a sample into a mathematical representation of the original and its storage in the form of a template or representation of the extracted biometric data which could then be used for later purposes.[61] Hence, such processing would in itself need to satisfy the requirements in the Regulation—a point to which we will return regarding the meaning of the reference to the processing of 'biometric data for the *purpose of uniquely identifying* a natural person' as a category of sensitive personal data mentioned in Article 9(1) of the GDPR.[62]

In addition, it should also be noted that there is a distinction to be made between a biometric sample and biometric data. The crux of this point is highlighted by the Article 29 Working Party opinion on the concept of personal data, which notes that:

> [h]uman tissue samples (like a blood sample) are themselves sources out of which biometric data are extracted, but they are not biometric data themselves (as for instance a pattern for fingerprints is biometric data, but the finger itself is not). Therefore the extraction of information from the samples is collection of personal data, to which the rules [...] apply.[63]

[60] Processing is defined in art 4(2) of the GDPR as 'any operation or set of operations which is performed on personal data or on sets of personal data, whether or not by automated means, such as collection, recording, organisation, structuring, storage, adaptation or alteration, retrieval, consultation, use, disclosure by transmission, dissemination or otherwise making available, alignment or combination, restriction, erasure or destruction'.

[61] Els J Kindt, *Privacy and Data Protection Issues of Biometric Applications* (Springer Netherlands 2013) 43–47.

[62] Art 9(1) of the GDPR (emphasis added).

[63] Article 29 Working Party, 'Opinion on personal data' (n 9) 9.

By building on the Working Party's example a further distinction can be made, in that although an extracted formatted representation of the fingerprint pattern is considered biometric data, a photograph of the fingerprint is not, despite its being personal data. Recital 51 specifically excludes photographs from systematically being considered as sensitive personal data with reference to the biometric data category and thus appears to implicitly acknowledge that personal images may not in themselves constitute sensitive personal data with reference to the other categories contained in Article 9(1). Nevertheless, this is not to say that such a photograph could not then later become biometric data as the photograph could (given the developments in technology) be used as a sample with specific technical processing then applied to extract the biometric data (or inferences as to other sensitive categories, see Subsection C.2 below).[64]

This differentiation between extracted biometric data and 'personal data […] relating to the physical, physiological or behavioural characteristics of a natural person' also highlights the breadth of the term 'information' in the definition of personal data. More specifically, although a photograph of a fingerprint will be considered personal data as it contains information which relates to an identifiable natural person, in order for it to be considered biometric data the extraction of data which 'allow or confirm the unique identification of that natural person' is necessary. Although there has been some academic debate regarding whether the differentiation between categories of data based on a technical process was appropriate, any alternative would arguably have been either over- or under-inclusive.[65] More specifically, I believe that regulating more strictly the potential for personal data to become biometric data, instead

[64] This point is reflected in Recital 51, which states, inter alia, that '[t]he processing of photographs should not systematically be considered to be processing of special categories of personal data as they are covered by the definition of biometric data only when processed through a specific technical means allowing the unique identification or authentication of a natural person'.

[65] In her analysis of this issue, Kindt notes that this differentiation on the basis of a technical operation in itself presents a risk to fundamental rights as the collection of facial images is not subject to the prohibition in art 9(1) given that such personal data have not undergone the process through which they are rendered biometric data as understood in the Regulation. The author questions the legislative choice made in the GDPR given that, in her view, such databases of images are often the precondition that allows for biometric identification. With this in mind, the author suggests that an approach built on 'the fitness of the data to be used by automated means for identification or identity verification purposes' should have been taken into account. Although there is certainly merit to Kindt's point, I believe that such an approach would have been overly broad given the potential effects of such an approach on the online ecosystem. To clarify, if the 'fitness' of the data for identification or identity verification purposes was used as the barometer for regulation, services such as Google Image Search or even a small website hosting photographs could seemingly be rendered unlawful given the impossibility of acquiring explicit consent from every data subject and the fact that images are often put online without the data subject's knowledge or input, thereby rendering such processing outside the 'manifestly made public' exception contained in art 9(2). Indeed, Kindt explicitly refers to Google and social networking sites to highlight the potential for far-reaching use given the developments in biometric technology with reference to the uploading of photographs. Kindt, 'Having Yes, Using No?' (n 55) 530.

of the data that has undergone the specific technical processing for instance, would have been over-inclusive and that the approach in the GDPR arguably better reflects the dynamic nature of personal data. The simple fact remains that the personal data capable of undergoing specific technical processing rendering it biometric data must still satisfy the requirements of the Regulation and when the specific technical processing occurs, it will be considered biometric data provided it allows or confirms 'the unique identification of that natural person'.

This final element, therefore, is effectively the qualitative condition to satisfy the definition of biometric data provided for in Article 4(14) and hangs on what is meant by the characteristics 'which allow or confirm the unique identification of that natural person'. A perhaps obvious preliminary point is that it is those personal data relating to the physical, physiological, or behavioural characteristics which undergo the specific technical processing which allows or confirms the unique identification of the data subject that are relevant, as opposed to the characteristics themselves in isolation. As such, it seems that it is the transformation of the personal data that is key to this definition and that, as the personal data must uniquely identify the data subject, its relational connection to the data subject rests with the 'content' aspect of this cumulative element of the definition of personal data.

However, as noted by the Article 29 Working Party, a 'peculiarity' of biometric data is that they can be 'identifiers' in the sense that they may establish a link between an individual and information (eg a person with these fingerprints touched this object).[66] Although the use of biometric data as an 'identifier' merely renders the data subject 'identifiable' it does so uniquely, as the data in question is linked specifically to that individual data subject (assuming that such characteristics do in fact uniquely identify natural persons in their content, or the very nature of the information itself). In contrast, as described in the previous section, the 'relate to' cumulative element in the definition of personal data is construed broadly by the court with information capable of relating to multiple natural persons in terms of its content despite the fact that it must relate in terms of either purpose or effect to an identifiable natural person.[67] Further complexity is added by the fact that (1) the definition of biometric data provided for in Article 4(14) refers to personal data which '*allow or confirm* the *unique identification* of that natural person';[68] and (2) Article 9(1),

[66] Article 29 Working Party, 'Opinion on personal data' (n 9) 8–9.
[67] *Peter Nowak v Data Protection Commissioner* (n 10).
[68] Art 4(14) of the GDPR (emphasis added).

which prohibits the processing of the categories of sensitive personal data, refers specifically to 'biometric data for the *purpose of uniquely identifying* a natural person'.[69] These points will now be explored.

(b) Allow or confirm and the purpose of uniquely identifying

It is important to highlight that there are uncertainties regarding the use of the terms 'allow or confirm' in Article 4(14) and its correlation with the more technical nomenclature used by the biometrics community. More specifically, Jasserand suggests that this uncertainty stems from the fact that identification in data protection law and in biometrics have distinct meanings.[70] Indeed, in biometrics identification is attributed a narrow meaning, referring to the process of establishing an individual's identity through the comparison of a biometric sample with a previously stored biometric template which may be located in one or various databases. This 'one-to-many' identity matching merely requires the singling out of an individual (ie you do not have to establish their legal identity), whereas identity verification (sometimes mistakenly referred to as identity authentication), in contrast, operates as a 'one-to-one' matching process and hence its purpose is not to identify the individual as such but instead to verify them against stored biometric information (eg on a passport or a database).

On this basis, Jasserand suggests that identification in the GDPR (ie to single someone out) has a broader meaning compared with biometric identification (to establish someone's identity) and that the provisions should be interpreted in this light.[71] Hence, through the inclusion of the terms 'allow or confirm' in the definition of biometric data the author argues that both biometric identification and identity verification come within the scope of the provision. I believe that although the author is correct in her conclusion that both biometric identification and identity verification come within the scope of Article 4(14), there is an alternative way to get to this conclusion. To clarify, the author potentially confuses the purposes that biometric data are used for and the 'identifiability' of the data subject. More specifically, it is questionable whether biometric data as a category of personal data are in fact afforded a specific definition by virtue of their highly 'identifying' nature as opposed to the purpose or function for which these data are used. This is exemplified by the reference to 'unique identification' but also reflects the fact that the protection of personal

[69] Art 9(1) of the GDPR (emphasis added).
[70] Jasserand, 'Legal Nature of Biometric Data' (n 58) 304–05.
[71] ibid 305.

data is closely connected to the desire to safeguard one's human identity and flourishing.[72] In short, therefore, it could be argued that it is not that identification has a broader meaning in the GDPR but rather that it is better categorized as 'identifiability', with biometric data for the purposes of Article 4(14) (at a minimum) *allowing* for the 'unique identification' of the data subject. This brings us to the second of the two points referred to: the specific mention of biometric data in Article 9(1).

To reiterate, Article 9(1) prohibits the processing of 'biometric data for the *purpose of uniquely identifying* a natural person'.[73] As one might expect, and in light of the analysis, there is uncertainty in relation to what is meant by a 'purpose of uniquely identifying' as the apparent trigger for the application of the prohibition on the processing of these data. Indeed, one can again question whether this provision is driven by (1) the purpose of a processing operation to uniquely identify in itself, or rather by (2) 'purpose' understood within the context of the 'relating to' element of the definition of personal data as a by-product of the means of determining the 'identifiability' of the data subject. To delineate these, one can understand identification 'purpose' to mean (1) the purpose of the processing in Article 5(1)(b) (ie the purpose limitation principle), or (2) as a required element for some other purpose (eg singling out a data subject to personalize content). The issue of course is that certain authors have already seen a reference to purpose through the use of the words 'allow or confirm the unique identification' within the definition of biometric data in Article 4(14).[74]

Hence, this again demonstrates the complexity in interpreting these different categories of biometric data as just one example of the types of personal data protected in the GDPR. To reiterate, three categories of biometric data can therefore be discerned, namely ordinary personal data that can be processed to extract biometric data, biometric data as defined in Article 4(14), and 'sensitive' biometric data falling under the prohibition contained in Article 9(1). Although this three-part categorization is uncontroversial, for Kindt only biometric identification and not identity verification as understood in the biometric research literature falls within this final sensitive category, as she reads the reference to purpose as limited in scope to one-to-many identity

[72] See Clifford, Richardson, and Witzleb (n 52).

[73] Art 9(1) of the GDPR (emphasis added).

[74] ie Kindt, 'Having Yes, Using No?' (n 55); Jasserand, 'Legal Nature of Biometric Data' (n 58). See also Catherine A Jasserand, 'Avoiding Terminological Confusion between the Notions of "Biometrics" and "Biometric Data": An Investigation into the Meanings of the Terms from a European Data Protection and a Scientific Perspective' (2015) 6 International Data Privacy Law 63.

matching.[75] In contrast, Jasserand suggests that both biometric identification and identity verification should come under the prohibition in Article 9(1), as these biometric processing purposes should be interpreted in light of the data protection framework and the meaning attributed to identification therein.[76] This is a strong argument, as rather than using these biometric practices as a means of reflecting upon the operation of the legal provisions, the legal provisions are instead used to determine the legality of the purposes, but it is still unclear.

Similarly to Kindt, however, Jasserand still interprets Article 9(1) as inherently dictated by the processing purpose of the biometric data, with this being the key determining factor in their categorization (or not) as sensitive personal data.[77] However, an alternative approach would suggest that this interpretation determines the categorization based on purpose rather than determining 'identifiability' with reference to the purposes of the processing, as is necessary under the interpretation of the definition of personal data adopted by the Court of Justice.[78] As biometric data and sensitive data must also clearly be personal data, it arguably makes sense to view them through this lens and as subsets of the more general overarching category of 'ordinary' personal data. Hence, although the three categories are accepted, it is debatable whether biometric data falling within the sensitive personal data processing prohibition require the unique identification of the data subject to be a by-product of the purpose rather than the purpose itself. This approach would differentiate the category from personal data that only come under the definition of biometric data but not the sensitive category. Indeed, although such information may relate to the data subject in both content and purpose, these data potentially only have to render that natural person uniquely 'identifiable' without necessarily identifying them.

This subtle distinction would make a significant difference. It would effectively broaden the types of biometric data that might come within the prohibition in Article 9(1), arguably better reflecting the focus of this provision in that the sensitivity of certain categories of information derives from the increased risk of harm affecting the autonomy, dignity, and personality of the data subject.[79] Recognizing that unique identification may be a by-product of a purpose as opposed to being *the* purpose would effectively focus the discussion on

[75] Kindt, 'Having Yes, Using No?' (n 55) 535.
[76] Jasserand, 'Legal Nature of Biometric Data' (n 58) 309–10.
[77] ibid.
[78] Case C-582/14 *Breyer*, ECLI: EU:C:2016:779.
[79] Clifford, Richardson, and Witzleb (n 52) 19, 34–37.

the nature of the personal data in question as opposed to that of the processing purposes, arguably reflecting the teleological goals of the GDPR. In breaking down the interpretative ambiguity, this extract from Article 9(1) must first be viewed within the overall provision and here it is important to note that the construction of 'biometric data for the *purpose of uniquely identifying* a natural person' is distinguishable, in that the other protected categories are unquestionably protected on the basis of their nature without any specific reference to purpose. Indeed, racial or ethnic origin, political opinions, religious or philosophical beliefs, trade union membership, genetic data, data concerning health, sex life, or sexual orientation are all prohibited on the basis of their categorization as opposed to the particular purpose of the processing. Despite these points, it must be acknowledged that there is no certainty, only complexity. In fact, for the purposes of this section, that ambiguity is the precise point being highlighted.

The more restrictive interpretation of what comes under the sensitive personal data prohibition may be the correct one even if I believe that the alternative reflects the meaning attributed to the terminology in the Regulation and not interdisciplinary insights. But what then are the implications of all this for E-AI? I will demonstrate these with three examples. First, irrespective of the various possible interpretations described, there appears to be a somewhat narrow prohibition provided for in Article 9(1). In the context of E-AI, the specific applications and, indeed, implementations will be significant. The narrower purpose-orientated understanding of biometric data will clearly limit the prohibition in Article 9(1) to 'unique identification' purposes, thereby seemingly excluding many (if not all) applications of E-AI from its scope.[80] Even with the broader interpretation, however, it appears that only purposes that uniquely identify the data subject in terms of a qualitative assessment of the personal data in question will invoke the prohibition in Article 9(1). Where the data subject remains merely 'identifiable' it will fall within the general provisions for the processing of personal data, thereby requiring the application of one of the conditions for lawful processing in Article 6.

For example, here we can refer to the singling out of natural persons through profiling for programmatic advertising purposes, where the unique identity of the data subject is not known despite the fact the biometric insights (ie behavioural insights) inferred may render this natural person *identifiable* given that they will be linked to a pseudonymous identifier. 'Identifiability' rests on the

[80] ie Kindt, 'Having Yes, Using No?' (n 55); Jasserand, 'Legal Nature of Biometric Data' (n 58). See also Jasserand, 'Avoiding Terminological Confusion' (n 74).

assessment of all the 'means reasonably likely to be used', and to assess whether something is reasonably likely 'all objective factors' should be explored including cost, the available technology (and any developments),[81] and the legality of the identification attempt.[82] Importantly, the definition in Article 4(1) focuses on the capacity to both 'directly' but also 'indirectly' identify the natural person through 'identifiers'. These identifiers can either refer to a specific attribute or collection of attributes which directly or indirectly identifies a natural person or renders the natural person identifiable. The definition specifically refers to examples such as 'an online identifier' and factors specific to a natural person (eg physical, physiological, or mental) but also, more broadly, to the fact that under the GDPR pseudonymous data are still considered personal.[83] It appears therefore that the processing of biometric data for such purposes will not come within the sensitive personal data category as the data subject will not be uniquely *identified* with respect to the type of personal data processed.

Secondly, for the purposes of the GDPR, biometric data must still be classified as personal data for the Regulation to apply. This seems like an obvious statement, but it is worth clarifying with an example, as there are limits to the definition of personal data (even in the GDPR).[84] In other words, what if the specific application of E-AI does not aim to single out a natural person by design or, alternatively, only aims to only single out specific individuals? A *potential* example of where E-AI is used but personal data are not processed is illustrated by the testing of the emotion-sensitive public advertising in 2015 developed by M & C Saatchi.[85] This test deployment took the form of a panel advertisement designed to be located in public areas such bus stops, with a camera installed to detect, inter alia, the emotions of passers-by via a Facial Action Coding System. As described by McStay, the first test deployment of

[81] More specifically, Recital 26 of the GDPR specifies that to determine whether a natural person is identifiable,

> account should be taken of all the means reasonably likely to be used, such as singling out, either by the controller or by another person to identify the natural person directly or indirectly. To ascertain whether means are reasonably likely to be used to identify the natural person, account should be taken of all objective factors, such as the costs of and the amount of time required for identification, taking into consideration the available technology at the time of the processing and technological developments.

See on this *Breyer* (n 78).

[82] See on this *Breyer* (n 78).

[83] See art 4(5) of the GDPR.

[84] Indeed, despite what Purtova thinks, I believe that the GDPR is not quite the law of everything. See Richardson and others (n 20); Dalla Corte (n 42).

[85] John Still, 'Is Artificial Intelligence the Next Step in Advertising?' *The Guardian* (27 July 2015) <www.theguardian.com/media-network/2015/jul/27/artificial-intelligence-future-advertising-saatchi-clearchannel> accessed 26 November 2018.

this technology allowed for the evolution of the advertising content over time (ie depending on the emotions of those viewing it in order to make itself gradually more effective) without the storage of any data or indeed the targeting of an identified or identifiable natural person.[86] Storage is arguably key to 'identifiability' as the longer data are stored, the more likely identification becomes. Put simply, the longer the period during which the data are kept, the longer there is an opportunity for them to satisfy the cumulative criteria contained in the definition of personal data.[87]

By relying on aggregate improvement, this example demonstrates how in public places such technologies may interact with society *arguably* without necessarily 'singling out' individuals and, hence, thereby *potentially* remaining outside the scope of the GDPR. More specifically, as claimed by the companies behind the pilot, the test technology simply reacted to facial expressions of up to 12 people at a time and did not store any information.[88] Moreover, if the categorical breakdown in such circumstances is based on age range, gender, and emotional status (eg happy, sad) etc, it is unclear whether such information is enough to truly render an individual identifiable in the traditional sense, given that the targeting would remain at an aggregate level. Although it may seem that I have chosen a particularly thorny example for dramatic effect, it does demonstrate the very real concerns with the surveillance of public spaces and the impact (or lack thereof) of data protection law. To recap, although the GDPR lists biometric data as falling within the prohibition against the processing of sensitive personal data in Article 9(1), for it to be classified as such it must (as a preliminary step) first come within the scope of the definition of personal data.

In contrast, thirdly, the processing of biometric data in smart devices for E-AI purposes may come within the scope of Article 9(1), as the very purpose of the processing may be to uniquely identify the emotions of the individual using their biometric data. Here one can refer to the use of smart watches, for instance, for *pseudo*-healthcare (well-being) purposes or the use of E-AI in a smart screen/television, for example, for interactive gaming purposes, where the natural person must inevitably be identified and, given the nature of personal data processed, this will clearly do so in a 'unique' manner. As such, the sub-purpose of uniquely identifying will come within the purpose of processing biometric data for the detection of the data subject's emotions. In this

[86] Andrew McStay, 'Empathic Media and Advertising: Industry, Policy, Legal and Citizen Perspectives (the Case for Intimacy)' (2016) 3 Big Data & Society 1, 6–8.
[87] Hon, Millard, and Walden (n 12) 213–14.
[88] Still (n 85).

regard, it is important to note that (1) information does not have to be accurate for it to be considered personal data,[89] and (2) the very purpose is to process biometric data that uniquely identifies the data subject in terms of the content element in the relational nexus for the purpose of offering them an insight into their emotions. As such, the unique identification of the data subject is a necessary component of the purpose as the data subject will be identified in order to achieve the purpose and the content of the biometric data processed achieves this identification in a unique manner.

Therefore, purpose seems to play an important role in delineating the biometric data that come within the Article 9(1) irrespective of how the category is approached, thus demonstrating its ambiguity. However, this role may relate to an assessment of the qualitative nature of the data and how the information relates to and identifies the natural person rather than what the data is used for specifically. This is in line with the definition of personal data provided for in Article 4(1), as opposed to the purpose of the processing (construed narrowly). Depending on whether one is trying to deploy E-AI through a smart device such as a smart watch compared with a smart television, or 'online' through behaviour and text analysis, or 'offline' in public or private spaces, the means of detection may vary. It is therefore arguable that establishing whether the data processed by E-AI falls into the personal or sensitive personal data category may potentially depend on the means of detection used: the use of biometric data (for E-AI, this could be images or audio collected by a smart device) may result in the processing of personal data, sensitive personal data, or arguably even non-personal data.

2. Inferences and sensitive data

From the analysis in the previous subsection, the purposes of the processing may also play a key role in determining whether sensitive personal data are processed. As will be demonstrated in this subsection, this may also be the case in terms of whether the inferences drawn fall into the sensitive personal data categories. The analysis will also highlight how the purposes of the processing may not, however, be definitive and therefore how sensitive inferences may be revealed indirectly through the processing of personal data.

[89] See Dara Hallinan and Frederik Zuiderveen Borgesius, 'Opinions Can Be Incorrect (in Our Opinion)! On Data Protection Law's Accuracy Principle' (2020) 10 International Data Privacy Law 1.

(a) *'Sensitive' purposes*

Although it is conceivable that a specific deployment of E-AI may only process personal data, it is important to note that the insights gathered may then be combined with the processing of personal data 'revealing' one of the sensitive categories mentioned in Article 9(1) depending on the purposes of the processing. Put simply, the detection of an individual's affective state will inevitably serve some ends and thus these ends may themselves invoke the prohibition. To demonstrate this point, reference can be made to a study conducted by Cabañas and colleagues, which demonstrated the capacity to target advertising on Facebook based on interests connected with personal attributes seemingly falling within Article 9(1) of the GDPR.[90] Indeed, from the authors' analysis it is demonstrably possible to target an individual based on their 'interest' (eg distilled from the fact they follow certain groups) in, for example, a particular religion or political party.[91] As a further illustration of this point, one can also refer to the *Cambridge Analytica* scandal,[92] where psychometric profiles were used to target people for political purposes on the basis of (and tailored towards) those individuals' perceived feelings towards a social issue under political debate.[93]

The purposes may therefore also be key as they may provide a clear link to the type of inference that may be drawn. Perhaps the best illustration of this point is the use of smart devices (such as smart watches) for *pseudo*-healthcare or well-being purposes. Article 4(15) defines data concerning health as 'personal data related to the physical or mental health of a natural person, including the provision of health care services, which reveal information about his or her health status'. This provision is further specified in the non-binding Recital 35 which stipulates, inter alia, that '[p]ersonal data concerning health should include all data pertaining to the health status of a data subject which reveal information relating to the past, current or future physical or mental health status of the data subject'. But then are insights that are garnered through E-AI for well-being (eg the quantified-self movement) purposes or for the purposes

[90] José González Cabañas, Ángel Cuevas, and Rubén Cuevas, 'Unveiling and Quantifying Facebook Exploitation of Sensitive Personal Data for Advertising Purposes' (Proceedings of the 27th USENIX Conference on Security Symposium, USENIX Association, 2018) <http://dl.acm.org/citation.cfm?id=3277203.3277240> accessed 4 October 2023.

[91] ibid.

[92] See 'The Cambridge Analytica Files' *The Guardian* <www.theguardian.com/news/series/cambridge-analytica-files> accessed 4 October 2023.

[93] Vian Bakir and Andrew McStay, 'Fake News and The Economy of Emotions: Problems, Causes, Solutions' [2017] Digital Journalism 1; Information Commissioner's Office, 'Investigation into the Use of Data Analytics in Political Campaigns' (*ICO*, 2018) <https://ico.org.uk/media/action-weve-taken/2259371/investigation-into-data-analytics-for-political-purposes-update.pdf> accessed 27 November 2018.

of advertising or marketing distinct from mental health data depending on the nature of the data and the potential to link such insights with an underlying mental illness? In essence, the question is what personal data come within this 'data concerning health' category and thus the prohibition contained in Article 9(1)? It is arguable that, given that the purpose is not to gain insights into the mental health status of the data subject, the personal data gathered would remain merely personal and not sensitive personal data.

However, in this regard it is interesting to refer in particular to the *Lindqvist* case, in which the Court of Justice found that the publishing of information relating to the fact that a woman had injured her foot came within the meaning of 'data concerning health' under the then Article 8(1) Directive 95/46/EC.[94] In its judgment the Court found that '[i]n the light of the purpose of the directive, the expression "data concerning health" used in Article 8(1) thereof must be given a wide interpretation so as to include information concerning all aspects, both physical and mental, of the health of an individual'.[95] Here it is also interesting to refer to the 2015 letter sent by the Article 29 Working Party to the European Parliament and the adjoining Annex on the scope of the 'data concerning health' category in the context of well-being applications and devices in light of Directive 95/46/EC, which was then in force.[96] In presenting a wide and dynamic interpretation of health data, the Working Party noted that 'health data (or all data pertaining to the health status of a data subject)' is a much broader term than the term 'medical' and also interestingly for the purposes of this analysis observes that data protection authorities have found that 'data about a person's intellectual and emotional capacity' concern the health of data subjects, thus coming within the 'data concerning health' category.[97]

The GDPR inserted a definition of 'data concerning health' for the first time and it appears from the broad language contained in Article 4(15) and Recital 35 that the expansive interpretation adopted by the Court has been explicitly incorporated in the Regulation. Interpreting the sensitive personal data categories in a broad manner to include information that 'indirectly' reveals such information was recently confirmed by the Court of Justice as the correct interpretation—again in circumstances dealing with the publication of information online.[98] Such an approach also appears consistent with the line of

[94] Case C-101/01 *Bodil Lindqvist*, ECLI:EU:C:2003:596.
[95] ibid 50.
[96] Article 29 Working Party, 'ANNEX—Health Data in Apps and Devices, to the Letter to European Commission, DG CONNECT on mHealth, Brussels, 05 February 2015'.
[97] ibid 2.
[98] Case C-184/20 *OT v Vyriausioji tarnybinės etikos komisija*, ECLI:EU:C:2022:601, paras 117–28.

argumentation adopted above in the previous section. However, it does raise a similar difficulty to that described in relation to the protection of biometric data in the determination of the precise boundaries between the personal and sensitive personal data categories. Indeed as noted by Malgieri and Comandé, when interpreting Article 4(15) and Recital 35, the question becomes one of how far the 'data revealing health' category stretches.[99] More specifically, the authors note that the determination of how to delineate those personal data which fall within the Article 9(1) prohibition and those that do not is precisely the key issue in scoping this prohibition. As one might imagine, there is certain information that will fall squarely within this category and here one can refer to Recital 35 in particular for examples.[100] Such personal data may relate to the medical information about an identified individual but may also, inter alia, include information regarding appointment times at a particular medical centre or the membership of a support group for those suffering from a particular illness. What becomes far more difficult to categorize, however, is the seemingly innocuous personal data, which although not health data by virtue of their content (ie their very nature) or even the purposes for which they are processed, may be considered as such due to inferences which can be drawn from their processing.

(b) *Indirectly revealing sensitive data*

In its decision in *Lindqvist*, the Court of Justice found that the publishing of information on a community church's website relating to the fact that a woman had injured her foot came within the meaning of 'data concerning health'.[101] Following the decision, there were concerns, for instance, that the publishing of virtually all personal images could be construed as sensitive personal data

[99] Gianclaudio Malgieri and Giovanni Comandé, 'Sensitive-by-Distance: Quasi-Health Data in the Algorithmic Era' (2017) 26 Information & Communications Technology Law 229, 231–37.

[100] This provision states that:

> [p]ersonal data concerning health should include all data pertaining to the health status of a data subject which reveal information relating to the past, current or future physical or mental health status of the data subject. This includes information about the natural person collected in the course of the registration for, or the provision of, health care services as referred to in Directive 2011/24/EU of the European Parliament and of the Council (1) to that natural person; a number, symbol or particular assigned to a natural person to uniquely identify the natural person for health purposes; information derived from the testing or examination of a body part or bodily substance, including from genetic data and biological samples; and any information on, for example, a disease, disability, disease risk, medical history, clinical treatment or the physiological or biomedical state of the data subject independent of its source, for example from a physician or other health professional, a hospital, a medical device or an in vitro diagnostic test.

[101] *Bodil Lindqvist* (n 94).

processing, given that such images often expose information regarding characteristics such as race, skin colour, and religion.[102] Although, as alluded to above in Subsection C.1(a), the specific issues associated with photographs have been dealt with in the reforms introduced by the Regulation, uncertainty remains as this represents just one type of exception for a particular form that information can take. In the more recent *OT* judgment dealing with the application of the sensitive personal data categories provided in the Regulation, for instance, the Court noted that publishing information of name-specific data online relating to an individual's spouse, cohabitee, or partner indirectly revealing the sexual orientation of the individual constituted the processing of sensitive personal data.[103] It is therefore clear from these judgments that the purpose of the processing does not always determine whether personal data falls within the scope of the Article 9(1) processing prohibition.

The question thus becomes one of how indirect this connection has to be for it to no longer disclose the sensitive insights for the purposes of Article 9 of the Regulation. If for instance (similarly to the definition of biometric data) some other technical process is required, it is very likely that the information in question will be merely personal but will become sensitive when it is processed to reveal the sensitive inferences. In other words, one must wonder what kind of separation results in information being classified as 'ordinary' personal data when it is only a short (perhaps, technical) step from one of the protected categories in Article 9(1).

As described in the previous section, it appears well established that in assessing the application of Article 9(1), one must have regard for both the 'raw' personal data (ie that which is collected either directly or indirectly from the data subject) and also the processed personal data and the inferences which may be derived indirectly. Indeed, the reference to the 'processing of personal data *revealing*' sensitive personal data in Article 9(1) arguably results in a blurring of the lines between the categories and the need to refer to inferred processed personal data in interpreting the application of the prohibition.[104] Although 'data concerning health' are somewhat differentiated from the other categories of sensitive personal data, the reference to personal data

[102] Lilian Edwards, 'Data Protection: Enter the General Data Protection Regulation' in Lilian Edwards (ed), *Law, Policy and the Internet* (Bloomsbury 2018) 89.

[103] *OT v Vyriausioji tarnybinės etikos komisija* (n 97).

[104] See eg Edwards, 'Data Protection' (n 102); Lilian Edwards, 'Data Protection and E-Privacy: From Spam and Cookies to Big Data, Machine Learning and Profiling' in Edwards (ed), Law, Policy and the Internet (n 97); Damian Clifford, 'Citizen-Consumers in a Personalised Galaxy: Emotion Influenced Decision-Making, A True Path to the Dark Side?' in Lilian Edwards, Burkhard Schafer, and Edina Harbinja (eds), *Emerging Technology, Regulation and Ethics* (1st edn, Edinburgh University Press 2020).

which 'reveal information about [the data subject's] health status' in the definition of data concerning health contained in Article 4(15), as supplemented by Recital 35, seems to point towards a similarly broad approach. This has been confirmed by the Court in the *OT* case, where the Court noted that although the word 'concerning' could be read as limiting the information coming within the scope of the category, this would be inconsistent with 'a contextual analysis of the provisions'.[105]

Here it is again interesting to refer to the Annex of the Article 29 Working Party letter to the Parliament mentioned in the previous sub-section, where it is noted that (1) personal data are health data where they are inherently medical data; (2) the personal data are raw sensor data that can be used (either by themselves or in combination with other data) to draw conclusions about the health status of a natural person; or (3) where such conclusions are drawn about a person's health status irrespective of, inter alia, the accuracy of these conclusions.[106] The first of these points is the easiest to categorize as such data will relate to the data subject's health in terms of its content. The second and third points are controversial as raw sensor data can increasingly be used to draw conclusions about an individual's health status, given the technological developments. Consequently, understanding the precise nature of the technical step required to transform this personal data into sensitive personal data is essential, and thus determining whether such personal data could relate to the health status of an individual will require a context-dependent assessment that will hinge in part on the scale of the processing. It is debatable whether reference should also be made to the purpose and effect of the processing in the assessment of how the personal data relate to the data subject. Indeed, although traditionally one would associate the sensitive personal data category with the content element,[107] in an era of 'big data' the automated processing of ordinary categories of personal data may often reveal sensitive personal data insights, particularly as data do not have to be accurate in order to be personal.

Hence, this capacity to infer should be taken into consideration and this is clearly an area where E-AI presents an excellent illustration of this need but also points to how the 'categories' approach evident in the Regulation struggles. To borrow and further expand upon an example from the Article 29 Working Party Annex, although it is clear that the posting of 'sad' messages on a social networking site will not amount to the processing of sensitive personal data,

[105] *OT v Vyriausioji tarnybinės etikos komisija* (n 97) para 124.
[106] Article 29 Working Party, 'ANNEX—Health Data in Apps and Devices' (n 95) 5.
[107] In this regard one can refer to the text of the GDPR itself and the listing of certain categories of data.

the further processing of this information to reveal whether a natural person suffers from depression would be prohibited subject to the exceptions contained in Article 9(2).[108] However, to further complicate this example, one may wonder whether the processing of these posts to reveal the emotional state of the individual for advertising purposes without processing them to reveal their mental health status would still come under Article 9(1). What if the controller only had a snapshot of the person's emotional state? And what if the interest that they were targeting had nothing to do with their emotional well-being? There are therefore important challenges associated with deciphering whether personal data processed by E-AI fall within the prohibition against the processing of sensitive personal data. Such considerations are key to determining the burden on controllers and hence, the level of protection afforded to the data subject.

The form E-AI takes is therefore important, but the purposes of the processing may also play a key role. To emphasize the importance of such considerations, one can refer to the fact that Facebook has previously been found to have facilitated the targeting of insecure youths with 'vulnerable' moods.[109] Although this example could be seen by some as an outlier, it does demonstrate the more abstract point. I believe that there are no obvious answers here as any assessment will be context dependent, but it is safe to conclude that much will hang on the scale of the processing and also whether the inference as to the data subject's health status could be (or indeed is) made without the need for an additional technical process. In this regard, however, it is important to emphasize the Article 29 Working Party's third example of when personal data are health data, namely where conclusions are drawn about a person's health status irrespective of the accuracy of these conclusions. This seems to point to the purpose and effect of the processing in terms of the triggering of the applicability of Article 9(1).[110]

Aside from the more general issues associated with the distinction between categories of data, therefore, the problem is potentially compounded by the

[108] Article 29 Working Party, 'ANNEX—Health Data in Apps and Devices' (n 95) 3.

[109] See Sam Levin, 'Facebook Told Advertisers it Can Identify Teens Feeling "Insecure" and "Worthless"' *The Guardian* (1 May 2017) <www.theguardian.com/technology/2017/may/01/facebook-advertising-data-insecure-teens> accessed 29 August 2017; Olivia Solon, '"This Oversteps a Boundary": Teenagers Perturbed by Facebook Surveillance' *The Guardian* (2 May 2017) <www.theguardian.com/technology/2017/may/02/facebook-surveillance-tech-ethics> accessed 29 August 2017; 'Facebook Research Targeted Insecure Youth, Leaked Documents Show' *The Independent* (1 May 2017) <www.independent.co.uk/news/media/facebook-leaked-documents-research-targeted-insecure-youth-teenagers-vulnerable-moods-advertising-a7711551.html> accessed 29 August 2017.

[110] An additional point of concern may relate to the potential negative impact such inaccuracies may have on the data subject—this will be described in more detail in Chapter 5.

fact that, depending on the purpose for which the E-AI technology is applied, the processing to develop the model may be completed in a product/marketing campaign development stage or even in academic or private research. This reflects the separation between the different ways that personal data may be processed in line with Figure 3.1. Such processing may therefore remain somewhat disconnected from any potential harm to the end-user, or indeed may arguably be compatible with the original purpose, given the special allowances afforded to repurposing for scientific research in the purpose limitation principle.[111] This also points to the potential challenge posed by what is known as 'function creep'.[112]

One must therefore wonder whether we should be focused on the protection of categories of information at all but instead on its uses—this is not a new debate. For instance, Bergkamp, writing in 2002 about EU Data Protection Directive 95/46/EC, questioned how governments were able to justify the adoption of such 'onerous, expensive, and paradoxical [...] regimes' in what he believed to be only on the basis of 'some vague notion of "fundamental right" and hypothetical risks'.[113] However, it seems unreasonable to suggest that these frameworks do not respond to genuine risks even if some of these are intangible. The question is more whether the frameworks respond appropriately to the risks posed. Personal data processing by its very nature involves risk.[114] For instance, the tangible risks associated with the potential for identity theft/fraud[115] exist irrespective of whether the personal data gathered may aim to detect the individual's emotions, whereas the potential negative effects associated with a data breach where the emotional insights reveal an underlying

[111] According to the purpose limitation principle, 'scientific research' is compatible with the initial purpose of the processing and thus no additional condition for lawful processing is required, provided the safeguards contained in art 89(1) of the GDPR are satisfied. Given that scientific research is not defined in the GDPR and further that Recital 159 of the GDPR indicates that it is to be 'interpreted in a broad manner', one must question how far this notion can stretch in the context of research conducted by private commercial entities, especially in light of the exemptions to the right to erasure (art 17(3)(d) GDPR) and the right to object (art 21(6) GDPR).

[112] Michael Curry, David Phillips, and Priscilla Regan, 'Emergency Response Systems and the Creeping Legibility of People and Places' (2004) 20 Information Society 357, 362. Function creep relates to a situation 'when a system developed for a particular purpose comes to be used for, or to provide the underpinnings for other systems that are used for, different purposes'.

[113] Lucas Bergkamp, 'EU Data Protection Policy: The Privacy Fallacy: Adverse Effects of Europe's Data Protection Policy in an Information-Driven Economy' (2002) 18 Computer Law & Security Review 31, 42.

[114] See Recital 71 of the GDPR: three particular risks specifically associated with profiling are provided in the GDPR, namely the risk of a data breach, the risk of errors, and finally the risk of discriminatory effects. However, and as will be clear from the analysis below, the risk of discriminatory effects is the only harm in this list, as the risk of data breach and the risk of errors are merely risks of data protection violations that are precursors to potential tangible and intangible harms.

[115] See Orla Lynskey, *The Foundations of EU Data Protection Law* (OUP 2016) 202–08.

mental health condition may be subjectively worse depending on the individual. Therefore, it is necessary to examine not only the application of technologies such as E-AI, but also the potential risks associated with personal data processing and E-AI more generally. This is certainly something the EU legislator is well aware of, given the regulation of E-AI in the Artificial Intelligence Act[116] and the banning of its use in certain contexts.

We can also consider risks more generally through a data protection law lens in order to discern the value of data protection law. In order to distil insights, information is collected through a variety of sensors and mechanisms and will therefore often incorporate the processing of large amounts of data.[117] Such personal data processing thus inherently incorporates the risk of both tangible and intangible harms. But what does this mean in a practical sense? In order to contextualize the debate, imagine John, who suffers from bipolar disorder, purchasing a smart device to track his emotions with the intention of improving his well-being.[118] To detect John's emotional state his smart device (let us assume it is a smart watch) captures a number of variables such as movement, heart rate, temperature, and galvanic skin response. This information is then transmitted to an application that John has downloaded on his phone allowing him to map his emotional states with reference to his calendar and geolocation and thus correlate the fluctuations with his scheduled events. Such insights can allow John to map his profile and alter his lifestyle to improve his well-being (leaving to one side the obvious doubts as to accuracy for now). But how and where are the data stored? How are they being processed? And for what purposes can John's information be used? Each of these questions is not specific to E-AI but does highlight the risk of harm which data protection law aims to mitigate.

Although the secure storage of data is of paramount importance given that, as with the above example, this may involve the processing of sensitive health data, it does not appear to raise unique difficulties from a security perspective when one considers the multitude of services gathering such sensitive data without a specific emotion-tracking component. However, one might question

[116] Proposal of the European Parliament and of the Council Laying Down Harmonised Rules on Artificial Intelligence (Artificial Intelligence Act) and Amending Certain Union Legislative Acts (COM (2021) 206 final).

[117] Detection mechanisms focus on a range of techniques, such as text analysis technology, speech emotional analytics technology, technology for quantifying emotions via the analysis of facial expressions/eye movement, and content consumption contextual triggers capable of inferring user moods based on usage patterns (eg media content provision services such as e-books, music, and video streaming)—see Chapter 4.

[118] See eg 'World's First Emotion Sensor & Mental Health Advisor' <www.myfeel.co/> accessed 30 August 2018.

the capacity to reveal particular emotional vulnerabilities, therefore potentially aggravating the associated harms. For example, assume that John keeps the fact that he suffers from bipolar disorder a secret to avoid what he believes would be a reputational harm if his work colleagues were to find out. Although this fear may not be a rational emotional response, in that a data breach and the disclosure of John's secret may not (in reality) have an effect on his reputation, the fear or anxiety attached to the perception of this potential harm qualifies as a potential intangible harm.[119] In his analysis of data processing harms, Calo decouples harm into two categories, namely subjective and objective. As described by the author, subjective harms are those that are 'internal to the person harm' or, in other words, those harms that 'flow from the perception of unwanted observation'.[120] Objective harms by contrast are those that are external to the person and involve 'the forced or unanticipated use of information about a person against that person',[121] ie even if they may also have a subjective impact. Positioning data protection law as having an affect-orientated/subjective impact appears to be well established in literature, and therefore John's fear or anxiety of negative consequences stemming from a potential data breach arguably justifies this affect-orientated conception and Calo's categorization of subjective harms. However, although John, in the example above, may feel anxious about the collection of his personal data and the security of the insights into his emotional well-being, this may not affect his decision to use the technology as his desire to improve his mental health might outweigh his assessment of the risks. This reflects the important role of choice, which will be discussed in the next chapter.

E-AI may also be just one feature of a product or service that is less directly linked to its purpose. For example, imagine Ruth who lives in a 'smart' home. To detect Ruth's emotions, devices within her home collect large amounts of data using voice and facial emotion recognition technology. Such technology is then utilized to adjust Ruth's living conditions based on her emotions (eg lighting or media consumption). In such circumstances, could intangible harms prevent those who visit Ruth from acting in particular ways in her home? This question alludes to the potential impact of surveillance and the resulting chilling effect on behaviour. Significantly, as noted by Calo, '[e]ven where we know intellectually that we are interacting with an image or a machine, our brains are hardwired to respond as though a person were actually there'.[122] This

[119] See Daniel Solove, '"I've Got Nothing to Hide" and Other Misunderstandings of Privacy' (2007) 44 The San Diego Law Review 745, 745–46.

[120] Ryan Calo, 'The Boundaries of Privacy Harm' (2011) 86 Indiana Law Journal 1142–43.

[121] ibid.

[122] ibid 1147.

observation contrasts strongly with the perspective of Posner, who argues that harm only occurs when an individual accesses and misuses information resulting in economic or physical harm and that therefore mere computerized observation is not enough to be categorized as a harm.[123] However, Posner's understanding is disputed strongly here and in other literature.[124] Certainly, I acknowledge that the mere trivial breach of data protection law will not generally result in legally cognizable damage,[125] but this does not mean that minor breaches do not cause some (even collective) harm, reflecting the fact that in any case they can still result in the imposition of penalties by Data Protection Authorities. Instead, it is argued that an affect-orientated conception of data protection allows for a deeper understanding of moral harm and its effect on actual individual behaviour, and this appears to be reflected in the research.[126] Consequently, the mere observation or perception of surveillance can arguably have a chilling effect on behaviour, thereby justifying statutory intervention.[127]

Moreover, such monitoring can also have an impact on an individual's ability to 'self-present'.[128] This refers to the ability of individuals to present multifaceted versions of themselves,[129] and thus behave differently depending on the circumstances.[130] As noted by Nissenbaum, informational norms 'circumscribe the type or nature of information about various individuals that, within a given context, is allowable, expected, or even demanded to be revealed'.[131] Although much of the discussion regarding an individual's capacity to self-present relates to anecdotal evidence in the context of the accessing of social media profiles by employers, one must acknowledge the potential impact given the controlling effect of being (or feeling as if one is being) monitored.[132]

[123] Richard A Posner, 'Privacy, Surveillance, and Law' (2008) 75 University of Chicago Law Review.

[124] See Calo (n 120) 1142–43.

[125] See eg Case C–300/21 *Österreichische Post*, ECLI:EU:C:2023:370.

[126] See Calo (n 120).

[127] One should also note that surveillance can have a chilling effect whether it is in the private or public domain; see Neil M Richards, 'The Dangers of Surveillance' (2013) 126 Harvard Law Review 1934, 1935: 'we must recognize that surveillance transcends the public/private divide. Public and private surveillance are simply related parts of the same problem, rather than wholly discrete. Even if we are ultimately more concerned with government surveillance, any solution must grapple with the complex relationships between government and corporate watchers.'

[128] Lynskey, *The Foundations of EU Data Protection Law* (n 115) 218.

[129] Richard Warner and Robert H Sloan, 'Self, Privacy, and Power: Is It All Over?' (2014) 17 Tulane Journal of Technology & Intellectual Property 8.

[130] James Rachels, 'Why Privacy Is Important' (1975) 4 Philosophy & Public Affairs 323, 323–33. The author goes on to discuss how we behave differently depending on who we are talking to; this has been argued as dishonest or a mask by certain authors, but the author disagrees, saying that these 'masks' are in fact a crucial part of the various relationships and are therefore not dishonest.

[131] Helen F Nissenbaum, 'Privacy as Contextual Integrity' (2004) 79 Washington Law Review 119, 120–21.

[132] Bentham refers to this as the 'consciousness of visibility' and it is the conceptual basis for the effectiveness of Bentham's Panopticon; see Jeremy Bentham, *Panopticon: Or The Inspection-House* (T Payne 1791).

For example, could the use of E-AI in Ruth's home prevent her friends and family from adopting the masks they present only to close friends and family? Behaviour or lifestyle may be masked in certain circumstances but so too are emotions and thus emotions that are 'felt' are often not 'displayed'.[133] Felt emotions (ie the actual emotional state of the individual) may be damaging to that person if expressed.[134] The erosion of the barrier between felt and displayed emotions or at least the perception of this erosion (given the clear accuracy concerns with E-AI) may present key challenges and, significantly, this view is given further weight by the potential to also deploy such technology outside the home and thus in so-called 'smart' environments.

E-AI provides an excellent illustrative example, as it arguably adds a layer of intimacy invasion via the perceived capacity not only to detect emotions as expressed, but also to detect underlying emotions that are being deliberately disguised (even if such technology may in practice only, for example, detect facial movements and not emotions, see Chapter 5). E-AI also challenges the division between personal and sensitive personal data as deployments may obviously rely on sensitive personal data in one context but not in another. Importantly, although there are significant doubts as to the accuracy of this technology which will be explored in detail in Chapter 5, it should be noted that even inaccurate inferences may be personal data and that the perception of accuracy may be just as harmful (or even more so) to individuals. Despite the uncertainties generated by the categories of information protected in the GDPR, therefore, it seems that protections of some kind are warranted.

D. Limits of the Challenge

The E-AI case study has demonstrated how objective categories of personal data can lead to inconsistencies. The treatment in different ways of what may appear to be the same risk arguably raises questions about the ongoing legitimacy of data protection law. However, although I believe there is a disengagement with the risks associated with the processing of personal data and that the reasons for this are arguably partly caused by these legislative frameworks, I also believe that data protection law responds to legitimate risks and has value. In this section, I will explore the ongoing utility of the 'categories'

[133] See eg Bella M Depaulo, 'Nonverbal Behavior and Self-Presentation' (1992) 111 Psychological Bulletin 203.

[134] eg in the workplace context one can imagine how masking your true emotions towards your employer or co-worker could be seen as a necessity in terms of career development.

approach in light of the criticism that focusing on the nature of information alone to determine the application of data protection laws (or indeed, the enhanced protections afforded to sensitive personal data in certain jurisdictions) fails to account for the subjectivity of data protection law.

I believe that the tangible and intangible, or objective and subjective, harms discussed legitimize the need for some form of statutory intervention imposing limits on the processing of personal data. Even in the US, for instance, where the adoption of data protection law to regulate the private sector has only recently emerged at the state level, the debate seems to be shifting from one about whether data protection laws are needed to a debate centred instead on the form that these hard law interventions should take.[135] Nevertheless, a key weakness of these laws is that they seemingly assume that the nature of particular types of information alone may automatically reveal whether they should be considered personal data or indeed be offered heightened protections as sensitive personal data. To illustrate, we can refer to (1) the exclusion of certain types of data from the scope of protection in certain jurisdictions, and (2) the separation of types of sensitive data, which are then subject to enhanced protections in various data protection laws.

1. Objective categories and personal data

The exclusion of publicly available information from the scope of protection in state consumer privacy laws in the US and also the debate regarding device-related information in Australia, mentioned in Section B above, are excellent illustrations of the first of these points. Such exclusions from the scope of protection create arbitrary lines disconnected from the subjective nature of the experience of data subjects. For example, assuming that the processing of publicly available information does not pose a risk simplifies the protections by providing one-size-fits-all rules that fail to account for the importance of context. In simple terms, the exclusion of this publicly available information fails to recognize that context is key. People may be happy to share their personal data online through social media platforms, for instance, but this does not mean that they are then happy with its use for all subsequently defined

[135] See the summary of the current debate amongst scholars in the US offered by Waldman: Ari Waldman, 'Privacy's Rights Trap' [2022] Northwestern University Law Review Online 90 <https://scholarlycommons.law.northwestern.edu/nulr_online/327> accessed 4 October 2023.

purposes, such as the development of large language models[136] or facial recognition technology.[137] Different uses and, indeed, different types of data can evoke varying emotional responses, which is logical: different uses and specific contexts raise different risks, thereby evoking different reactions.

As will be described in Chapter 6, such exclusions from the scope of data protection law reflect the challenges in appropriately describing the various interests at stake when analysing its underlying conceptual values. Simply put, the problem with creating objective exclusions from the scope of personal data is that, irrespective of the nature of the particular information, there may be strong interests associated with its protection.[138] I believe, therefore, that the broader definition of personal data in the GDPR is preferable as it is better aligned with the risks and is also adaptable to the subjective expectations of the public. It certainly offers more room for context and, to the extent possible, seemingly avoids somewhat arbitrary lines. Although Purtova's critical characterization of the GDPR as 'the law of everything' thus has some merit, the broad approach may be necessary in light of the risks of rather arbitrary under-inclusion, especially as there are other limits to the scope of application of data protection law (see Chapter 6).[139] The law and emotion challenge to data protection must therefore recognize the legitimacy of data protection law's objectives.

2. Objective categories and sensitive data

The demarcation of certain categories of personal data as sensitive arguably suffers from the same problems, in that this separation also seemingly relies on the nature of the information in question to afford additional protection, ie even if there is inconsistency in terms of their precise form. Sensitivity in data protection law derives from the increased risk of harm.[140] In the GDPR, more specifically, Recital 51 recognizes the risks that the processing of these data poses for fundamental rights and freedoms. One can imagine, for instance, the

[136] See eg the controversy regarding ChatGPT: Matt Burgess, 'ChatGPT Has a Big Privacy Problem | WIRED' (*Wired*, 4 April 2023) <www.wired.com/story/italy-ban-chatgpt-privacy-gdpr/> accessed 12 July 2023.

[137] See eg the controversy regarding Clearview AI: Office of the Australian Information Commissioner, 'Clearview AI Breached Australians' Privacy' (*OAIC*, 10 March 2023) <www.oaic.gov.au/newsroom/clearview-ai-breached-australians-privacy> accessed 13 July 2023.

[138] Daniel Solove, *Understanding Privacy* (Harvard University Press 2010) 69.

[139] I think this is also the case because Purtova exaggerates the point somewhat. See Richardson and others (n 20).

[140] Clifford, Richardson, and Witzleb (n 52) 19, 34–37.

illegitimate processing of sensitive personal data such as health information evoking strong emotional reactions, with such a reaction stemming not only from any potential economic loss but also from the very intimate nature of the information itself and the stigma associated with certain illnesses.[141] Similarly, in the modernized Convention 108 +, the link between the risk of harm and the categories of sensitive personal data is emphasized through the explicit reference to the risks posed to 'the interests, rights and fundamental freedoms of the data subject, notably a risk of discrimination'.[142]

In analysing these categories and the differences between jurisdictions, Solove has argued that the information included is often arbitrary.[143] For example, some data protection laws include protections for geolocation information, others do not. On this basis, Solove then questions these inclusions and exclusions and also argues that the differences between these lists demonstrates their randomness.[144] I believe that three points can be made in this respect. First, variations in these lists are to be expected given the potential for cultural differences across jurisdictions. In fact, this was presented as a reason why the OECD Guidelines avoided providing additional safeguards for sensitive personal data categories and the Convention 108 (and indeed the modernized Convention 108 +) list is left open-ended for states to modify as they see fit.[145] Secondly, data protection law is not the only means of designating certain data (or indeed uses of data) as sensitive. We can refer to a range of sector-specific legislation in this regard, with Ohm's examination of sensitive data categories in the US being a clear example of such an analysis.[146] These sector-specific legislative interventions are often not fully considered in the assessment of lists such as those provided in the GDPR. Arguably, therefore, sensitivity may have different slants in its meaning in data protection laws; but data protection law does not exist in a vacuum. And, thirdly, if it is accepted that data protection law (at least in some jurisdictions) overlaps closely with the safeguarding of human identity and flourishing, it can be argued that there is a spectrum of harms that can be suffered which seem to be inherently connected to the protection of fundamental rights and freedoms, thereby justifying their inclusion.

[141] In this regard, the absence of a category such as financial information is not surprising as it is less tied to the individual's personality (albeit potentially revealing aspects of it).

[142] Modernized Convention for the Protection of Individuals with Regard to the Processing of Personal Data (Convention 108 +), art 6(2).

[143] Solove, 'Data Is What Data Does' (n 47) 29–30.

[144] ibid.

[145] For a discussion, see McCullagh (n 52).

[146] See Paul Ohm, 'Sensitive Information' (2014) 88 Southern California Law Review 1125.

As I have argued elsewhere with colleagues, here we can refer to the potential for physical or economic, social or political, and spiritual forms of harm.[147]

Despite the objective reasons for such protections, Solove does make an important point that the inclusion/exclusion of certain types of personal data from the categories of sensitive personal data may at times seem somewhat arbitrary. This is hardly a new concern, however, and even in Europe where such lists seemingly originated there was significant variation across jurisdictions prior to the adoption of the GDPR and even more so before the enactment of Data Protection Directive 95/46/EC.[148] Moreover, it is undoubtedly true that providing additional safeguards for certain categories of information fails to account for the fact that the experience of privacy is subjective and that therefore any such list will always be somewhat arbitrary as a one-size-fits-all approach. The sensitivity of data is relative to the individual and a function of the context and/or purposes for which the data are used.[149] Attempts to categorize particular data sets as sensitive need to take into account that the prospect of harm cannot solely be attributed to the nature of the information but also depends on the contexts in which, and indeed the purposes for which, this information is processed.[150] Arguably, if context and/or purposes are key then these lists should be avoided in favour of sector-specific rules that allow for a greater appreciation of contextual factors.[151] Prohibitions on the processing of sensitive personal data such as that contained in the GDPR certainly seem to send an unrealistic message given that, as noted by Simitis, '[a]ll they can ask for is an adequate protection'.[152] In the EU, this has led in Lynskey's words to the 'ad hoc rationalisation of the law to accommodate' business models and the reading down of the provision as a right instead of as a prohibition.[153] I believe, however, that framed as 'a mere alarm device' the categorization of certain information as sensitive serves a useful purpose in that it signals the risks of discrimination and harms to fundamental rights and freedoms.[154] Objectively, certain types of information can result in a higher risk of harm. Hence, as these lists merely add an additional layer of protection (and there is seemingly good

[147] See Clifford, Richardson, and Witzleb (n 52).

[148] For a discussion of the differences in the implementation of the old Data Protection Directive 95/46/EC, see Douwe Korff, 'EC Study on Implementation of Data Protection Directive 95/46/EC' (2002) <https://papers.ssrn.com/abstract=1287667> accessed 12 July 2023.

[149] McCullagh (n 52) 197.

[150] Clifford, Richardson and Witzleb (n 52) 36.

[151] Spiros Simitis, 'Revisiting Sensitive Data' 9 <www.coe.int/t/dghl/standardsetting/dataprotection/Reports/Report_Simitis_1999.pd> accessed 9 February 2016.

[152] ibid 8.

[153] Orla Lynskey, 'Complete and Effective Data Protection' [2023] Current Legal Problems 21 <http://eprints.lse.ac.uk/120212/> accessed 25 September 2023.

[154] Simitis (n 151) 8.

reason for this even if more could be added), the arbitrariness arguably mostly relates to interpreting them as closed lists and their treatment in a 'mechanical black-letter' manner.[155]

In line with Simitis, I believe that the lists of sensitive personal data should be merely indicative even if I may be relatively more enthusiastic as to their value.[156] The need for flexibility also links to the fact that although providing categories may on paper achieve legal certainty, the reality is that precisely determining what fits into the categories at the fringes is far more ambiguous, given the capacity for inferences to be drawn from seemingly innocuous personal data. The emergence of data-intensive processing that can reveal sensitive insights without necessarily having access to sensitive personal data arguably undermines the utility of these protections. Although it appears that classifying what comes within the remit of such provisions is a simple task, the rise of analysis-intensive processing methods has arguably blurred the lines between the personal and sensitive personal data categories.[157] The crux of the matter relates to how closely drawn the connected inferences are to the protected categories. In this vein, one must wonder whether the ability to target advertising, for example, based on interests seemingly connected to these categories results in the processing of sensitive personal data.[158] To explain this in less abstract terms, let us again refer to the example of Sarah described above in Section B. We know from her browsing habits that she is receiving advertisements for baby products, but should we classify this information as sensitive if the obvious inference is that Sarah is pregnant (ie even if this is incorrect) given that health-related information is generally a sensitive category of personal data? In addition, does the answer change or remain the same if Sarah starts to receive advertisements relating to pregnancy? In practice, the separation between personal and sensitive personal data may be dynamic. This highlights the clear potential to make sensitive inferences from ordinary personal data that arguably further contributes to the undermining of the categories-based approach common to data protection law. Indeed, as noted

155 Clifford, Richardson, and Witzleb (n 52) 34.

156 Simitis (n 151) 9.

157 Paul De Hert and Vagelis Papakonstantinou, 'The Proposed Data Protection Regulation Replacing Directive 95/46/EC: A Sound System for the Protection of Individuals' (2012) 28 Computer Law & Security Review 130.

158 See Cabañas, Cuevas, and Cuevas (n 89). As a further illustration of this point, one can also refer to the *Cambridge Analytica* scandal. This highlights the potential for a psychometric profile to be used to target an individual for political purposes on the basis of (and tailored towards) that individual's perceived feelings towards a social issue under political debate, which again is often included in these categories of sensitive personal data. See Bakir and McStay (n 92); Information Commissioner's Office (n 92).

by Edwards, '[g]iven the increasing power of [machine learning] algorithms, this might lead us to the inexorable conclusion that not only is "everything personal data" as per Purtova, but perhaps even, 'everything is special category data'.[159] As described in the previous section (see Subsection C.2), EU case law suggests that where there appears to be a reasonably likely possibility that sensitive inferences will be able to be drawn then it will fall within the scope of protection.[160] These are also issues that were discussed in more recent reforms in other jurisdictions, but they have been dealt with in varying ways.

For instance, as noted above in Section B, in the California Consumer Privacy Act inferences are specifically included as personal information.[161] However, the Act remains silent as to whether inferences may also be considered sensitive. In addition, the right of consumers to limit the use and disclosure of sensitive personal information contained in the Act excludes 'sensitive personal information that is collected or processed without the purpose of inferring characteristics about a consumer'.[162] This suggests a potential qualification constraining the regime's regulation of sensitive data.[163] But assuming that sensitive inferences do come within the scope of the sensitive personal information, what does this mean in terms of the protections afforded? If it is the inferences that may come within the categories, should we then treat the 'ordinary' personal data used to reveal such insights as sensitive at the outset in all circumstances? It appears relatively uncontroversial to suggest that by virtue of its content certain information will come within the scope of the sensitive personal data category and that personal data processing that is aimed at exploiting sensitive characteristics through inference, as demonstrated by the purpose of the processing, will also come within the categories of sensitive personal data. In contrast, suggesting that processing which reveals information through which inferences may be made regarding sensitive characteristics irrespective of the purposes or intention of the controller falls within these categories is a far more provocative contention as it may further blur the lines between personal and sensitive personal data and give rise to clear legal certainty concerns. These concerns have led certain scholars to question the continuing utility of the sensitive personal data category.[164] Solove in particular is very critical of what he believes are fixed categories because of the capacity for

[159] Edwards, 'Data Protection' (n 102) 90.
[160] *Bodil Lindqvist* (n 94).
[161] California Consumer Privacy Act of 2018 s 1798.140.V.1.(k).
[162] ibid s 1798.121.
[163] Clifford, Richardson, and Witzleb (n 52) 37–38.
[164] Edwards, 'Data Protection' (n 102) 90; Quinn and Malgieri (n 53); Solove, 'Data Is What Data Does' (n 47); Wachter and Mittelstadt (n 53).

inferences to undermine the boundaries between personal and sensitive personal data.[165]

Certainly, maintaining the sensitive data categories will potentially lead to the proliferation of the processing of this type of personal data, requiring adherence to stricter rules, and then, as argued by Quinn and Malgieri, potentially devaluing the concept.[166] However, as I have argued elsewhere, together with colleagues, the categories also certainly protect individuals from even more pointed risks of harm, and thus a focus on harm alleviation can help inform policymakers and judges when dealing with inferred data.[167] Treating harm alleviation as a guiding consideration in the assessment and regulation of sensitive data, including with respect to inferences, is in my view the sensible way forward as it affords a way in which these categories can be interpreted flexibly. In this regard, it seems practical to draw a distinction between personal data that *could* be used to infer attributes relating to the data subject and personal data that *will* be processed to reveal, or at least *reasonably risks* the revealing of, such attributes through its processing.[168]

For reasons connected with the aim of achieving fairness and justice (but also for practical reasons), therefore, objective categories of information seem necessary, even if arbitrary lines should be avoided as much as possible in order to afford flexibility in relation to the context and purposes of the processing. In saying that, however, I believe that sensitive data categories are different from 'ordinary' personal data as these speak to circumstances in which additional protections are merited in response to an increased risk of harm and not protections in general. Provided there is flexibility in the application of these categories at the fringes and a reasoned approach in terms of the protections provided, I believe that they have ongoing utility. However, I acknowledge that a very broad definition of personal data and the blurring of the personal and sensitive personal data categories may arguably contribute to the desensitizing of individuals to the risks posed by personal data processing. This relates to the fact that there are limits to the extent to which individuals can act in their own interest without becoming disengaged from the risks. It is arguable that the challenge to focus on, however, is not whether personal and sensitive personal data should be protected but rather whether positioning the data subject as a

[165] See Solove, 'Data Is What Data Does' (n 47).
[166] ibid.
[167] Quinn and Malgieri also argue that the concept of sensitive data should be preserved. See Quinn and Malgieri (n 53).
[168] See Clifford, Richardson, and Witzleb (n 52).

key decision-maker at the centre of the framework is fundamentally flawed. This is the focus of the next chapter.

E. Conclusion

The key theme of this chapter has been that the 'categories' approach to data protection law arguably exacerbates emotional disengagement from the dangers associated with intensive data processing. The analysis has explored how the pervasive gathering of personal data allows for the generation of detailed sensitive inferences about individuals. I have demonstrated how these interact with data protection law and how such sensitive inferences may or may not be classified as sensitive personal data depending on the circumstances. Through the use of E-AI as a case study and using the GDPR as the high-water mark example of these laws, I have further demonstrated how different types of E-AI with the same inherent purpose may interact with the GDPR in different ways. Some may clearly involve the processing of sensitive personal data whereas others arguably may not.

Such inconsistencies raise doubts that I believe demonstrate the emotional disconnect between our feelings towards certain types of data processing and their genuine risks. However, I still see an important role for data protection law. I believe it aims to mitigate the subjective and objective risks of harm associated with personal data processing. Therefore, at the end of this chapter, we are at a point in the analysis where we need to consider whether the problem is less the focus on the protection of (sensitive) personal data and more the focus on the role of individual data subjects as the key decision-makers required to navigate the complex data processing ecosystems.

4

The Challenge to Individual Choice

A. Introduction

Data protection law is designed to safeguard the personal data of the 'data subject'. This natural person is presumed to be an active participant in the protection of their own interests with the capacity to make informed rational choices. This is reflected in the role of consent in many data protection laws.[1] It is also evident in the role played by data subject control rights as balancing mechanisms designed to allow individuals the qualified capacity to choose (or not) to exercise control over their personal data.[2] However, scholars have repeatedly criticized the reliance on choice as a key justifying element in data protection law, and for good reasons. There have certainly been several examples of how privacy policies can be used to exploit data subjects, ranging from the inclusion of publicity stunt clauses (eg the requirement to surrender your first-born child[3] or to clean the city sewers[4]) to the more practical difficulties connected to the complex legalese and lengthy texts used.[5] Such examples illustrate how privacy policies and data subject consent for instance, are an easy target for critics, given their apparent futility in their primary function of providing data subjects with information as to how their personal data are processed.

Although the existing literature provides valuable analysis of the problems posed by a legislative framework designed around the rational data subject as an active market participant, I believe that the literature does not fully account

[1] Daniel J Solove, 'Murky Consent: An Approach to the Fictions of Consent in Privacy Law' (22 January 2023) <https://papers.ssrn.com/abstract=4333743> accessed 11 June 2023; Daniel J Solove, 'Introduction: Privacy Self-Management and the Consent Dilemma' (2013) 126 Harvard Law Review 1880.

[2] Ari Waldman, 'Privacy's Rights Trap' [2022] Northwestern University Law Review Online <https://scholarlycommons.law.northwestern.edu/nulr_online/327> accessed 4 October 2023; Daniel Solove, 'The Limitations of Privacy Rights' (2023) 98 Notre Dame Law Review 975.

[3] Leyden John, 'Consumers Agree to Give up First-Born Child for Free Wi-Fi—Survey' (30 September 2014) <www.theregister.co.uk/2014/09/30/free_wi_fi_survey/> accessed 17 February 2018.

[4] Alex Hern, 'Thousands Sign up to Clean Sewage Because They Didn't Read the Small Print' *The Guardian* (14 July 2017) <www.theguardian.com/technology/2017/jul/14/wifi-terms-and-conditions-thousands-sign-up-clean-sewage-did-not-read-small-print> accessed 17 February 2018.

[5] See eg the Norwegian consumer authority live-streaming the reading of the terms of smartphone applications: 'Norway Stages 32-Hour App Term Reading' *BBC News* (25 May 2016) <www.bbc.co.uk/news/world-europe-36378215> accessed 17 February 2018.

Data Protection Law and Emotion. Damian Clifford, Oxford University Press. © Damian Clifford 2024.
DOI: 10.1093/oso/9780192845863.003.0004

for the subjective importance of consent and control rights. The purpose of this chapter, therefore, is to explore the role of choice in data protection law. Section B explores the challenge of exercising choice in data protection law by analysing the behavioural criticisms levelled against the protections provided. Although individuals are afforded the capacity to make subjective choices in theory, the analysis will demonstrate that they are arguably incapable of doing so in practice. The challenge is that although data protection law provides subjective control rights so that we can make our own choices, it assumes data subjects' objective rational capacity to make them and fails to account for how people actually reach decisions in reality. The section also highlights, however, the role played by the rational data subject as a fiction that serves a normative function, and how the varying standards of protection provided in data protection laws raise questions about how far the critique of choice goes. It is arguable that the behavioural critique is less significant in the more modern data protection laws as they have been developed with at least some understanding of the challenges of operationalizing choices in practice. The chapter will test this contention and develop the problem of failing to properly provide for the role of choice in data protection law through the lens of the Emotional Artificial Intelligence (E-AI) case study introduced in Chapter 1.

More specifically, similar to the previous chapter, Section C builds on this analysis by offering E-AI as a case study to demonstrate the practical challenges associated with relying on subjective rights in practice. In this section, I will again refer exclusively to the protections afforded in the General Data Protection Regulation (GDPR) as the high-water mark example of data protection law in order to analyse the challenge in detail. I will demonstrate that although there are clear limits to the mechanisms for choice, they have also been a driving force for change. Section D explores the limits of the challenge to the role for individual choice evident in data protection law by demonstrating why the rational data subject is a necessary fiction, while exploring alternatives before introducing the significance of accountability mechanisms in providing the environment in which we can make choices and thus ensuring fair personal data processing.

B. Affective Features of the Challenge

From a formal legal perspective, we 'choose' to give up our personal data. We make such 'choices' multiple times a day. We are often the actors positioned to determine when, how, and in what circumstances our personal data may be processed through the role of consent and the data subject control rights provided in these frameworks. Such empowerment mechanisms rely on individual decision-making as a means of mitigating the risks associated with personal data processing and require the active participation of individuals. The ability to make decisions through the control rights provided in data protection law represents the importance of subjective choices. Data protection is a response to the power and information asymmetries between data subjects and controllers. It aims, therefore, amongst other things, to establish the conditions in which data subjects may be able to make effective subjective choices.

However, although our capacity to make subjective choices through the control rights and consent requirements provided in data protection law may have theoretical significance, practically exercising choice seems to require significant effort and is arguably becoming increasingly difficult.[6] The challenge is that although data protection law provides for subjective control rights and consent so that we can make our own choices, it assumes data subjects' rational objective capacity to make them in the protections it provides. Arguably, given the extensive literature undermining this assumption, the legitimacy of these mechanisms is undercut. This objectivization of choice pushes data protection law into assumptions and hierarchies, in that the manifestation of choice seemingly trumps actual knowledge.[7] It is for these reasons that more collective protections are provided in these frameworks (see Chapter 5). Importantly, however, as I will argue, when criticizing the role of choice we must be mindful of the normative role of rationality and the varying objective standards of protection provided in different jurisdictions. The analysis will (1) explore the limits on our capacity to choose as characterized by the complexity of the regulatory environment and our bounded rational capacity to make choices. It will then (2) examine the normative role played by the fiction of the rational data subject and how variations in the standards of protection across jurisdictions must be acknowledged in our assessment of the role of choice in data protection law.

[6] For a discussion, see eg Bert-Jaap Koops, 'The Trouble with European Data Protection Law' (2014) 4 International Data Privacy Law 250; Solove, 'The Limitations of Privacy Rights' (n 2); Waldman, 'Privacy's Rights Trap' (n 2).

[7] This point has been adapted from the same one made by Sally Wheeler in relation to decisions to give up data as applied to common law contract law doctrine. See Sally Wheeler, 'Data in a Relational Setting' in Damian Clifford, Jeannie Marie Paterson, and Kwan Ho Lau (eds), *Data and Private Law* (Hart 2023).

1. Complexity and bounded rationality

There are both behavioural and technological aspects to the limits of our capacity to make choices.[8] There is an extensive body of literature highlighting these limits inspired by economic theory.[9] The criticisms reflect the impact of (1) information asymmetries and uncertainties, and (2) our bounded rationality and the heuristics and biases we rely upon to make choices. These two points will now be analysed in turn.

(a) Asymmetries and uncertainties

The digital environment is characterized by information asymmetries and complexity. As a consequence, the effectiveness of data protection law has been repeatedly questioned as asymmetry diminishes the legitimacy of user participation, presents barriers to finding businesses accountable, and also clearly impacts the data subject's bargaining power.[10] Data subjects are presented with complex choices as their options are often characterized by unknowns.[11] For example, data subjects may only have a vague understanding of their options, these options may have unpredictable consequences, their desired option and/or adequate information on how to exercise that choice may be missing, and their choice may be a by-product of another transaction and thus may be bundled.[12] Due to such uncertainties, it can be difficult for a data subject to make an informed choice based on the risks and benefits of data processing as they may have no awareness of the potential outcomes. It is hard to understand the consequences of decisions to give up personal data as some of the potential harms are intangible and typically involve trade-offs.[13]

[8] Bart Custers and others, 'Consent and Privacy' in Andreas Müller and Peter Schaber (eds), *The Routledge Handbook of the Ethics of Consent* (Routledge 2018) 251–54.

[9] Koops, 'The Trouble with European Data Protection Law' (n 6); Waldman, 'Privacy's Rights Trap' (n 2); Solove, 'The Limitations of Privacy Rights' (n 2); Solove, 'Murky Consent' (n 1); Solove, 'Introduction' (n 1); Woodrow Hartzog, 'Opinions—The Case Against Idealising Control' (2018) 4 European Data Protection Law Review 423; Elettra Bietti, 'Consent as a Free Pass: Platform Power and the Limits of the Informational Turn' (2020) 40 Pace Law Review 307.

[10] Orla Lynskey, 'Deconstructing Data Protection: The "Added-Value" of a Right to Data Protection in the EU Legal Order' (2014) 63 International & Comparative Law Quarterly 569.

[11] See Alessandro Acquisti and Jens Grossklags, 'What Can Behavioral Economics Teach Us about Privacy?' in Alessandro Acquisti and others (eds), *Digital Privacy: Theory, Technologies, and Practices* (1st edn, Auerbach Publications 2007).

[12] ibid 367–68.

[13] Alessandro Acquisti, Laura Brandimarte, and George Loewenstein, 'Privacy and Behavioral Economics' in Bart P Knijnenburg and others (eds), *Modern Socio-Technical Perspectives on Privacy* (Springer International 2022) 64 <https://doi.org/10.1007/978-3-030-82786-1_4> accessed 12 September 2023.

In addition, as described in the previous chapter through the examples of profiling and inferences, personal data may be generated by a controller without the knowledge of the data subject, and, although a data subject may not agree to the use of their personal data to help develop a profile, it may still be applied to them later. These examples demonstrate the 'sociality' of data,[14] the limits of our choices, and thus how our decisions can also negatively affect others, thereby reflecting the challenge of applying a control-rights approach to address societal problems.[15] The difficulties of exercising choice through control rights and consent are therefore certainly amplified due to the complexity caused by the uncertainty of the regulatory environment.[16] The contextual nature of the decisions also plays an important role in that there are a multitude of inconspicuous factors which may shape these decisions.[17] The significance of these points is amplified when we consider that even a well-intentioned controller may find it difficult to provide all the information that a data subject would need in order to make an informed choice—at least in an accessible form. Shorter, more user-friendly information may lack the necessary detail,[18] but as noted by Barocas and Nissenbaum, even the most savvy users would be overwhelmed by full information disclosure.[19] There is therefore no agreement on how complex information can be communicated to data subjects effectively, albeit authors tend to disagree on the extent of the problem with disclosure, some highlighting the role of enforcement authorities and civil society and pointing out that data subjects are not the only audience for this information.[20]

Leaving this point to one side, however, there is certainly a clear consensus that data subjects do not read this information.[21] Even when they do, they may not understand the information provided, or even if they do understand it, they may lack the knowledge necessary to make informed choices or they may not be offered the option that reflects their preference.[22] Even aside from the information transparency issues, however, data subjects may also be uncertain as to their preferences.[23] Due to the lack of data subject awareness and

[14] See Salomé Viljoen, 'A Relational Theory of Data Governance' (2021) 131 The Yale Law Journal 573.
[15] Solove, 'The Limitations of Privacy Rights' (n 2) 984.
[16] Acquisti and Grossklags (n 11) 362–68.
[17] Acquisti, Brandimarte, and Loewenstein (n 13) 67–70.
[18] Solove, 'Murky Consent' (n 1) 28.
[19] Solon Barocas and Helen Nissenbaum, 'Big Data's End Run around Anonymity and Consent' in Julia Lane and others (eds), *Privacy, Big Data, and the Public Good: Frameworks for Engagement* (CUP 2014) 58–59.
[20] See Mike Hintze, 'In Defense of the Long Privacy Statement' (2016) 76 Maryland Law Review 1044.
[21] For a discussion, see Wheeler (n 7).
[22] Custers and others (n 8) 253.
[23] Acquisti, Brandimarte, and Loewenstein (n 13) 64–67.

understanding, it can therefore also be difficult for responsible controllers to distinguish their personal data processing practices and for data subjects to exercise choice based on the level of protection afforded. It has been suggested that this can result in a so-called 'market for lemons' in which low-quality options win out over high-quality alternatives due to data subject ignorance, thereby resulting in a race-to-the-bottom.[24] This is particularly problematic in an environment dominated by market effects, user lock-in, and asymmetries in that take-it-or-leave-it offers do not facilitate any real choice for individuals.[25] The asymmetric transaction costs[26] and the inability to recognize bad practices are also of significance in relation to the ways in which controllers can manipulate choice and how design can thus be used to trick, confuse, and obscure options.[27] Even if individuals had access to complete information, however, our bounded rationality means that our capacity to assess all information rationally is limited. This reflects the popular behavioural critique of data protection law.

(b) Heuristics and biases

Behavioural law economics research emerged as a challenge to classical law and economics (ie rational choice theory). In simple terms, rational choice theory assumes that individuals are rationally self-interested and make choices to maximize their own welfare. Behavioural economics is based on rational choice theory but challenges the rationality assumption inherent in rational choice theory and aims instead to explore the consequences of actual rather than hypothetical human behaviour by integrating evidence from individual, cognitive, and social psychology.[28] The appeal of rational choice theory is its simplicity: by holding that individuals make decisions that maximize their own well-being, policymakers should only intervene to counteract a market failure.[29] Behavioural economics questions this simple understanding of

[24] For a discussion in a privacy context, see Frederik J Zuiderveen Borgesius, 'Behavioural Sciences and the Regulation of Privacy on the Internet' in Alberto Alemanno and Anne-Lise Sibony (eds) (Hart 2015) 188–89.

[25] See Damian Clifford, Inge Graef, and Peggy Valcke, 'Pre-Formulated Declarations of Data Subject Consent—Citizen-Consumer Empowerment and the Alignment of Data, Consumer and Competition Law Protections' (2019) 20 German Law Journal 679.

[26] For a discussion, see Borgesius (n 24) 190–92.

[27] See Ari Waldman, 'Cognitive Biases, Dark Patterns, and the "Privacy Paradox"' (2020) 31 Current Opinion in Psychology 105.

[28] See Acquisti and Grossklags (n 11).

[29] David J Arkush, 'Situating Emotion: A Critical Realist View of Emotion and Nonconscious Cognitive Processes for Law and Legal Theory' [2008] Brigham Young University Law Review 1275, 1331.

individual behaviour and tests 'the central ideas of utility maximization, stable preferences, rational expectations, and optimal processing of information'.[30]

Given the strong link between rationality and the autonomy of individual decision-making, any such deviations from the standard rational approach are significant in terms of the continuing relevance of such protections. In essence, therefore, the behavioural economics literature challenges rational choice theory and contests the notion of unbounded rationality, will-power, and self-interest.[31] The scholarship also opposes two other neo-classical assumptions, namely (1) that individuals learn from their mistakes, inevitably resulting in a market learning effect; and (2) that only rational actors will survive in the market, hence reducing irrationality.[32] Due to our bounded rationality, behavioural economics literature argues that our capacity to act rationally is exhaustible and we often rely on mental heuristics as shortcuts in place of rational analyses of available options. For example, research suggests that the framing of a problem or question affects how individuals respond to it, which brings into question how information on personal data processing is presented to data subjects.[33] The behavioural economics scholarship therefore challenges the legitimacy of rational maximizing behaviour (ie rational choice theory) at the root of the economic principles underlying the standard law and economics approach.[34]

To explain, behavioural economics research generally divides decision-making into rational and irrational. Reference can be made here to the work of Kahneman, who differentiates between 'System 1 reasoning' and 'System 2 reasoning'. System 1 reasoning is 'fast, automatic, effortless, associative, and often emotionally charged' whereas System 2 reasoning is 'slower, serial, effortful, and deliberately controlled'.[35] This suggests, therefore, that a failure to

[30] Christine Jolls, Cass R Sunstein, and Richard H Thaler, 'A Behavioral Approach to Law and Economics' (1998) 50 Stanford Law Review 1471, 1476.

[31] ibid.

[32] Iain Ramsay, *Consumer Law and Policy: Text and Materials on Regulating Consumer Markets* (Hart 2012) 56.

[33] Acquisti and Grossklags (n 11) 370–72.

[34] Although less developed, similar concerns have also been raised in law and neuroscience theory more broadly. In short, law and neuroscience theory emerged as another challenge to the existing rational choice theory alongside behavioural law and economics and essentially aims to use the insights from neuroscientific research to gather a more accurate understanding of human reasoning and what it means for the law. Although it remains out of the scope of this book to delve further into the genesis and practical mapping of how and to what extent these theories are reflected in current legal protections, it is important to note that, practically speaking, behavioural law and economics literature in particular has gained a huge amount of popularity.

[35] Daniel Kahneman, 'Maps of Bounded Rationality: Psychology for Behavioral Economics' (2003) 93 The American Economic Review 1449, 1451, as referred to by Dan M Kahan, 'Emotion in Risk Regulation: Competing Theories' in Sabine Roeser (ed), *Emotions and Risky Technologies* (Springer Netherlands 2010) 161–62. As noted by Sunstein, System 2 is therefore more deliberative relative to the

protect data subjects against System 1 style reasoning may lead to consumption-distorting behaviour. In substantiating their criticism of rational choice theory, proponents of behavioural economics have also relied on research revealing a number of biases and other anomalies via experimental studies that contradict the underlying principles of rational choice theory.[36] The literature argues, for example, that biases affect the manner in which we analyse options and assess risks. Behavioural insights have been used to help explain phenomena such as the privacy paradox.

More specifically, an inconsistency between an individual's stated preference in terms of the importance of privacy (ie their attitude) and their behaviour can reasonably be understood as paradoxical when we view that individual as a rational agent with the capacity to consider their options and choose effectively. In addition, explanations of the inconsistency which highlight the role of 'privacy calculus', and thus the benefits of disclosure outweighing privacy, demonstrate a similar rational actor/cost-benefit analysis logic. Referring to this dichotomy between attitude and behaviour as a paradox is misleading, however, when one considers literature exploring how technology has been integrated into our daily lives as a habitual interaction designed to constrain our behaviour, with community-based norms and contextual factors informing our willingness to share.[37] The biases that impact our decision-making capacity are also of significance in this regard. Indeed, behavioural insights have also been used to demonstrate the incapacity of data subjects to act in their own best interests, thereby calling into question reliance on the rationality of individual decision-making and the role of control rights.[38] The significance of this research can be demonstrated by two examples of biases discussed in the

more error-prone System 1, which is based on heuristic reasoning. Cass Sunstein, *Laws of Fear: Beyond the Precautionary Principle* (CUP 2009) 65, as referred to by Kahan 161–62.

[36] In terms of biases one can refer, inter alia, to the following biases: fairness and behaviour (Colin Camerer and Richard H Thaler, 'Anomalies: Ultimatums, Dictators and Manners' (1995) 9 Journal of Economic Perspectives 209); loss aversion (Daniel Kahneman and Amos Tversky, 'Prospect Theory: An Analysis of Decision under Risk' (1979) 47 Econometrica 263); inability to predict experience utility (Daniel Kahneman, 'New Challenges to the Rationality Assumption' (1994) 150 Journal of Institutional and Theoretical Economics (JITE)/Zeitschrift für die gesamte Staatswissenschaft 18); over-optimism (Neil D Weinstein, 'Unrealistic Optimism about Future Life Events' (1980) 39 Journal of Personality and Social Psychology 806); hindsight bias (Baruch Fischhoff, 'Hindsight Is Not Equal to Foresight: The Effect of Outcome Knowledge on Judgment under Uncertainty' (1975) 1 Journal of Experimental Psychology: Human Perception and Performance 288); availability heuristic (Amos Tversky and Daniel Kahneman, 'Judgment under Uncertainty: Heuristics and Biases' (1974) 185 Science 1124).

[37] See Daniel Solove, 'The Myth of the Privacy Paradox' [2020] GW Law Faculty Publications & Other Works <https://scholarship.law.gwu.edu/faculty_publications/1482> accessed 4 October 2023.

[38] See Waldman, 'Privacy's Rights Trap' (n 2); Waldman, 'Cognitive Biases, Dark Patterns, and the "Privacy Paradox"' (n 27); Solove, 'The Limitations of Privacy Rights' (n 2); Borgesius (n 24).

literature: (1) present bias, and (2) status quo bias or inertia, but many more, such as framing as mentioned earlier in this section for instance, are relevant.[39]

'Present bias' relates to how people tend to focus more on the present than on the future, thereby opting for immediate gratification and ignoring future costs, whereas 'status quo bias' or inertia relates to the fact that most people do not change from the default option.[40] Regarding the first of these, present bias is significant for data protection as we arguably do not immediately feel the costs of data tracking and because of this we tend to overvalue the benefits of simply using the associated service.[41] Borgesius offers the example of take-it-or-leave-it personal data processing in the context of the provision of online consumer services reliant on behavioural advertising as an example of where this bias may seemingly play a role.[42] For the second, the significance of default settings explains the importance of 'status quo bias' or inertia and the fact that most people do not change from the default option. In the data protection context this explains the significance between opt-in and opt-out consent in particular,[43] but also the challenge of effectively implementing the control rights provided in data protection law. It could be argued, therefore, that having data subject choice as an important feature of some of data protection law is fundamentally flawed.

Data protection law provides subjective control rights so that we can make our own choices but then it assumes data subjects' objective rational capacity to make them and fails to account for how people actually make decisions. Arguably, this undercuts the legitimacy of consent and control rights. To explore the significance of this criticism, however, we must understand the normative role the rational data subject plays in data protection law.

2. Subjective rights and objective choices

The consequences of the limits of data subjects' capacity to make decisions differ depending on whether you treat the rational data subject as an empirical or a normative standard. I believe that the rational data subject is a normative fiction in data protection law that serves a function and that we must assess

[39] eg Waldman discusses five such biases: anchoring, framing, hyperbolic discounting, overchoice, and metacognitive processes in decision-making. See Waldman, 'Cognitive Biases, Dark Patterns, and the "Privacy Paradox"' (n 27).

[40] For a more extensive discussion, see Borgesius (n 24).

[41] Waldman, 'Privacy's Rights Trap' (n 2) 95.

[42] Borgesius (n 24) 23.

[43] ibid 20.

the criticisms of choice in that light. It is necessary, therefore, to understand both (1) the nature of the challenge of accounting for decision-making and the role of rationality more precisely, and (2) that, despite similarities in structure and form, there are varying levels of protection provided in data protection law across jurisdictions.

(a) Understanding the challenge

Rationality requires an objective assessment of decision-making that does not correspond to our subjective intentions, understandings, or indeed limitations. Although the behavioural law and economics literature aims to better reflect the actual decision-making of individuals, it retains rationality at its centre. This reflects the point that this construct plays the role of a functional normative fiction in law, including data protection law. It also aims to encourage people to be 'rational', thereby acting as a positive standard.[44] When assessing the effectiveness of the mechanisms for choice in data protection law we have to keep this normative role in mind. In this regard, reference can also be made to libertarian paternalism, or 'nudging', to counteract the mental heuristics and biases which give rise to irrational behaviour and thus the aim in policymaking of improving the decision-making of individuals to encourage 'rational' choices.[45] The point here is that it is important to note that even behavioural economics has a rather restrictive understanding of decision-making, since it retains rationality at its core, with the liberatarian paternalism literature, for instance, advocating nudges back to 'rationality'.

The failure to account for a broader perspective on individual decision-making is perhaps best characterized by the fact that although Adam Smith, the father of modern economics, highlighted the importance of emotion in decision-making over 250 years ago, this aspect of Smith's writing was largely ignored.[46] The interpretation of Smith's work that has gained most notoriety

[44] See Gillian K Hadfield, 'The Second Wave of Law and Economics' (1996) 46 The University of Toronto Law Journal 181.

[45] Richard H Thaler and Cass R Sunstein, *Nudge: Improving Decisions about Health, Wealth, and Happiness* (Yale University Press 2008).

[46] Indeed, attention has focused on the invisible hand theory. Smith, the father of modern economics, first referred to the invisible hand theory to describe the unintended benefits of self-serving individual actions in his work *The Theory of Moral Sentiments* (1759). Adam Smith, *The Theory of Moral Sentiments* (6th edn, 1690) 165 <www.ibiblio.org/ml/libri/s/SmithA_MoralSentiments_p.pdf> accessed 4 October 2023. Despite being developed more thoroughly in Smith's magnum opus, Adam Smith, *Wealth of Nations* (Wordsworth Editions, 2012), it took more than a century for his reflections to be fully appreciated and understood. This theory dominated the economic policy of Western countries during the nineteenth century. Although this dominance has evolved somewhat through the emergence of consumer mobilization in the second half of the twentieth century (in response to the acknowledgement of consumer-business asymmetries), the theory still provides the bedrock upon which the current economic realities are based, having been embedded in Western socio-economic thought. See

is seemingly at odds with his more general contentions in *The Theory of Moral Sentiments*.[47] The popular interpretation of Smith's *invisible hand* theory forms the basis of rational choice theory and teaches that a competitive free market is *Pareto optimal*, meaning that when an economy is in equilibrium the economic welfare of every citizen is impossible to improve, as any interference will result in negative consequences for at least a portion of that citizenship.[48] As a result, according to this theory, specific protections for individuals are for the most part deemed unnecessary as such interventions would act as a restriction on the freedom to trade, thereby denying individuals the chance to improve their circumstances.[49] Smith's theory focuses on contractual autonomy and thus the notion that the more individuals are free to choose, and hence reap the rewards of their efforts (via the division of labour), the more the state benefits in turn. Although the *modern* interpretation of Smith's theory does recognize the possibility of impediments to its success—such as the effects of externalities, bad distributions of income, and that markets can become anti-competitive—it rests on the capacity of the individual to act rationally in their own best interests.[50]

On the basis of such an understanding, although subjective or emotional elements may be the goal of decisions (ie the use of the word goal is to be understood synonymously with preferences, utility, and welfare), they play no rational role in the making of decisions themselves and are instead viewed as undesirable and, indeed, exceptional in decision-making.[51] Certainly, as described, although the insights provided by behavioural economics research are significant, it also demonstrates a constrained interpretation of the role of emotion in decision-making. This is evident through the continued focus on dichotomizing emotion and rationality/reason, or the subjective and objective. More specifically, the conception of emotion as a primitive reaction

Simon Clarke, 'The Neoliberal Theory of Society' in Alfredo Saad-Filho and Deborah Johnston (eds), *Neoliberalism: A Critical Reader* (Pluto Press 2005).

[47] To clarify, in contrast with the rational self-interest espoused in *The Wealth of Nations*, The *Theory of Moral Sentiments* argues for a theoretical approach to human behaviour determined on the basis of a struggle between what Smith referred to as 'passions' and the 'impartial spectator'. See generally Stefano Fiori, 'Individual and Self-Interest in Adam Smith's Wealth of Nations' (2005) 49 Cahiers d'économie politique 19; Amartya Sen, 'Adam Smith and the Contemporary World' (2010) 3 Erasmus Journal for Philosophy and Economics 18; Karl Moene, 'The Moral Sentiments of Wealth of Nations' (2011) 6 The Adam Smith Review 109.

[48] George Akerlof and Robert Shiller, *Phishing for Phools: The Economics of Manipulation and Deception* (Princeton University Press 2015) 5.

[49] Iris Benöhr, *EU Consumer Law and Human Rights* (OUP 2013) 12–13.

[50] Akerlof and Shiller (n 48) 5.

[51] For a discussion, see Arkush (n 29); Jeremy A Blumenthal, 'Emotional Paternalism' (2007) 35 Florida State University Law Review 1; Kahan (n 35).

rather than as a variety of mental states has resulted in their being classified as irrational. This reflects the historical weight attributed to the mechanistic view of emotions as opposed to the cognitive one that receives broad support in the contemporary interdisciplinary research on emotion: behavioural economics divides decision-making into rational (cognitive) and irrational (including emotional).

Reference can be made, for instance, to the fact that emotion is seen to pervade forms of Kahneman's heuristic System 1 reasoning, with the literature suggesting not only that this type of reasoning is less accurate than calculative reasoning, but also that such reasoning can displace reflective thinking, resulting in behaviour which deviates from what the individual in question would deem to be the best course of action if they were in a cold deliberative state.[52] A failure to protect individuals against System 1 style reasoning, and thus emotionally driven decision-making as an example, may lead to consumption-distorting behaviour.

However, insights from neuroscientists and psychologists have established that emotions are an integral part of all decision-making (ie that they are not just an irrational bias).[53] For example, in their critical analysis of the psychological research detailing the role of emotion in decision-making, Lerner and colleagues summarize it by stating that, '[p]ut succinctly, emotion and decision making go hand in hand' with 'many psychological scientists now assum[ing] that emotions are, for better or worse, the dominant driver of most meaningful decisions in life'.[54] Furthermore, important work in the field of neuroscience has also led to the conclusion that emotions are essential to decision-making.[55] Indeed, as noted by Phelps and colleagues, this contrasts with the traditional view that the 'limbic system' drives emotion.[56] Hence, it appears uncontroversial to say that conventional interdisciplinary understanding does not view emotion and cognition as separate systems. Emotions are understood, therefore, as powerful influences on cognition and behaviour.[57] Interestingly, it

[52] Kahan (n 35) 161–62.

[53] Robin Markwica, *Emotional Choices: How the Logic of Affect Shapes Coercive Diplomacy* (OUP 2018) 7.

[54] Jennifer S Lerner and others, 'Emotion and Decision Making' (2015) 66 Annual Review of Psychology 799, 801.

[55] Antonio R Damasio, *Descartes' Error: Emotion, Reason and the Human Brain* (Quill 2004); Joseph Le Doux, *The Emotional Brain: The Mysterious Underpinnings of Emotional Life* (Simon & Schuster 1996). Moreover, Schacter has shown that this can have an effect even when we are not paying attention and can interact with our emotional memory stores, see Daniel L Schacter, *Searching For Memory: The Brain, the Mind, and the Past* (Basic Books 1996).

[56] Elizabeth A Phelps, Karolina M Lempert, and Peter Sokol-Hessner, 'Emotion and Decision Making: Multiple Modulatory Neural Circuits' (2014) 37 Annual Review of Neuroscience 263, 265.

[57] Jennifer S Lerner and others, 'Emotion and Decision Making—Supplementary Text' (2015) 66 Annual Review of Psychology 1, 3.

appears that the reverse is also true, with research showing that cognitive processes can play a modulating role on emotions.[58]

The key takeaway, therefore, is that although behavioural economics research recognizes that people do not always act rationally, the theory appears to maintain the assumption that emotions act as values to be weighed by individuals in their pursuit of welfare maximization or, alternatively, that emotion is predominantly an irrational force which interferes with decision-making (albeit accepting that this occurs frequently).[59] More specifically, in the context of research explaining the privacy paradox, emotion is viewed as an irrational influence on behaviour, with the research indicating that this 'affect infusion bias' influences the assessment of risk and willingness to disclose.[60] This bias refers to the fact that, in general, those in positive moods are more easily persuaded than those in negative moods as they tend to rely on heuristics.[61] This research sits within a broader literature examining how emotions influence how individuals process information and affects whether they do so superficially or in detail.[62]

However, viewing emotion as a purely irrational bias or the pursued outcome of a decision does not reflect contemporary interdisciplinary research. Indeed, it has been argued that the idea of competing rational and irrational (ie emotional) parts of the brain does not make much sense.[63] According to Stark, despite the valuable contributions of behavioural economics, it therefore 'has difficulty transcending its own frame of reference to offer broader insights on the subjective experience of online life, and why people act in the "irrational" ways that they do'.[64] This arguably calls into question the extent to which the

[58] ibid.

[59] This delineation between rationality and emotion also seems inherent in much of the law and neuroscience literature. See eg Terrence Chorvat, Kevin McCabe, and Vernon Smith, 'Law and Neuroeconomics' (2005) 13 Supreme Court Economic Review 35; Kevin McCabe and Laura Inglis, 'Using Neuroeconomics Experiments to Study Tort Reform' [2007] Mercatus Policy Series George Mason University 25. Indeed, as noted by Pardo and Patterson, the idea of competing rational and irrational (ie emotional) parts of the brain does not appear to make much sense and therefore '[t]he current neuroeconomic explanation of decision making misguidedly ascribes psychological attributes to the brain (e.g., deciding, reasoning, adjudicating) that only make sense when attributed to the person. This confusion undermines attempts to draw conclusions for law.' Michael S Pardo and Dennis Patterson, *Minds, Brains, and Law: The Conceptual Foundations of Law and Neuroscience* (OUP 2013) 70.

[60] See eg Joseph P Forgas, 'Mood and Judgment: The Affect Infusion Model (AIM)' (1995) 117 Psychological Bulletin 39.

[61] ibid.

[62] Craig R Hullett, 'The Impact of Mood on Persuasion: A Meta-Analysis' (2005) 32 Communication Research 423.

[63] Pardo and Patterson (n 59) 70.

[64] Luke Stark, 'The Emotional Context of Information Privacy' (2016) 32 The Information Society 14, 16.

behavioural limits can be unreservedly used to criticize choice in data protection law. More specifically, viewing all non-privacy-preserving behaviour as irrational appears to acknowledge that in certain circumstances it may be highly rational to avoid the complex trade-offs and resign oneself to the inevitability of information sharing. Importantly in this regard, it should be noted that the behavioural economics literature itself also suggests that heuristics may be helpful in decision-making.[65]

Due to limitations of time and willpower, heuristics may be positioned as necessary and efficient strategies to ignore certain information (rational ignorance).[66] In addition, it is clear that there are rational benefits to information sharing, such as the desire to be a part of a community—in fact this is very much part of the design of many online services.[67] Due to the subjective nature of decisions, we cannot therefore automatically assume that non-privacy-preserving decisions are irrational.[68] It is also difficult to determine the impact of biases as there may be several possible heuristics or biases impacting any one decision.[69] Nevertheless, as outlined by the law and emotion literature, by retaining rationality as an anchor, behavioural economics also has limitations in terms of how it explains decision-making.

(b) Varying objective standards

Although the critique of the separation between reason and emotion in law and emotion theory is often central to the contribution of this body of literature, I believe that it is not destructive to the normative construct of the 'rational' data subject. This is despite the fact that it has implications for how we understand the capacities of the data subject (and how we might design regulation for the protection of their personal data—see Section D and Chapter 6). The rational decision-maker is a necessary fiction in law, as is the objective approach

[65] See Acquisti and Grossklags (n 11) 369.

[66] See Jan Trzaskowski, 'Behavioural Innovations in Marketing Law' in Hans-W Micklitz, Anne-Lise Sibony, and Fabrizio Esposito (eds), *Research Methods in Consumer Law* (Edward Elgar 2018) 322. Those authors who see heuristics as both positive and negative forces advocate the studying of heuristic strategies to determine whether the outcome as opposed to the procedure was good, with regulators needing to take the environment into account in order to determine whether individual behaviour is biased or whether an unbiased mind is trying to align with the environment (so-called 'ecological rationality'). See Mark Leiser, 'The Problem with "Dots": Questioning the Role of Rationality in the Online Environment' (2016) 30 International Review of Law, Computers & Technology 191, 200–01.

[67] Christoph Lutz and Pepe Strathoff, 'Privacy Concerns and Online Behavior—Not so Paradoxical after All? Viewing the Privacy Paradox Through Different Theoretical Lenses' (15 April 2014) <https://papers.ssrn.com/abstract=2425132> accessed 22 September 2023.

[68] See Solove, 'Introduction' (n 1).

[69] Acquisti and Grossklags (n 11) 372–73.

more generally.[70] The reliance on a fictional rational data subject is certainly not designed to mimic actual behaviour, even if in behavioural economics the aim is to better approximate it. It is thus a normative construct designed not only for practical and pragmatic considerations, such as the need for legal certainty, but also for reasons concerned with achieving an objective standard of fairness for everyone. Adopting an approach that assumes the rational capacity of individuals means that we as individual data subjects are best placed to decide what we want. It also means, however, that our actions should be assessed objectively to ensure consistent and fair outcomes both for data subjects and controllers (and processors). Objective approaches pervade the common law for these reasons.[71]

Therefore, although the law and emotion criticisms of rationality are valid, they must be understood through the lens of what role this notion plays functionally. This, at least to some extent, places not only the behavioural law and economics literature and the prioritizing of Kahneman's System 2 reasoning, but also the criticism of choice in data protection law more specifically, in a different light. The assessment of the effectiveness of rationality must therefore be considered for what it is: a fiction with a function. In order to examine the effectiveness of choice in data protection law, we must recognize that despite the significant similarities in the types of protections afforded in data protection laws across different jurisdictions, significant variation exists in the levels of protection provided. It must be acknowledged when criticizing data protection law, therefore, (1) that not all data protection laws rely on the same standards of protection, and thus the related point, (2) that insights from behavioural economics have in fact already played some role in shaping the nature of the protections provided in certain jurisdictions. Indeed, the establishment (and 'stickiness') of default settings for consent,[72] the legitimacy of 'informed consent' for legalese-illiterate internet users,[73] the capacity to withdraw

[70] Antoinette Rouvroy, 'The End(s) of Critique: Data Behaviourism versus Due Process' in Katja de Vries and Mireille Hildebrandt (eds), *Privacy, Due Process and the Computational Turn* (Routledge 2013) 157–58. In reaching this conclusion the author relies on the work of several authors including Jacques Derrida, 'Force of Law: The "Mystical Foundation of Authority"' (1990) 11 Cardozo Law Review 920.

[71] eg contract law formation (ie *consensus ad idem*) and contract construction are two specific examples of the judicial preference for objective assessments of individual behaviour. Reasonableness standards that apply throughout the common law in areas such as contract, tort, equity, and administrative law are another excellent example.

[72] Cass R Sunstein, 'Impersonal Default Rules vs. Active Choices vs. Personalized Default Rules: A Triptych' (2013) Social Science Research Network Scholarly Paper ID 2171343 <https://papers.ssrn.com/abstract=2171343> accessed 31 August 2018; Lauren E Willis, 'Why Not Privacy by Default?' (2014) 29 Berkeley Technology Law Journal 61.

[73] Matthew Kirsch, 'Do Not Track: Revising the EU's Data Protection Framework to Require Meaningful Consent for Behavioral Advertising' (2011) 18 Richmond Journal of Law & Technology 2.

consent,[74] the role and importance of manipulative design practices,[75] and the consequences of power and information asymmetries more generally, have all been clear points of contention in policymaking debates for some time. Such insights have been significant in the adoption or updating of data protection laws.

Variations in the manner in which data protection frameworks were adopted and the substantive standard and role of consent demonstrate the important differences evident in data protection laws. For instance, in the United States (US), the soft law manifestation of the FIPPs regulating the private sector at the federal level has been characterized as a 'notice and choice'-based framework, whereby companies are required to provide a privacy policy, and data subjects are given the choice of either accepting this policy or rejecting it and using other websites.[76] This has been heavily criticized in the literature and represents a far more formalistic approach to protection.[77] In contrast, the Australian Privacy Act 1988 (Cth), for example, regulates both the private and federal public sector in hard law. The Act only provides for a limited role for consent but, similarly to the US, contains a rather weak standard of consent.[78] Different again is the approach taken in Singaporean Personal Data Protection Act, where, in addition to the notion of consent that is generally required, there is also 'deemed consent'. This arises when (1) an individual 'voluntarily provides' personal data to an organization for a purpose, provided it is reasonable;[79] (2) it is necessary for the formation or conclusion of a contract;[80] or (3) notice is given and the individual does not opt out of the collection, use, and disclosure of their personal data.[81]

In contrast to these examples, in the European Union (EU) there is a far more robust standard of consent provided for in the GDPR (see Section C), which has inspired reform in several jurisdictions, leading towards the requirement for a more explicit standard. This is particularly evident in the US, with

[74] See eg Marcu Florea, 'Withdrawal of Consent for Processing Personal Data in Biomedical Research' (2023) 13 International Data Privacy Law 107.

[75] Colin M Gray and others, 'Dark Patterns and the Legal Requirements of Consent Banners: An Interaction Criticism Perspective' (Proceedings of the 2021 CHI Conference on Human Factors in Computing Systems, CHI '21, Association for Computing Machinery, New York, NY, USA, 2021) art 172, 1–18.

[76] For a discussion, see Waldman, 'Privacy's Rights Trap' (n 2); Margot Kaminski, 'The Case for Data Privacy Rights (Or "Please, a Little Optimism")' (2022) 97 Notre Dame Law Review Reflection 385.

[77] For a discussion, see Waldman, 'Privacy's Rights Trap' (n 2); Kaminski (n 76).

[78] See Damian Clifford and Jeannie Paterson, 'Consumer Privacy and Consent: Reform in the Light of Contract and Consumer Protection Law' (2020) 94 Australian Law Journal 741.

[79] Personal Data Protection Act 2012, s 15(1).

[80] ibid s 15(3).

[81] ibid s 15(A).

the adoption of a range of consumer privacy laws at the state level.[82] These reforms aim to bolster the level of protection by providing for a stronger definition of consent, similar to that provided in the GDPR, and an expanded list of rights such as the right to non-discrimination in the exercising of data subject rights.[83] In this regard, it is interesting to note that control rights are somewhat difficult to classify within data protection laws in an absolute way. More specifically, in the Organisation for Economic Co-operation and Development (OECD) Guidelines 'individual participation' is included as a specific principle,[84] as supplemented by the 'openness' principle which in essence encourages transparency. In contrast, in Convention 108 there is no specific reference to individual participation as a principle, but instead Article 8 includes 'additional safeguards for the data subject' and this separation of these subjective control rights is also evident in the GDPR (see Section C).

Despite these differences, however, there is substantive similarity in the control rights provided in data protection law's foundational instruments, namely a right to be informed and to access their personal data, in addition to the right to have it corrected/rectified or deleted. In later data protection laws such as the GDPR, the various consumer privacy Acts adopted at the state level in the US, and indeed the modernized Convention 108 + amongst many others, these rights have been expanded significantly. For example, in addition to those in the 1981 Convention, Convention 108 + includes the right not to be subject to automated decision-making, the right to object, the right to have a remedy following violations of rights, and the right to assistance from a supervisory authority in exercising one's rights.[85] These 'new' control rights were inspired—or rather driven—by those included in the GDPR. Indeed, although, as noted in Chapter 2, Convention 108 inspired the approach taken in the old Data Protection Directive 95/46/EC and in the development of the right to data protection in Article 8 of the EU Charter, it is difficult to underestimate the significance of the role played by EU law in the development of Convention 108 as well. Importantly, this is not limited to the updating of the Convention in the

[82] See Virginia Consumer Data Protection Act (2021), Utah Consumer Privacy Act (2022), Texas Data Privacy and Security Act (2023), Tennessee Information Protection Act (2023), Montana Consumer Data Privacy Act (2023), Iowa Consumer Data Protection Act (2023), Indiana Consumer Data Protection Act (2023), Connecticut Data Privacy Act (2022), and Colorado Privacy Act (2021).

[83] eg legislation such as the California Consumer Privacy Act has expanded and bolstered this list of rights by providing them in hard law and including rights such as the right to non-discrimination in the exercising of data subject rights.

[84] The Guidelines on the Protection of Privacy and Transborder Flows of Personal Data (OECD) 1980, para 13.

[85] See modernized Convention for the Protection of Individuals with Regard to the Processing of Personal Data (Convention 108 +), art 9.

form of Convention 108 + but is also evident, for instance, in the adoption of the Additional Protocol[86] to the old Convention requiring limitations on data transfers and supervisory authorities, so as to better align it with the old Data Protection Directive 95/46/EC. Both of these have now been incorporated into Convention 108 + and are a clear demonstration of the influence of the EU but also the increasing strength of data protection laws.

Despite these general moves towards heightened levels of protection, however, the higher standards do not necessarily mean that data protection law does not still struggle to afford individuals the capacity to make subjective choices in practice. The question, therefore, is whether the assumed rationality of the data subject actually functions as a normative fiction in frameworks that provide such heightened protections or whether the continued criticism is justified. This will be explained in the next section through the use of E-AI as a case study, with the GDPR as the specific framework to be analysed.

C. Investigating the Features—Choice and E-AI

The analysis in this section will explore the role of choice and the effectiveness of the mechanisms that facilitate it in the system of checks and balances provided by the GDPR. To understand more fully the role played by the data subject, it is necessary to appreciate how and where they fit within the regulatory framework. The analysis in the previous chapter revealed that we may often seem emotionally disengaged from the risks associated with personal data processing. It could therefore be argued that having data subject choice as an important feature of the GDPR is fundamentally flawed. There has certainly been ongoing criticism of the role of choice in data protection law even with respect to the reforms introduced by the Regulation that have aimed, at least in part, to account for the limits of data subjects' decision-making capacity.[87] The question therefore is whether the assumed rationality of the data subject actually functions as a normative fiction in the GDPR or if this criticism is justified.

E-AI provides an excellent case study to demonstrate the challenges associated with data subjects exercising choices regarding the protection of their personal data and thus to examine this question. As applications of E-AI will

[86] Council of Europe Additional Protocol to the Convention for the Protection of Individuals with regard to Automatic Processing of Personal Data regarding supervisory authorities and transborder data flows, Strasbourg, 8 November 2001.

[87] For an excellent example of such critical scholarship, see Koops, 'The Trouble with European Data Protection Law' (n 6).

frequently require the processing of sensitive personal data, explicit consent will often be required. This is particularly the case when E-AI is deployed in the context of the provision of consumer goods and services. This section will therefore explore whether the assumed rationality of the data subject actually functions as a normative fiction in the GDPR specifically, in order to better contextualize the critique of individual participation through a specific example. I will first outline the role for choice in the GDPR, the importance of consent, and also controller attempts to avoid data subject choice. I will then highlight how control rights have been used to provide collective benefits even if data protection law more broadly may not be the framework through which certain societal/collective risks of harm may best be addressed.

1. Desensitizing data subjects

Exercising individual choice through the conditions for lawful processing and data subject control rights are important manifestations of the role of data subject participation. The Regulation is not consent-based and data subject choice does not always play a role in the application of the conditions provided for lawful processing. From the perspective of the data subject, therefore, in an *ex post* sense data subject control rights are a particularly important example of the opportunity for data subject choice. However, as will be explored, although consent often appears to be the default condition for lawful processing, controllers have seemingly tried to avoid (or at least to limit) the circumstances in which they give data subjects choices.

(a) *Defaulting to consent*

Data protection scholars have repeatedly criticized interpretations of the GDPR that describe it as a 'notice and consent' framework.[88] They retort that consent is only one of the conditions for lawful processing contained in Article 6(1) and that there is no hierarchy contained in this provision. The purposes, means, and nature of the data used in E-AI will effectively determine what condition for lawful processing (Article 6(1)) or indeed, what exception from the general prohibition against the processing of sensitive personal data (Article

[88] For a discussion of the broader interests evident in the GDPR, see Claudia Quelle, 'Not Just User Control in the General Data Protection Regulation' in Anja Lehmann and others (eds), *Privacy and Identity Management. Facing up to Next Steps: 11th IFIP WG 9.2, 9.5, 9.6/11.7, 11.4, 11.6/SIG 9.2.2 International Summer School, Karlstad, Sweden, August 21–26, 2016, Revised Selected Papers* (Springer International 2016) <https://doi.org/10.1007/978-3-319-55783-0_11> accessed 23 September 2023.

9(2)), applies in a given context. The application of a condition or an exception is essential to the legitimization of the processing which underlies the purpose for which the E-AI may be deployed.

Only two of the conditions (consent—Article 6(1)(a)) and contract—Article 6(1)(b)) and one of the exceptions (explicit consent—Article 9(1)(a)) are directly connected to the data subject's capacity to make choices. The other conditions and exceptions can hence operate independently of the data subject's choice albeit the data subject may still exercise the choice to invoke (or not) their data subject rights. Each of the conditions for lawful processing provided for in Article 6(1) of the Regulation plays a distinct and delineated role. In the context of E-AI, we can see, for instance, how consent and contract may be important in the provision of services requested by the data subject.[89] Leaving aside the questions relating to the appropriateness of the balance struck,[90] it is conceivable that a controller may also in certain circumstances aim to legitimize personal data processing as being in the public interest (Article 6(1)(e)). We can imagine here the example of deployments of E-AI in publicly accessible spaces for public safety purposes. We can also imagine how a controller may aim to rely on legitimate interests (Article 6(1)(f)) to justify the use of the technology in public or at least publicly accessible private spaces such as shopping centres for commercial purposes, for example. The more general point, therefore, is that the purpose of the personal data processing, the means employed to achieve this purpose, and the interests at stake determine the applicability (and indeed which of these conditions may be suitable) in a given situation.

However, although I have sympathy for the view that the GDPR is not consent-based in that it is demonstrably correct from reading the provisions of the Regulation, I also believe that this simply ignores the implicit hierarchy that has been created through the Regulation's provisions (and those of the ePrivacy Directive), interpretative guidance,[91] and case law.[92] Indeed, in the context of the processing of personal data for consumer products/services although consent, contract, or legitimate interests may be relied on, it has been repeatedly stated that, for higher risk processing, consent may in fact be the

[89] See Damian Clifford, 'Citizen-Consumers in a Personalised Galaxy: Emotion Influenced Decision-Making, A True Path to the Dark Side?' in Lilian Edwards, Burkhard Schafer, and Edina Harbinja (eds), *Emerging Technology, Regulation and Ethics* (1st edn, Edinburgh University Press 2020).

[90] It is debatable whether any such deployment could in fact be considered proportionate.

[91] See European Data Protection Board, Opinion 5/2019 on the interplay between the ePrivacy Directive and the GDPR, in particular regarding the competence, tasks and powers of data protection authorities (adopted 12 March 2019).

[92] See Case C–252/21 *Meta Platforms v Bundeskartellamt*, ECLI:EU:C:2023:537.

only suitable condition.[93] I believe that this seemingly well-accepted point in the guidance literature and scholarly analysis reflects the importance of consent in the GDPR and is illustrative of an underlying tension. The simple fact of the matter is that although the GDPR is not consent-based, the higher the risk, the more likely it is that you will be required to rely on the consent of the data subject. Indeed, it has been repeatedly stated by the Article 29 Working Party (as replaced by the European Data Protection Board through the Regulation) that where large amounts of personal data are processed, consent will often be the only available condition.[94] The prioritization of consent is evident in at least two ways: (1) the narrow interpretation of the word 'necessary' in the alternative conditions for lawful processing in Article 6(1), and (2) the positioning of consent as a condition/exception/exemption in situations where the legislature believed there was a specifically identified high risk.

Regarding the first of these points, the necessity test at the core of each of these conditions for lawful processing has been construed restrictively to mean that the processing must be understood as being required from a practical perspective.[95] For instance, in the *Meta Platforms and Others* case, the Court of Justice found that to come within contract as a condition, the processing 'must be objectively indispensable for a purpose that is integral to the contractual obligation intended for the data subject'.[96] In addition, regarding the legitimate interests condition, the Court stated that the processing must be strictly necessary for the purposes of that legitimate interest and, amongst other things, effectively found that personalized advertising could not amount to such a legitimate interest pursued by *Meta*.[97] Put simply then, the higher the risk, the

[93] Although in contexts outside the provision of consumer products and services other conditions for lawful processing may be relevant (eg a public authority relying on the public interest condition in art 6(1)(e)), data subject consent will therefore often be the only legitimate option open to controllers.

[94] See Article 29 Working Party, 'Opinion 02/2010 on online behavioural advertising' (2010) WP 171 <http://ec.europa.eu/justice/policies/privacy/docs/wpdocs/2010/wp171_en.pdf> accessed 3 November 2012; Article 29 Working Party, 'Opinion 06/2014 on the notion of legitimate interests of the data controller under Article 7 of Directive 95/46/EC' (European Commission 2014) WP 217 <http://ec.europa.eu/justice/data-protection/article-29/documentation/opinion-recommendation/files/2014/wp217_en.pdf> accessed 10 September 2014.

[95] eg in relation to contract as a condition, the processing must be necessary for the formation or performance of the contract—such as the processing of personal data in payment or delivery details in the context of online shopping. Regarding legitimate interests, case law interpretation suggests that the processing must be required to achieve the process so that if there is an alternative way which is less of an interference with the data subject's right to data protection then the processing will fail to meet the necessity test in art 6(1)(f). Case C–524/06 *Heinz Huber v Bundesrepublik Deutschland* ECLI:EU:C:2008:724, para 62. For a discussion, see Irene Kamara and Paul De Hert, 'Understanding the Balancing Act behind the Legitimate Interest of the Controller Ground' in Evan Selinger, Jules Polonetsky, and Omer Tene (eds), *The Cambridge Handbook of Consumer Privacy* (CUP 2018) 14.

[96] *Meta Platforms v Bundeskartellamt* (n 92) para 98.

[97] ibid para 117.

more likely it is that consent will be required. Consent's role as the go-to condition for higher risk processing is thus ingrained through the meaning of 'necessary' processing in the alternatives.[98]

For the second of the points listed, we can use a range of examples. For instance, even in contexts such as the use of technologies in state schools during the early days of the Covid-19 pandemic there has been some conflicting messaging from data protection authorities (DPAs) regarding the need for consent.[99] This further reflects the point that, practically, the operation of the public interest exception to the prohibition on the processing of sensitive personal data, for instance, requires a basis in Union or Member State law under Article 9(2)(i) of the Regulation and therefore that there can be built-in legislative hurdles that prioritize consent. The importance of consent outside this more public interest-based setting is further demonstrated through its key positioning of consent in three other ways. First, the processing of information (such as cookies) for non-functional purposes coming within the scope of the *lex specialis* requirement for consent in Article 5(3) of the ePrivacy Directive 2002/58/EC will require consent (see Subsection C.2 below).[100] Secondly, according to Article 22 of the GDPR, profiling or automated individual decision-making may require the data subject's (explicit) consent. And thirdly, the processing of sensitive personal data is prohibited, but the *explicit* consent of the data subject can be used to legitimize it in the context of the provision of consumer products or services, but neither legitimate interests nor contract will be sufficient as they are not included in the exceptions listed in Article 9(2).

To contextualize these points, imagine once again the example of Ruth who lives in the smart home as described in Chapter 3. To detect Ruth's emotions, devices within her home collect large amounts of data using, for example, facial analysis to adjust her living conditions. It is clear in such circumstances that sensitive personal data may be processed, as facial action coding for emotion

[98] Both contract and legitimate interest are available when the processing is necessary for the 'performance of a contract' or for the 'purposes of the legitimate interests pursued'.

[99] eg the Italian Data Protection Authority, in their response to the pandemic and move to online teaching and learning, noted that consent is not appropriate as the processing is linked to the functions assigned to educational institutions. See 'Provvedimento del 26 marzo 2020—"Didattica a distanza: prime indicazioni" [9300784]' <www.garanteprivacy.it:443/home/docweb/-/docweb-display/docweb/9300784> accessed 1 July 2020. However, in contrast, a recent decision of the Belgian DPA held that parental consent under the GDPR was required when a mental health survey was conducted in schools. This decision appears to have been inherently linked to the fact that the DPA considered such information to be sensitive personal data under art 9(1), which then limited the available means to legitimize such processing. See 'APD/GBA—31/2020' (*GDPRhub*, 2 July 2020) <https://gdprhub.eu/index.php?title=APD/GBA_-_31/2020> accessed 8 July 2020.

[100] For a discussion of the relationship between the ePrivacy Directive and the GDPR, see European Data Protection Board, Opinion 5/2019 (n 91).

recognition will require the use of biometric data as protected in Article 9(1) of the Regulation. Similarly, take the hypothetical example of John and the tracking of his mental well-being through an application on his smart watch described in the previous chapter. This would seem to require the processing of 'data concerning health', again as protected in Article 9(1). It appears, therefore, that the explicit consent of the data subject in Article 9(2)(a) would be required. However, even aside from any potential processing of sensitive personal data, any accessing of or placing of information on John's device would also seem to trigger the application of Article 5(3) of the ePrivacy Directive, thereby requiring consent—unless these were for purely functional purposes.[101]

Consequently, although the processing of the (sensitive) personal data in the examples provided could be understood as being 'necessary' for the performance of a contract, the explicit consent or at least ordinary consent of the data subject will be required as an exception to the prohibition on the processing of sensitive personal data. This also appears to be the case where there are multiple purposes—the purpose of delivering the service requested (eg adjusting Ruth's living conditions or monitoring John's emotional well-being) but also, for instance, using this data for advertising and marketing purposes. Importantly, although explicit consent does not seem to present much of a barrier where such processing is necessary to provide a service requested by a data subject (ie through the purchase of a device or application), in order to repurpose such insights for other commercial purposes the explicit consent of the data subject will be required. This explicit consent will also need to satisfy the conditions for consent contained in the GDPR, which seem to prohibit take-it-or-leave-it trade-offs.[102]

Hence, where sensitive personal data are processed, and the only available exception is explicit consent, this is required even if such processing is necessary in order to provide a service requested by the data subject. To reiterate, there is no equivalent to Article 6(1)(b) which recognizes the legitimacy of processing 'necessary for the performance of a contract' in Article 9(2). This

[101] The 'functional purposes' exemption applies if the information (1) is used 'for the sole purpose of carrying out the transmission of a communication over an electronic communications network' or (2) the cookie is 'strictly necessary in order for the provider of an information society service explicitly requested by the subscriber or user to provide the service'. In its opinion on the exemptions, the Article 29 Working Party has noted that these exemptions should be interpreted narrowly and that, for instance, cookies for, inter alia, user tracking, third-party advertising, or first-party analytics therefore do not come within their scope. Article 29 Working Party, 'Opinion 04/2012 on cookie consent Exemption' (2012) WP 194 9–11. See also Article 29 Working Party, 'Opinion on online behavioural advertising' (n 94); Article 29 Working Party, 'Opinion 16/2011 on EASA/IAB best practice recommendation on online behavioural advertising' (2011) WP 188.

[102] For a detailed discussion, see Clifford, Graef, and Valcke (n 25).

distinction is further reflected in Article 22(4), which specifies that contract as referred to in Article 22(2)(a) cannot be utilized to legitimize automated individual decision-making, including profiling based on the processing of sensitive personal data. Instead, and by cross-reference to Article 9(2)(a), explicit consent appears to be the only exception allowing for such processing. We can refer again to the example of John and his smart watch tracking his emotional well-being. Let us assume that a health insurance provider is given access to John's personal data and then uses this to incentivize John to exercise by tracking his step-count and offering him a small discount on his premium when he completes a certain number of steps. Assuming that this example fits within the scope of Article 22 of the Regulation, it would appear that this could amount to the processing of sensitive health data, thereby requiring the explicit consent of the data subject.

Explicit consent, or at least the ordinary notion of consent contained in Article 6(1)(a), will often be required, therefore, even if the GDPR is not consent-based. Controllers have interpreted the provisions differently, however, and seemingly in a manner designed to avoid the role of data subject choice in practice. This demonstrates that although there are significant issues with effectively exercising consent and control rights in the GDPR, the outlook might not be quite as bad as the critical scholars suggest, since arguably the difficulty has related to the effective implementation of consent and data subject control rights and not the data subject's limited capacity to exercise them.[103]

(b) Take-it-or-leave-it or object

Requiring consent through an interpretation of the legislative framework seems to indicate that the higher the risk, the more likely it is that consent will be required. This is evident even in the separation between explicit consent in Article 9(2)(a) and the ordinary consent as a condition for lawful processing in Article 6(1)(a), with the processing of the sensitive personal data categories obviously requiring more than the processing of ordinary personal data requiring consent, even of this separation itself causes uncertainty. The point, therefore, is that in many respects the practical operation of the framework in the context of the provision of consumer products and services is consent-based. Despite the fact that I believe that my interpretation of the provisions in the GDPR is reasonable, in practice there appears to have been far more uncertainty. There has been an apparent move towards relying on contract and/or legitimate

[103] See *Meta Platforms v Bundeskartellamt* (n 92).

interests in response to the industry concerns regarding the high standard of consent provided for in the Regulation.[104]

Article 7 in particular is a key innovation of the Regulation, and this provision has caused significant concern. Article 7 aims to further specify the need to respect each of the conditional elements contained in the definition of consent (freely given, specific, informed, and unambiguous) and appears to establish amongst other things a burden of care on controllers regarding their responsibility to ensure that data subjects have been fairly informed and that they have understood the information provided. These provisions have caused significant concern amongst controllers given the robust standard stipulated. The meaning of Article 7(4) in particular has led to an intense debate regarding the availability of contract (Article 6(1)(b)) and legitimate interest (Article 6(1)(f)) as two of the six conditions for lawful processing provided for in the GDPR.

In addition, poor legal advice and the fear of fines led to a deluge of emails being sent to customers to renew consents following the adoption of the GDPR,[105] with the effects of this certainly entering the public consciousness. Ironically, many of these requests were themselves seen as violations of the Regulation and were indicative of the sheer panic associated with the Regulation's entry into force.[106] Services also began blocking those trying to access their websites in the EU with pop-up messages.[107] These examples reflected the very real impact of the Regulation and the fear of fines, which stoked controller anxiety. The avoidance of consent and the reliance on legitimate interests or contract as the condition for lawful processing instead is significant. Where controllers rely on contract, data subjects are effectively given a take-it-or-leave-it choice, and the use of legitimate interests results in the role of individual choice shifting to *ex post* data subject rights and, in particular, the right to object.

Despite the legislative moves towards more robust opt-in controls introduced by the GDPR, therefore, at least in some respects there has been a shift to requiring data subjects to opt out or, in practice, simply walk away to exercise choice.[108] Given the stickiness of default settings, these points are significant

[104] For an example here, reference can be made to the changes in Meta's policy: see 'How Meta Uses Legal Bases for Processing Ads in the EU' (*Meta*, 4 January 2023) <https://about.fb.com/news/2023/01/how-meta-uses-legal-bases-for-processing-ads-in-the-eu/> accessed 14 September 2023.

[105] See Alex Hern, 'Most GDPR Emails Unnecessary and Some Illegal, Say Experts' *The Guardian* (21 May 2018) <www.theguardian.com/technology/2018/may/21/gdpr-emails-mostly-unnecessary-and-in-some-cases-illegal-say-experts> accessed 19 June 2023.

[106] ibid.

[107] See 'GDPR: US News Sites Unavailable to EU Users under New Rules' *BBC News* (25 May 2018) <www.bbc.com/news/world-europe-44248448> accessed 19 June 2023.

[108] However, in this regard, it would appear from the Court of Justice's decision against Meta that these approaches to the requirements are increasingly in doubt. See *Meta Platforms v Bundeskartellamt*

despite the emergence of more granular options available for the exercising of the right to object, also due to the fact that the effective implementation of data subject rights remains a significant issue of concern.[109] For example, in the context of E-AI, these challenges to implementation may relate to the fact that consumer devices may rely on inferences derived from information taken from a variety of sensors using proprietary technologies and evolving machine learning techniques. Although, according to recital 63 of the Regulation, such concerns should not result in 'a refusal to provide all information to the data subject', the example nevertheless demonstrates the need to balance the interests at stake in such circumstances. Another example is evident, for instance, in the balance that may need to be struck when a data subject is requesting access to personal data that may relate to more than one person. Here we can think of E-AI deployed in smart speakers and how a balance may need to be struck regarding the operation of the right to access ambient personal data. Although these examples are not unique to E-AI, they do demonstrate the challenge of effectively exercising data subject control rights.

That being said, however, it is important to note that there have been a number of complaints brought both in respect of the implementation of the rights provided but also through their use as tools to reveal compliance issues, thereby allowing data subjects to monitor controller activities.[110] In particular, the right of access has been used as a means of verifying compliance, with Max Schrem's actions against *Meta* being an excellent illustration of this function.[111] However, although control rights may have theoretical significance and there are some high-profile examples of how they have been invoked, their practical operation seemingly requires significant effort and is arguably becoming increasingly difficult.[112] The challenge here in part relates to issues of scale and the desensitizing effects of requiring data subjects to make choices. In analysing control rights, Solove, for instance, argues that they are ill-equipped to provide protection as they represent 'an endless burden of chores' that are

(n 92). See also Meta's evolving response to this issue: 'How Meta Uses Legal Bases for Processing Ads in the EU' (n 104).

[109] See Jef Ausloos, Réne Mahieu, and Michael Veale, 'Getting Data Subject Rights Right A Submission to the European Data Protection Board from International Data Rights Academics, to Inform Regulatory Guidance' (2020) 10 Journal of Intellectual Property, Information Technology and Electronic Commerce Law <www.jipitec.eu/issues/jipitec-10-3-2019/5031> accessed 4 October 2023.

[110] For an early discussion of this aspect, see Jef Ausloos and Pierre Dewitte, 'Shattering One-Way Mirrors—Data Subject Access Rights in Practice' (2018) 8 International Data Privacy Law 4.

[111] Ausloos, Mahieu, and Veale (n 109) 285.

[112] See Bert-Jaap Koops, 'On Decision Transparency, or How to Enhance Data Protection after the Computational Turn' in Hildebrandt and Vries (eds) (n 70) 199; Solove, 'The Limitations of Privacy Rights' (n 2); Waldman, 'Privacy's Rights Trap' (n 2).

incapable of being invoked in a systematic way that will control how personal data is processed and that this results in individuals being blamed for failing to exercise their rights.[113] Although there are certainly examples of control rights being used systematically by civil society organizations in the EU, Solove has a point that, due to the scale of personal data processing activities, these rights would need to be exercised with respect to 'hundreds if not thousands of organisations'.[114]

The critical point, therefore, is that data subjects are overwhelmed by the choices that they have to make in order to be fully informed and this may actually be worsened where consent is required. For example, although one could argue that meaningful information about the logic involved in an automated decision and the personal data processed (as required through Articles 13, 14, 15, and 22) could stimulate informed data subject consent, there are a number of limitations to such a claim.[115] First, it is uncertain whether it is in fact possible to explain certain types of machine learning processes.[116] Secondly, it is debatable whether such transparency requirements actually remedy the problems, such as those associated with inaccuracy that will be discussed in Chapter 5. Thirdly, for the meaningful information requirement to have any impact there needs to be scepticism about the trade secrecy claims of commercial operators,[117] which is a very controversial issue.[118] And, fourthly, consent needs to be meaningful (ie the conditions for consent must be respected), a point which goes to the core of the debate presented in this chapter. It is therefore questionable whether transparency as to process will entirely alleviate the problems outlined notwithstanding the data subject's right to contest and express their point of view as per Article 22(3), since in commercial contexts the provision will still ultimately hang on the capacity of the data subject to make an informed choice. As Cohen observes more generally, therefore, it is unclear how individuals would benefit from this added layer of complexity in terms of information.[119]

Even where we are presented with *ex ante* choices we may be overwhelmed by the repeated and seemingly constant nature of the requests for consent. Although consent fatigue has been pointed to as a consequence of the

[113] Solove, 'The Limitations of Privacy Rights' (n 2) 984.
[114] ibid 985.
[115] See Julie E Cohen, 'Turning Privacy Inside Out' (2019) 20 Theoretical Inquiries in Law 32.
[116] See Frank Pasquale, *The Black Box Society: The Secret Algorithms That Control Money and Information* (Harvard University Press 2014).
[117] Cohen, 'Turning Privacy Inside Out' (n 115) 8.
[118] See Gianclaudio Malgieri, 'Trade Secrets v Personal Data: A Possible Solution for Balancing Rights' (2016) 6 International Data Privacy Law 102.
[119] Cohen, 'Turning Privacy Inside Out' (n 115) 8.

introduction of the GDPR, its risks were well known long before the adoption of the Regulation.[120] Consent request overload combined with information overload and a lack of meaningful choice was described by Schermer and colleagues as a recipe for 'consent desensitization' with this in turn leading to the potential lowering of the standard of protection provided by the framework and a disregard for what they refer to as the 'bilateral nature of consent transactions'.[121] The authors were writing in 2014, but I believe that their concerns were legitimate and have been realized in practice. There was significant anxiety surrounding the implementation of the Regulation and the potential fines for infringements. This clearly incentivized compliance and, in light of the complexity of the framework, I believe it led to a situation in which consent was relied upon and indeed (re-)requested, even in situations where (1) it was not required, (2) the (re-)request itself actually demonstrated an original violation of the former Data Protection Directive 95/46/EC, and (3) extensive privacy and cookies policies were created which worsened the issues associated with information overload. These circumstances also appear to have incentivized the use of consent management providers as a response.[122] This is particularly obvious with the example of cookies and similar technologies and, thus, their regulation.

2. Objectified collective benefits

The most common example of consent requests is actually mandated by EU law through Article 5(3) of the *lex specialis* ePrivacy Directive. Article 5(3) of the ePrivacy Directive provides that consent, as defined under the *lex generalis* GDPR, is required for the 'storing of information, or the gaining of access to information already stored, in the terminal equipment' of the user for non-functional purposes.[123] Cookie consent requests are the punchline in jokes about the effectiveness of the GDPR even if they were required prior to the

[120] See eg Bart W Schermer, Bart Custers, and Simone van der Hof, 'The Crisis of Consent: How Stronger Legal Protection May Lead to Weaker Consent in Data Protection' (2014) 16 Ethics and Information Technology 171.

[121] ibid.

[122] See Wheeler (n 7).

[123] As described by the Article 29 Working Party, art 5(3) of the ePrivacy Directive allows for processing to be exempt from the requirement of consent, if one of the following criteria is satisfied (1) technical storage or access 'for the sole purpose of carrying out the transmission of a communication over an electronic communications network' or (2) technical storage or access which is 'strictly necessary in order for the provider of an information society service explicitly requested by the subscriber or user to provide the service'. See Article 29 Working Party, 'Opinion 04/2012 on cookie consent exemption' (n 101).

entry into force of the Regulation and exist as *lex specialis* rules that do not hinge on whether personal data are in fact processed.[124] Indeed, Article 5(3) of the ePrivacy Directive refers to 'information' as opposed to the narrower category of personal data as protected in the GDPR, meaning that it is not a prerequisite that the information be classified as personal to invoke the applicability of the provision.[125]

Consequently, it is information considered to be in the 'private sphere of the users' that triggers the application of Article 5(3) and, hence, not if the information is classified as personal data even if cookies are generally understood to be a category of personal data.[126] Leaving this more pedantic point to one side, the fact that we encounter these requests on *every* website we visit has undoubtedly led to consent request overload, and this could be seen as a deliberate design feature of cookie banners. The regulatory history of cookies is an interesting example of the sliding scale towards more protective legislative interventions accompanied by industry pushback. More specifically, before the update to the Directive in 2009 the use of cookies was 'opt-out'.[127] Despite the European Parliament proposal to require consent, this was watered down by the Council and Parliament in the final version of the 2002 ePrivacy Directive after significant industry lobbying.[128] This decision was then reversed in the 2009 update to the Directive, but these changes failed to have the intended effect, arguably due to the manner in which this requirement was implemented and thus European authorities' failure to persuade US companies to introduce the requirement in a meaningful manner.[129] In the reforms adopted by the GDPR, emphasis was placed on provisions such as data protection by design and by default in Article 25 of the Regulation as a potential solution to this problem. Cookie-consent banners and their design, however, have remained a significant problem (which will be discussed in Chapter 5).

[124] See Damian Clifford, 'EU Data Protection Law and Targeted Advertising: Consent and the Cookie Monster-Tracking the Crumbs of Online User Behaviour' (2014) 5 Journal of Intellectual Property, Information Technology and Electronic Commerce Law 194.

[125] Article 29 Working Party, 'Opinion on online behavioural advertising' (n 94); Article 29 Working Party, 'Opinion 16/2011 on EASA/IAB best practice recommendation on online behavioural advertising' (n 101).

[126] Indeed, as per the European Data Protection opinion on the relationship between the GDPR and the ePrivacy Directive, where it is noted that it is only when the information for the purposes of art 5(3) ePrivacy in question also constitutes personal data that the GDPR also applies. European Data Protection Board, Opinion 5/2019 (n 91) 13–14.

[127] For a discussion, see Ian Brown and Christopher T Marsden, *Regulating Code: Good Governance and Better Regulation in the Information Age* (The MIT Press 2013) 56–57.

[128] ibid.

[129] ibid 165.

Certainly, technology is necessarily designed in a manner which constrains our choices and this reflects well-established accounts of the regulatory impact of technology.[130] However, research on the use of dark patterns or manipulative design strategies, for example, suggests that user interface and user experience design is being used to manipulate data subjects into giving more personal data and to undermine the availability of choice.[131] The precise consequences of the information asymmetries combined with unilateral power to design the interactions with data subjects thus raise important concerns. This is particularly the case as controllers are aware of the mental heuristics and biases we rely upon to make choices.[132] These factors thus increase the risk, given that data subjects often authorize the extensive use of their personal data as disclosed in privacy and cookies policies provided by clicking 'accept'. Such practices are gaining increasing attention in academic research,[133] policymaking, and law reform,[134] and, importantly, at the enforcement level.[135] This is an important and welcome development, but it should also be acknowledged that standard form policies are the norm due to practical realities even if the mechanisms used to gather the consents are obviously ineffective. Controllers are required to inform data subjects, and the scale of data processing operations necessitates the pre-formulation of detailed information to comply with the transparency requirements mandated in the GDPR. Given the detailed information to be communicated to the data subject, standard form texts are a necessity.[136] In this manner, it should be understood that lengthy and even vaguely worded privacy policies may also have been encouraged through the adoption of the GDPR. This may seem counterintuitive at first glance, given that the Regulation and

[130] Famously, see Lawrence Lessig, *Code: And Other Laws of Cyberspace* (Basic Books 1999); Lawrence Lessig, *Code: Version 2.0* (Basic Books 2006).

[131] See Gray and others, 'Dark Patterns and the Legal Requirements of Consent Banners' (n 75).

[132] See Ryan Calo, 'Digital Market Manipulation' (2014) 82 George Washington Law Review 995.

[133] Christoph Bösch and others, 'Tales from the Dark Side: Privacy Dark Strategies and Privacy Dark Patterns' (2016) 2016 Proceedings on Privacy Enhancing Technologies 237; Colin M Gray and others, 'The Dark (Patterns) Side of UX Design' (Proceedings of the 2018 CHI Conference on Human Factors in Computing Systems—CHI '18, ACM Press, 2018) <http://dl.acm.org/citation.cfm?doid=3173574.3174108> accessed 25 April 2019.

[134] See California Consumer Privacy Act of 2018.

[135] 'When digital services employ dark patterns to nudge users toward sharing more personal data, the financial incentive has taken precedence over respecting users' right to choose. The practice of misleading consumers into making certain choices, which may put their privacy at risk, is unethical and exploitative.' Forbrukerrådet (Norwegian Consumer Council), 'Deceived by Design: How Tech Companies Use Dark Patterns to Discourage Us from Exercising Our Rights to Privacy' (*Forbrukerrådet*, 2018) 5 <https://fil.forbrukerradet.no/wp-content/uploads/2018/06/2018-06-27-deceived-by-design-final.pdf> accessed 25 April 2019.

[136] See Clifford and Paterson, 'Consumer Privacy and Consent' (n 78); Damian Clifford and Jeannie Marie Paterson, 'Data Rights and Contract Law: Formation, Incorporation and Vitiating Factors' in Clifford, Paterson, and Lau (eds (n 7).

guidance seem to encourage short, precise, and understandable information and even the use of icons.[137] However, in light of the anxiety and uncertainty caused by some of the GDPR's provisions, it can hardly been surprising that there is scholarly research suggesting that these documents appear to be becoming increasingly complex.[138]

Such policies can certainly be used to disadvantage data subjects. We can refer back to the hypothetical example of John and the use of his smart watch to track his emotional well-being. Although we can imagine that John may be aware of the risks associated with the secure storage of such sensitive data concerning his health, given the repeated and well-publicized data breaches, he may not have anticipated the on-selling of his data to the insurance company. But even if he is aware of the abstract risk of such a thing happening he might not feel emotionally connected to this risk due to the multiplicity of requests for consent he receives. This point reflects the fact that the value that we attach to our personal data may vary. Indeed, despite the wide range of literature examining the economic value of personal data and essentially the pricing of information, such efforts arguably fail to fully reflect the inherent subjective value attached to such information which may be difficult if not impossible to quantify, given the unavoidably subjective nature of such considerations.[139] In simple terms, the value one attaches to one's personal data may not correspond to the commercial economic valuations derived from a mere *macro*-level market analysis. Commercial valuations of personal data reflect its positioning as an asset, and such an approach fails to account for the subjective valuations of the data subject to whom the personal data relate. This point is perhaps compounded by the fact that people may only feel the sting of this subjective valuation when they have experienced a harm such as a data breach.[140] This risk arguably remains unaddressed by the individual participation rights-based approach evident in data protection law and the failure to align the reality of individual and, indeed, societal risks posed by personal data processing with data subject behaviour.[141]

137 See Radim Polčák, 'Article 12 Transparent Information, Communication and Modalities for the Exercise of the Rights of the Data Subject' in Christopher Kuner and others (eds), *The EU General Data Protection Regulation (GDPR): A Commentary* (OUP 2020).

138 See Shmuel I Becher and Uri Benoliel, 'Law in Books and Law in Action: The Readability of Privacy Policies and the GDPR' in Klaus Mathis and Avishalom Tor (eds), *Consumer Law and Economics* (Springer International 2021).

139 For a discussion of this point, see Oscar H Gandy, *The Panoptic Sort: A Political Economy of Personal Information* (Westview 1993).

140 Stark (n 64) 22.

141 On the relational nature of personal data, see Viljoen (n 14); Wheeler (n 7).

However, this point arguably fails to account for the fact that data subject control rights can (and do) have societal/collective impacts. Indeed, the very objectification of compliance efforts ensures that when a particular personal data processing management mechanism is found to be unfair, the consequences are by definition societal. For example, although there are significant issues with the cookies consent-rule processes for compliance, (1) these concerns are well known; (2) they have been the topic of discussion and the subject of complaints for some time; and (3) they are seemingly on their last legs in part due to the regulatory reforms to consent introduced by the GDPR, the enforcement actions being taken against the IAB's standard, and the resulting regulatory and civil society pressure.[142] This example further demonstrates how individual control rights and individual rights of action can be used for targeted litigation and how a complaint can turn an industry practice on its head. We can also refer here to the impact of the *Google Spain* case[143] but also of course the various complaints that have been made against *Meta* and, in particular, the Court of Justice's ruling in the *Meta* case.[144] Indeed, Meta has come under significant scrutiny regarding its reliance on contract and legitimate interests as conditions for lawful processing instead of consent, with the company announcing its plans to move to a consent-based approach to legitimize behavioural advertising in response to significant pressure and enforcement actions.

The use of control rights by civil society has certainly been a feature of data protection law enforcement in the EU, and therefore it is incorrect to conclude that individual rights cannot have a societal impact. It is an oversimplification to say that the choice mechanisms in the GDPR are futile attempts to empower the data subject. Our measure for the success or failure of the mechanisms for choice must account for the fact that the Regulation provides for an objectified approach to the manner in which our choices are given an instrumental role. The effectiveness of choice in the GDPR, therefore, may arguably be more accurately assessed if we examine the rational data subject as a fiction that serves a function as opposed to a construct that is designed to mirror the actual subjective capacities of data subjects. Certainly, there are ongoing issues. Many of the criticisms outlined in the critical literature are valid and

[142] See eg 'The BE DPA to Restore Order to the Online Advertising Industry: IAB Europe Held Responsible for a Mechanism that Infringes the GDPR | Autorité de Protection des données/ Gegevensbeschermingsautoriteit' <www.dataprotectionauthority.be/citizen/iab-europe-held-responsible-for-a-mechanism-that-infringes-the-gdpr> accessed 23 September 2023.

[143] Case C-131/12, *Google Spain SL and Google Inc. v Agencia Española de Protección de Datos (AEPD) and Mario Costeja González*, ECLI:EU:C:2014:317.

[144] *Meta Platforms v Bundeskartellamt* (n 92).

hard to dispute—there is significant evidence supporting them after all. There are quite obviously information and power asymmetries, market effects, manipulative design practices, and cognitive capacity issues at play. Put simply, actual human behaviour is very different from the assumptions found in data protection law. The problem with relying on data subjects to exercise choice then is that arguably our capacity to choose only exists in theory—in a formal and not a substantive sense. However, when we understand the rational data subject as a fiction that serves a specific normative function, we can see how control rights (and, indeed, the data subject's direct right of action) have been used in particular. Although these examples alone certainly do not mean that the choice mechanisms are functioning, we can see how they have been used to generate more meaningful protection for all data subjects, thus serving not only as a mechanism of choice and control but also as means of holding controllers to account.[145]

To be clear, however, the way in which the exercising of choice can have collective/societal benefits does not negate the point that the GDPR may be ill-suited to regulating some types of societal/collective harms. Indeed, control rights arguably fail to account for societal risks and the relational or social nature of the information economy. This problem is not solved by the way in which mechanisms for choice can be used for collective benefit. Our individual choices may negatively affect others. To demonstrate this point, we can consider for instance how E-AI poses significant societal risks that may be unaddressed. Aside from the accuracy issues (see Chapter 5), an E-AI example here might be the potentially manipulative effects of the technology when it is used to profile data subjects for advertising and marketing purposes. The emergence of E-AI and the harnessing of emotional insights for commercial purposes certainly raises key concerns regarding individual autonomy, in that they could arguably exacerbate the issues regarding the continuing reliance on the rationality paradigm and, hence, self-determination and individual autonomy as core underlying rationales of legal protections.

Such risks are compounded by the fact that, although we may be well positioned to accept or reject the risks of sharing our sensitive health information with the provider of an application, arguably we are simply incapable of navigating the complex issues at play in ecosystems such as online advertising in order to understand the significance and effects of our consent, but also as our personal data may not have been used to develop the profile that may be applied to us subsequently. When there are a whole range of actors, purposes,

[145] See Quelle (n 88).

and interests at stake and we are asked to make these decisions repeatedly, we may have a very limited capacity to choose, and also our choices may have a limited effect on the overall development and deployment of the technology. Importantly, however, and as will also be explored in Chapter 5, although data protection law arguably struggles to counteract these risks, the GDPR does not prevent additional regulatory interventions providing enhanced protections.[146] It is therefore debatable whether removing the role for subjective choice is the best means of addressing these more collective harms. This is particularly the case as the criticisms of choice arguably fail to fully account for the more complex realities.

D. Limits of the Challenge

The mechanisms of choice provided for in data protection law are the means through which individuals are afforded the capacity to make subjective choices. Removing them would therefore further objectify the protections. Neatly dividing behaviour into either rational or irrational does not reflect the more complex reality. These points refer to the fact that although the contribution of the behavioural critique of choice is of significant importance, we still need to recognize not only that reasonable people can disagree on what they deem to be a legitimate use of their personal data,[147] but also that even the behavioural economics account of decision-making itself has shortcomings.

Emotion plays a role in all decision-making and it therefore undoubtedly also impacts our decisions to give up our data. The rational and seemingly emotionless data subject empowered to protect themselves through calculated choices seems to contrast with the practical reality. Although there has been some discussion of the need to protect against the 'subjective' emotional harms risked by surveillance (as distinct from objective harms—see Chapter 3),[148] there is a continuing need for research that attempts to connect how the 'lived nuances and messy complexities' described by Stark[149] impact individual

[146] eg we can refer to the EU's AI Act and the banning of certain applications of E-AI, but also more generally the role of areas of law such as consumer law, as clear examples of this room for alternative forms of regulation.

[147] This is a point that is recognized even by some of the strongest critics of consent and control rights. See Solove, 'Murky Consent' (n 1); Solove, 'Introduction' (n 1).

[148] See generally Daniel J Solove and Danielle Keats Citron, 'Risk and Anxiety: A Theory of Data Breach Harms' (2016) Social Science Research Network Scholarly Paper ID 2885638 <https://papers.ssrn.com/abstract=2885638> accessed 4 October 2023; Ryan Calo, 'The Boundaries of Privacy Harm' (2011) 86 Indiana Law Journal 1131.

[149] Stark (n 64) 16.

participation in data protection law. Explanations of the privacy paradox, as an example, therefore seem to oversimplify certain factors and the preferences and/or failure to properly account for the role of emotion and thus how emotional ties and norms influence decision-making.[150] As such, there is a need for a fuller account of the role of emotion in decision-making in data protection law. The simple fact is that advancements in understanding the role and importance of emotion across various disciplines suggests that emotion and cognition are not separate, with emotion understood as being inherently intertwined with decision-making irrespective of whether one's decisions are good, bad, or indifferent.[151]

Emotions are therefore indispensable to our capacity to choose in that they allow us to best exercise 'the instruments of logic'.[152] However, just because emotion is key to decision-making does not mean that (1) all emotions we experience are rational in terms of their normative acceptability, nor does it mean that (2) they cannot negatively affect the reasoning process. Indeed, with this in mind one can refer to Nussbaum's positioning of irrational emotions, which she defines in terms of thought and thus from the perspective of normative irrationalities based on false information or values.[153] Irrational emotions will result from an incorrect assessment of a situation or when the person's underlying value system is somehow flawed.[154] Nussbaum offers the example of racism resulting in an irrational emotional response based on flawed information or values. In the context of data protection, one can imagine how false information or values can have an impact on data subject trust, appetite for risk, and thus fear, in relation to decisions to surrender personal data or not. To demonstrate this it must be understood that although emotions are necessary for decision-making, this does not mean that emotions do not mislead

[150] See Lutz and Strathoff (n 67).

[151] Lerner and others, 'Emotion and Decision Making' (n 54) 801.

[152] Ronald De Sousa, *The Rationality of Emotion* (MIT Press 1987) xii.

[153] Martha Craven Nussbaum, *Hiding from Humanity: Disgust, Shame, and the Law* (Princeton University Press 2004) 11–12. As noted by the author:

> in terms of thought that is bad thought in some normative sense. Thus, the person who says that two plus two is five, even after repeated teaching, is irrational, because he thinks badly. So, too, in a different way, we typically hold that racism is irrational, based on belief that are false or ungrounded [. . .]. Of course many particular instances of anger or fear may indeed be irrational in the normative sense. They may be based on false information . . . [or] false values, as would be the case if someone reacted with overwhelming anger to a minor insult. (Aristotle's example of this is anger at people who forget one's name).

[154] In contrast, irrationality in terms of behavioural economics refers more to flawed decision-making, mental heuristics, and bounded rationality. Irrationality here should be construed as referring to a decision that an individual would not have made if they were informed and had alternative choices (ie if informed afterwards they would wish to change their choice). Cass R Sunstein, 'Nudging: A Very Short Guide' (2014) 37 Journal of Consumer Policy 583; Cass R Sunstein, 'Fifty Shades of Manipulation' [2016] Journal of Marketing Behaviour 213, 213; Jolls, Sunstein, and Thaler (n 30).

us—a computer scientist might overlook risks due to their enthusiasm about something they have built, a policymaker might overlook risks because of the promise of economic prosperity, or the public might focus on risks and overlook the benefits of a particular technology because of a particular worldview. The point then is that although all those listed might not be 'rational', emotion may be expressive of our values rather than necessarily being an irrational influence. Emotions can however certainly 'cause havoc in the processes of reasoning',[155] and this reflects the second of the points above.

The key takeaway, therefore, is that there are no such cold deliberative 'rational' states and that decision-making and emotion go hand in hand.[156] Although the need for a rationality paradigm as a normative construct is defended in this book, there are those who suggest abandoning it. For instance, Arkush suggests that libertarian paternalism (or nudging) in behavioural economics literature is inherently flawed, as proponents of the theory retain the idea that through our choices we reveal our preferences, despite destabilizing the decision-making capacity of individuals to effectively pursue their preferences and well-being.[157] Such criticism reflects the tightrope walking between autonomy and paternalism evident in the behavioural economics (nudging literature). Indeed, because behavioural economics retains this idea that our choices reveal our preferences but simultaneously undercuts the legitimacy of the capacity of individuals to pursue their preferences, libertarian paternalism can only offer piecemeal progress. Nudging policies are therefore only adopted in areas that are intuitively problematic for autonomy and aim to improve 'rational' decision-making. Without rationality as a normative anchor, the law would have to assume that data subjects are not able to choose for themselves and thus arguably then make all choices for them. Indeed, it must be emphasized that any move from a rationality-based approach in legal protections would be far more epistemologically challenging than other alternatives[158] and would seemingly change the role of regulation as it is currently conceived.

In simple terms, the use of rationality as a functional fiction rests on the conceptual starting point that individuals are best placed to decide on their preferences. Although this is certainly a fiction, doing away with the rationality paradigm would undermine the very roots of autonomy and effectively lead to a far more paternalistic form of governance whereby the legislature would

155 Damasio (n 55). xii.

156 Kathryn Abrams and Hila Keren, 'Who's Afraid of Law and the Emotions' (2009) 94 Minnesota Law Review 1997, 1999.

157 Arkush (n 29) 1343.

158 Abrams and Keren (n 156) 1999.

seemingly be required to decide how individuals' welfare and preferences should be formulated. One must really question whether such an approach would be desirable *in every context*, especially in light of the fact that emotions affect the decision-making of all individuals, including the legislator (see Chapter 6). To help explain this, let us imagine what would happen if the legislative interventions such as those provided in consumer law, as a different area of law with substantive similarities in its underlying assumptions, simply assumed that individuals could not act rationally at all. How would this affect legislative interventions, such as those provided in statutory protections against the use of unfair terms? If consumers cannot be trusted to make choices, then would we not need legislative interventions dictating the terms of consumer agreements and not just those that exclude unfair ones? How would this approach be scalable, particularly in today's digital economy, and what would it mean for the role of rationality as the fundamental unit of liberalism?

I do not think there is a good wholesale answer to these questions that is feasible from a policymaking perspective; after all, data subjects continue to struggle to exercise their subjective control rights even in data protection frameworks such as the GDPR that provide for the most robust levels of protection. This struggle is unavoidable as data protection law necessarily provides for protections constrained by objective standards and not subjective ones. Controllers make decisions and design their interactions with the data subject, and data subjects are then inevitably left to make sense of them. Instead, therefore, it may be that minor modifications of existing theories are necessary—instead of viewing emotion as a purely irrational influence on decision-making, it must also be seen as a component of rationality. In a data protection context, understanding the role of emotion as a component of rationality may require further reflection on the precise role of mechanisms such as individual consent without necessarily envisaging no role for it. I believe, in line with Schermer and colleagues, that this may cause us to reflect more on the circumstances in which consent for instance is required if it is the legislator's intent that requiring consent should signal a particularly risky use of personal data.[159] This is not to say that consent does not play a useful role in data protection law, but rather that to ensure its effectiveness we may need to think more about the circumstances in which it may or may not provide meaningful protection and the mechanisms that may be used to bolster its effectiveness or provide alternative forms of protection.

[159] Schermer, Custers, and van der Hof (n 120).

In this regard, Solove, for instance, proposes 'murky consent', which aims to embrace the problems associated with consent.[160] The proposal recognizes these problems expressly by providing for a weak basis for the processing of personal data in data protection law, with in-built fiduciary obligations to protect the interests of data subjects and a hodgepodge of protections already found in statutes such as the GDPR and also taken from the law of equity.[161] Solove's proposal therefore seems to be a more protective version of the notion of 'deemed consent' in the Singaporean PDPA, or something between contract and legitimate interests in the GDPR, given how the fairness principle also requires the interests of data subjects to be factored in, and how these conditions are narrowed by the 'necessity' test as will be explored in Chapter 5. Irrespective of such proposals, I believe more generally that there is an oversimplification in the literature criticizing the enhanced role of choice in frameworks such as the GDPR which may weigh on the merits of any one proposed reform over another. As the analysis in the previous section has demonstrated, any criticism must account for the fact that there are clear signs that controllers have tried to rely on alternatives to consent and also that data subject rights and, indeed, the individual right of action provided for in the GDPR have been used to engender significant changes. The reality is that the problems may be more in the nature of challenges associated with compliance as opposed to necessarily being issues with the mechanisms for choice provided in data protection law.

Several authors have highlighted that reliance on an 'atomistic' data subject fails to address the societal implication[162] of many of decisions regarding data but also 'discipline networked processes at scale'.[163] However, describing the data subject as an atomistic individual arguably belies the fact that individual participation is generally just one of the components of these frameworks. Indeed, as will be described in Chapter 5, data protection laws generally rely on a number of principles that aim at constraining the behaviour of controllers in order to ensure a *fairer* personal data processing environment, thus serving these frameworks' key tenet of controller responsibility.[164] To a certain extent, and as will be explained further in the next chapter, the GDPR already aims to create an environment in which consent can function through a range of

[160] Solove, 'Murky Consent' (n 1).

[161] ibid 37–44.

[162] See Solove, 'The Limitations of Privacy Rights' (n 2); Julie E Cohen, 'How (Not) to Write a Privacy Law' (2021) 21 Knight First Amendment Institute <https://knightcolumbia.org/content/how-not-to-write-a-privacy-law> accessed 4 October 2023; Ari Ezra Waldman, 'The New Privacy Law' (2021) 55 UC Davis Law Review Online 19.

[163] Cohen, 'How (Not) to Write a Privacy Law' (n 162).

[164] For a description in the context of the GDPR, see Chapter 5 but also Quelle (n 88).

accountability mechanisms such as the requirements to conduct a data protection impact assessment/privacy impact assessment or the requirement for data protection/privacy by default and by design. Indeed, as noted by Quelle, a data subject cannot 'consent away' the principles for lawful processing at least in frameworks provided for in hard law such as the GDPR.[165]

For me, the question then becomes to what extent these requirements already require those processing personal data to develop mechanisms that allow for meaningful and valid choice. Reference here can be made to the emergence of consent management mechanisms and the role of browser settings, for instance, in the management of cookie requests but also more data subject-friendly developments such as Apple's App Tracking Transparency (ATT) Framework which has provided an excellent example of how design can be harnessed in a privacy-preserving manner. More specifically, Apple switched tracking for targeted advertising from an opt-out to an opt-in basis. However, in contrast to the cookies example, Apple implemented this change through user-friendly design thereby demonstrating the potential of consent for enthusiasts.[166] The predominant focus of data protection guidance on process as opposed to substantive fairness, as well as on collection of data as opposed to use, will be developed in Chapter 5, in particular through an analysis of the role of impact assessments, but here it must be acknowledged that these processes of compliance do objectify the data subject.

To explain, although individuals are afforded the right to consent or not in legislative instruments such as the GDPR, and individual data subject rights such as the right not to be subject to an automated decision that allow them on paper to make subjective choices, the law will assess their conduct objectively, and compliance efforts will be designed for the world at large and with a managerialized slant.[167] Take, for instance, the example of Meta services like Facebook, where its privacy and cookies policies and terms and conditions and pre-formulated declarations of consent will always by necessity be in standard form. Even in the context of data subject rights where individuals request the access to or erasure of their data, there will also always be standardized approaches. In short, we need to account for the fact that the role for subjective choice is increasingly objectified through compliance mechanisms in a world

[165] ibid 146.

[166] For more, see Cristobal Cheyre and others, 'The Impact of Apple's App Tracking Transparency Framework on the App Ecosystem' (19 May 2023) <https://papers.ssrn.com/abstract=4453463> accessed 22 September 2023.

[167] See Julie E Cohen, *Between Truth and Power: The Legal Constructions of Informational Capitalism* (OUP 2019); Ari Ezra Waldman, 'Outsourcing Privacy' (2021) 96 Notre Dame Law Review Reflection 194.

of technologically mediated choices. As will be described in the next chapter, this may be exacerbated by compliance in process and not substance in particular. We therefore need to consider the role of accountability and the responsibility of those processing personal data to do so *fairly*.

E. Conclusion

The analysis in this chapter has demonstrated that there is an important critical literature that challenges the rationality assumption evident in data protection law. Although this literature offers important critiques of the role of choice, and thus the assumed rationality of the data subject, I believe that the challenge has limits. The analysis has demonstrated how interdisciplinary insights on decision-making call into question some of the regulatory choices made by the legislature. In particular, I have demonstrated how the failure to account for how people make decisions in reality may have knock-on effects in terms of the legitimate use of specific technologies. Emotions and decision-making go hand in hand, but rationality is a necessary functional fiction in law and should not be disregarded.

Through the use of E-AI as a case study, I developed the identified challenge by exploring how the GDPR could be seen as the ready-made solution to the risks posed by this technology and questioned the Regulation's capacity to appropriately respond to the limitations of relying on data subject choice. In doing so, I explored how the changes introduced by the GDPR have had an impact and questioned whether the problems associated with effectuating choice may in fact be more in the nature of challenges associated with compliance as opposed to necessarily being entirely issues with the mechanisms for choice provided in the Regulation. We must therefore now turn our attention to the accountability mechanisms that are designed, at least in part, to ensure a fair environment in which the data subject can act in their own interest.

5

The Challenge to Fairness

A. Introduction

Data protection law requires fair personal data processing. Those processing personal data have the responsibility of complying with the framework and, where they are provided for, applying some core accountability mechanisms to achieve this in practice. These accountability mechanisms may vary, but requirements to conduct impact assessments in particular are common in many data protection laws. Fairness and accountability therefore go hand in hand.[1] Certainly, oversight mechanisms and the role of enforcement authorities are significant for compliance. As discussed in Chapter 2, the reforms introduced by the General Data Protection Regulation (GDPR) and the bolstering of the enforcement stick wielded by data protection authorities (DPAs) caused significant anxiety amongst controllers. However, it is questionable whether the threat of this stick has merely resulted in compliance in form as opposed to in substance. This challenge to the effective operation of controller accountability is a key criticism of the reliance on the notion of control in data protection law and the data subject rights-orientated approach evident in these frameworks.

Those processing personal data are not invested in compliance, and, perhaps more fundamentally, the complexities of the framework require this level of commitment given the vagueness of what is considered fair and/or unfair. The affective feature of this challenge then is that although data protection law aims to provide an environment in which data subjects can make subjective choices, it affords controllers significant latitude and arguably allows them the scope not to comply in a meaningful manner. The purpose of this chapter is to explore this disconnect through the lens of fairness and accountability mechanisms in data protection law. Again, Emotional Artificial Intelligence (E-AI) will be used as a case study, with a focus in this chapter on how its purported inaccuracy interacts with the rights and requirements embedded in the GDPR

[1] See Hielke Hijmans and Charles D Raab, 'Ethical Dimensions of the GDPR' in Mark Cole and Franziska Boehm (eds), *Commentary on the General Data Protection Regulation* (Edward Elgar 2018) <https://papers.ssrn.com/abstract=3222677> accessed 3 September 2018.

Data Protection Law and Emotion. Damian Clifford, Oxford University Press.
DOI: 10.1093/oso/9780192845863.003.0005

in particular. Concerns with the accuracy of E-AI are widely referenced in the academic literature and in popular culture and it therefore provides an excellent lens through which to analyse the affective features of the challenge.

Section B explores the affective features of the problem through an analysis of data protection law's failure to achieve meaningful compliance. Section C builds on this analysis by offering E-AI as a case study to demonstrate how this challenge manifests itself in practice through the lens of the GDPR. Section D then explores the limits of the challenge to controller accountability and the application of key accountability mechanisms. In essence, I argue that data protection's failure to reach 'the hearts and minds' of those regulated, as noted by Koops,[2] can hardly been seen as a problem that is unique to data protection law. However, I also demonstrate that the open-textured nature of the fairness principle in the GDPR in particular may exacerbate the issues associated with failing to comply in substance as opposed to in process and that there may be a role for other areas of law to provide a more precise indication of what may be unfair in certain circumstances.

B. Affective Features of the Challenge

Data protection law aims to protect against both tangible and intangible risks of harm. It establishes both proactive and reactive rights and obligations. However, it arguably struggles to achieve this aim. The challenge is that although data protection law aims to provide an environment in which data subjects can make subjective choices, it affords controllers significant latitude in terms of their compliance with the objective standards. Arguably, this allows controllers the scope not to comply in a meaningful manner and to embed their subjective interpretations of the requirements to suit their own ends.[3]

Importantly however, as will be demonstrated, when criticizing the key role played by the controller we must be mindful of the varying objective standards of 'fairness' in different jurisdictions, and also the role played by the key accountability mechanisms provided for in data protection law which aim to embed the fairness checks and balances in practice. The analysis in this section will therefore explore the role of the controller in providing an environment in which the data subject can meaningfully make choices by analysing the role

[2] Bert-Jaap Koops, 'The Trouble with European Data Protection Law' (2014) 4 International Data Privacy Law 250.

[3] ibid.

of (1) the fairness checks and balances provided in data protection law, and (2) the varying standards of fairness evident in these laws.

1. Checks, balances, and compliance

Data protection law is inherently intertwined with the notion of fairness, and there is an obvious link to the historical development of the data protection principles or fair information practice principles (FIPPs). For example, as discussed in Chapter 2, the FIPPs developed in the US and at the national level in Europe had an obvious influence in the development of the key international instruments: the Organisation for Economic Co-operation and Development (OECD) Guidelines and Convention 108. Consequently, almost all data protection laws globally have been adopted with similar FIPPs included and therefore they are also often centred around this (or at least *a*) notion of fairness.[4] Describing the data subject as an atomistic individual, therefore, arguably belies the fact that individual participation is generally just one of the components of these frameworks.[5] Data protection laws constrain controllers by requiring adherence to principles.

The Collection Limitation,[6] Purpose Specification,[7] and Use Limitation[8] principles, for instance, are important examples. Although Convention 108, and indeed, the updated Convention 108 + also split these parts (albeit in different and slightly differing manners), it is possible to understand these three principles as different aspects of the same thing—the purpose limitation principle.[9] As described in Chapter 2, the purpose limitation principle requires that personal data should only be collected for specified and legitimate purposes and not further processed for incompatible purposes. The principle seems to be of universal importance.[10] Purpose limitation essentially aims to restrict the

[4] Despite its widely accepted importance, there are examples of data protection laws that do not refer to fairness. For example, see: the Singaporean PDPA and the Canadian Privacy Act, which regulates how the federal government handles personal data. Privacy Act (RSC 1985, c P-21).

[5] As described in Chapter 4, these individual participations may be included as one of the principles or through some other means.

[6] The Guidelines on the Protection of Privacy and Transborder Flows of Personal Data (OECD) 1980, para 7.

[7] ibid 9.

[8] ibid 10.

[9] Lee A Bygrave, *Data Protection Law: Approaching Its Rationale, Logic and Limits* (Kluwer Law International 2002) 61.

[10] eg in the OECD Guidelines this principle seems to be spread across principles 7, 9, and 10: see The Guidelines on the Protection of Privacy and Transborder Flows of Personal Data (OECD) 1980. In contrast, see art 5(b) of the Convention for the Protection of Individuals with Regard to Automatic Processing of Personal Data (Council of Europe) 1981 (Convention 108) and art 5(b) of Directive 95/46/EC of the European Parliament and of the Council of 24 October 1995 on the protection of individuals

processing of personal data for purposes other than those originally specified. The specification of the purpose is a prerequisite for applying the principles/requirements, ie the purpose should be made clear before the data processing takes place and the subsequent use limited to the fulfilment of only compatible purposes.[11] This aim is strongly connected to the limited retention principle and the principle of data minimization, which are also common in many data protection laws. In simple terms, these principles require 'minimality',[12] in that data gathering should be strictly constrained to that which is necessary for the purpose pursued by the processing and that personal data no longer required should be erased or anonymized. Convention 108 and Convention 108 + specifically recognize the limited retention principle in Article 5(e) and Article 5(4)(e) respectively, and Article 5(1)(e) of the GDPR recognizes the substantively similar storage limitation principle, with Article 5(1)(c) providing for the data minimization principle. Although the data minimization principle was recognized by the Court of Justice of the European Union (Court of Justice) under the old Data Protection Directive 95/46/EC, prior to the adoption of the GDPR it was not expressly provided for in EU data protection law.[13] Neither of these principles, however, is expressly included in the OECD Guidelines.

In addition to principles dealing with the how, why, and what of data processing, there are also common principles dealing with the quality of the data and its security and, more broadly, accountability. The security principle requires those processing personal data to implement the necessary organizational and technical measures to ensure the protection of that personal data and to prevent accidental loss and unauthorized disclosure and use. At the national level and in the GDPR and modernized Convention 108 +, for instance, these requirements are then often further developed through mechanisms such as breach notification obligations and requirements to conduct impact assessments. These requirements are in turn connected to accountability, which is expressly included as a principle in the OECD Guidelines, the Asia-Pacific Economic Cooperation (APEC) Privacy Framework, and also the GDPR, the

with regard to the processing of personal data and on the free movement of such data [1995] OJ L281/31–50. This also represents the approach adopted in the GDPR, for instance, where the purpose limitation principle is provided in art 5(1)(b) of the Regulation in addition to the lawfulness, fairness, and transparency principles in art 5(1)(a).

[11] Article 29 Working Party, 'Opinion 03/2013 on purpose limitation' (2013) WP 203.

[12] Bygrave (n 9) 60.

[13] The principle was however, implied by certain requirements; see Case C–274/99 P *Connolly v Commission* [2001] OJ C173/13; Case C–131/12 *Google Spain SL and Google Inc v Agencia Española de Protección de Datos (AEPD) and Mario Costeja González*, ECLI:EU:C:2014:317.

Singaporean Personal Data Protection Act (PDPA),[14] and the Canadian Act regulating the private sector, for example.[15] Although the data quality principle varies considerably across both Convention 108 and the OECD Guidelines and also the various national implementations in terms of its scope and stringency,[16] both state that personal data should be accurate, complete, and, where necessary, kept up-to-date.

This is just a sampling of the key principles that are common across most data protection laws that form part of the checks and balances which, as described in Chapter 4, also include a role for grounds for processing such as consent and also control rights. However, pessimistic interpretations of the role of data protection see the effectiveness of data protection as being impacted not only by its focus on data subject consent and subjective control rights, but also through its seemingly unrealistic view of controllers' willingness and, arguably, capacity to comply with data protection law's principles and rules and, thus, accountability mechanisms. Certainly, there have been repeated criticisms of some of the principles outlined. For example, as described in Chapter 2, it has been suggested that data gathering in the big data environment appears to be almost inherently in contradiction with the data minimization and purpose limitation principles,[17] and data security is also becoming gradually more difficult as demonstrated by well-publicized data breaches. This has led some scholars to question not only the ongoing utility of these principles but also the role of the various accountability mechanisms provided in data protection law.

Indeed, as explained in Chapter 2, there appears to be a more collective aspect to the notion of control that is embedded in EU data protection law in particular, but also frameworks in other jurisdictions, that relates to the creation of an environment in which an individual can 'choose'. Even in the United States (US) where there is no federal data protection/privacy statute like the GDPR, privacy impact assessments (PIAs) are required under the 2002 E-Government Act, and, through the exercising of its powers under the Federal Trade Commission Act,[18] the Federal Trade Commission, for instance, may

[14] See Advisory Guidelines on Key Concepts in the Personal Data Protection Act (Personal Data Protection Commission 2013) 151–55 <www.pdpc.gov.sg/-/media/Files/PDPC/PDF-Files/Advisory-Guidelines/AG-on-Key-Concepts/Advisory-Guidelines-on-Key-Concepts-in-the-PDPA-1-Oct-2021.pdf?la=en> accessed 19 June 2023.

[15] Personal Information Protection and Electronic Documents Act (SC 2000, c 5) sch 1.

[16] Bygrave (n 9) 62.

[17] Valerie Verdoodt, Damian Clifford, and Eva Lievens, 'Toying with Children's Emotions, the New Game in Town? The Legality of Advergames in the EU' (2016) 32 Computer Law & Security Review 599.

[18] The Federal Trade Commission Act of 1914.

require entities who have signed a consent order to undergo monitoring and reporting for up to twenty years.[19]

However, Waldman argues that many of the mechanisms established by data protection laws, such as impact assessments, audits, and policies, are examples of 'compliance in name only'.[20] He also points to what he considers to be a dangerous trend—the outsourcing of compliance efforts to third-party technology vendors resulting in the narrowing of the legislative rules and principles into its 'codable pieces' and the recasting of the focus from the risks posed to individuals to the mitigation of the regulatory/corporate risks.[21] Indeed, scholars have pointed to the role and impact of managerial values, where managerialized data protection is focused on minimizing the effects of the law rather than adherence to its goals.[22] This criticism also imports a discussion of the role of individual data subjects as active market participants capable of holding controllers accountable for their actions and arguably means that these managerialized structures are complicit in increasing the power of those processing the data.[23] Certainly, such developments risk undermining core aspects of data protection law that are context-dependent in terms of applications such as the requirements for *fair* personal data processing. But what does fairness actually mean in the checks and balances provided by data protection law?

2. Varying standards of fairness

Early discussions of the need for data protection frameworks such as the 1973 and 1974 Council of Europe Resolutions,[24] the 1980 OECD Guidelines, and key reports such as the 1978 United Kingdom (UK) Lindop Report[25] focused on the fair *collection* of personal data. In the OECD Guidelines, for instance, 'fair and lawful' is only referred to within the collection limitation principle.[26]

[19] See Ari Ezra Waldman, 'Outsourcing Privacy' (2021) 96 Notre Dame Law Review Reflection 194, 199.

[20] ibid 195.

[21] ibid 205–07.

[22] See Julie E Cohen, *Between Truth and Power: The Legal Constructions of Informational Capitalism* (OUP 2019); Waldman, 'Outsourcing Privacy' (n 19).

[23] Cohen (n 22) 154–64.

[24] Council of Europe—Committee of Ministers, Resolution (73) 22 on the Protection of the Privacy of Individuals Vis-à-Vis Electronic Data Banks in the Private Sector (26 September 1973); Council of Europe—Committee of Ministers, Resolution (74) 29 on the Protection of the Privacy of Individuals Vis-a-Vis Electronic Data Banks in the Public Sector (20 September 1974).

[25] See Norman Lindop, *Report of the Committee on Data Protection, Chairman: Norman Lindop* (Her Majesty's Stationery Office 1978) 11.

[26] The Guidelines on the Protection of Privacy and Transborder Flows of Personal Data (OECD) 1980, para 7.

This is also the case in the APEC Privacy Framework, which is unsurprising given the influence of the OECD Guidelines in their development.[27] These examples of FIPPs are based on procedural fairness and aimed at rebalancing asymmetries; in many of these laws, the notion of fairness provided for seems inherently connected to the collection of personal data. Given the influence of the OECD Guidelines (see Chapter 2) at the national level, jurisdictions such as Australia,[28] New Zealand,[29] and Canada (in its Act regulating the private sector)[30] have also historically limited the role of 'fair and lawful' to the collection of personal data.[31]

However, this procedural focus and collection-orientated approach is not universal and there is a clear emphasis in some jurisdictions on more substantive protections, with broader notions of risk that recognize the role for impact assessments and design requirements and a seemingly more substantive notion of fairness. This broader focus is evident in the requirement for fair 'processing', which is a more expansive term that includes, but is not limited to, collection. This broader approach is evident in the European Union (EU) (see Section C) and also Convention 108 +, which states that personal data should be 'obtained and processed fairly and lawfully'. Processing in the GDPR[32] or 'data processing' in Convention [33]108 +, for example, are defined similarly in both frameworks and, given the breadth of the definition, it is hard to imagine an activity not falling within their scope.[34] In other words, personal data can only be collected and/or processed for legitimate purposes and be justified

[27] See Collection Limitation Principle in Asia-Pacific Economic Cooperation (APEC) Privacy Framework <www.apec.org/docs/default-source/Publications/2017/8/APEC-Privacy-Framework-(2015)/217_ECSG_2015-APEC-Privacy-Framework.pdf> accessed 4 October 2023

[28] Privacy Act 1988 (Cth).

[29] Privacy Act 2020.

[30] Personal Information Protection and Electronic Documents Act (SC 2000, c 5).

[31] However, it should be noted that this is a specific area for reform currently under debate in Australia in terms of the introduction of a 'fair and reasonable' requirement. See 'Privacy Act Review: Discussion Paper' (Australian Government, Attorney-General's Department 2021) <https://consultations.ag.gov.au/rights-and-protections/privacy-act-review-discussion-paper/user_uploads/privacy-act-review-discussion-paper.pdf> accessed 4 October 2023. See Proposal 12.1: 'Government Response to the Privacy Act Review Report' (Australian Government 2023) <www.ag.gov.au/rights-and-protections/publications/government-response-privacy-act-review-report> accessed 4 October 2023.

[32] Art 4(2) of the GDPR: '"processing" means any operation or set of operations which is performed on personal data or on sets of personal data, whether or not by automated means, such as collection, recording, organisation, structuring, storage, adaptation or alteration, retrieval, consultation, use, disclosure by transmission, dissemination or otherwise making available, alignment or combination, restriction, erasure or destruction.'

[33] Art 2(b) of Convention 108 + '"data processing" means any operation or set of operations performed on personal data, such as the collection, storage, preservation, alteration, retrieval, disclosure, making available, erasure, or destruction of, or the carrying out of logical and/or arithmetical operations on such data.'

[34] The application of the frameworks thus largely comes down to the notion of personal data as discussed in Chapter 3.

either through the consent of the data subject or some other 'fair and lawful' basis laid down by law. In the modernized Convention 108 +, the references to fairness appear to indicate that it has grown in significance and emerged as a principle not strictly connected to the notion of lawfulness. More specifically, Article 5(1) of Convention 108 + stipulates that a 'fair balance' must be struck between all interests, rights, and freedoms concerned when personal data are processed—demonstrating a requirement to ensure processing is proportionate. In addition, Article 5(4)(a) states that personal data must be 'processed fairly and in a transparent manner'. This suggests that fairness plays a role in terms of its collection and also its use, deletion, transfer etc, but also with respect to the exercising of data subject rights. Certainly, through such formulations, fairness shows a strong connection to proportionality and thus the balancing of fundamental rights and interests.[35] There appears to be some connection between this broader notion of fairness, therefore, and the more rights-based data protection laws that have been adopted in Europe. This will be explored further in the next section through the lens of EU law and the GDPR specifically, but it seems apparent that the European Convention on Human Rights and the EU Charter of Fundamental Rights are significant in shaping the interpretation of fairness in Convention 108 + and the GDPR respectively. Understanding this more expansive role for fairness is important as law reform in several jurisdictions appears to be looking towards a more expansive role for fairness, even in jurisdictions that seemingly lack the same commitment in hard law to fundamental rights.[36]

A more optimistic interpretation of data protection law then may thus look to the role of fairness more specifically, and indeed its potential violation, as a means through which meaningful engagement with requirements could be encouraged and understood. Significantly, as noted by Bygrave, fairness is important not just at the individual level but also in terms of how underlying information systems are designed and structured.[37] Indeed, the idea of privacy by design developed by Cavoukian, the former Information and Privacy Commissioner of Ontario, effectively requires the implementation of the FIPPs.[38] Therefore, fairness also seemingly plays an important role in the

[35] See Gianclaudio Malgieri, 'The Concept of Fairness in the GDPR' (Proceedings of FAT* '20, 27–30 January 2020).

[36] See eg the discussion regarding the reform of the Australian Privacy Act 1988 (Cth) and the proposed insertion of a 'fair and reasonable' test. 'Privacy Act Review: Discussion Paper' (n 31). See also Proposal 12.1: 'Government Response to the Privacy Act Review Report' (n 31).

[37] Bygrave (n 9) 58.

[38] Indeed, according to Cavoukian, privacy by design is achieved by taking into account the following seven Foundational Principles: (1) Proactive not Reactive, Preventive not Remedial; (2) Privacy as the Default Setting; (3) Privacy Embedded into Design; (4) Full Functionality (Positive-Sum not

accountability mechanisms such as the requirement to conduct and impact assessment and privacy/data protection by design, which aim, at least in part, to foster meaningful compliance and embed the values of data protection law in the operation of its requirements.[39] Despite these developments, however, the higher standards of protection through the expanded role for the fairness principle do not necessarily mean that data protection law does not still struggle to afford individuals safeguards in practice. Scholars have highlighted the uncertainty of the meaning of fair personal data processing in EU law[40] and have questioned whether too much faith is placed in controllers' capacity and willingness to comply with data protection law in a *meaningful* manner.[41]

In his critical analysis of EU data protection law, Koops suggests that there has been a failure to reach 'the hearts and minds' of controllers to ensure an approach to implementation that moves beyond mere compliance.[42] Instead, there is what he refers to as a '[p]rocedure followed, problem solved' approach to requirements such as the obligation to conduct a data protection impact assessment.[43] The problem is that to apply the requirements in the Regulation wholeheartedly, it is arguably necessary to understand its logic and rationale. However, it is argued by Koops, for instance, that the 'attitude, vision and mindset' necessary to achieve meaningful compliance are not fostered through the framework.[44] Arguably, this is the key challenge to the effectiveness of data protection law. The question therefore is whether the fairness checks and balances actually function as the means through which the hearts of controllers are reached and if a more substantive notion of fairness allows for the embedding of these values in practice. This will be explained in the next section again through the use of E-AI as a case study, with the GDPR as the specific framework to be analysed.

Zero-Sum); (5) End-to-End Security (Lifecycle Protection); (6) Visibility and Transparency; and (7) Respect for User Privacy. See 'Privacy by Design (Cavoukian 1995–2013) Archives' (*Global Privacy and Security by Design Centre*) <https://gpsbydesigncentre.com/portfolio-types/privacy-by-design-cavoukian-1995-2013/> accessed 23 September 2023. However, these principles are strikingly similar to the FIPPs.

[39] Karen Yeung and Lee A Bygrave, 'Demystifying the Modernized European Data Protection Regime: Cross-Disciplinary Insights from Legal and Regulatory Governance Scholarship' (2022) 16 Regulation & Governance 137, 141–42.

[40] See Damian Clifford and Jef Ausloos, 'Data Protection and the Role of Fairness' [2018] Yearbook of European Law 1; Malgieri (n 35); Michael Butterworth, 'The ICO and Artificial Intelligence: The Role of Fairness in the GDPR Framework' (2018) 34 Computer Law & Security Review 257.

[41] Koops, 'The Trouble with European Data Protection Law' (n 2).

[42] ibid.

[43] ibid.

[44] ibid.

C. Investigating the Features—Inaccuracy and E-AI

The GDPR certainly aims to provide an environment in which data subjects can make subjective choices. However, it arguably affords controllers significant latitude and thus allows them the scope not to comply in a meaningful manner in practice. The Regulation is designed to empower data subjects and bolster their capacity to act in their own best interest.[45] The question, therefore, is whether the protections provided actually function or if the criticism is justified. The principles-based, risk-based, and rights-based approaches, with rather open-textured definitions of core concepts such as personal data (see Chapter 3), certainly mean that there is significant latitude afforded to controllers to define the impact of the application of the GDPR in specific contexts. The analysis in this section will explore the role of the fairness principle and its relationship to the accountability principle in the GDPR. To understand the intersections between fairness and accountability in more detail, it is necessary to understand the role for fairness in the requirements provided in the GDPR and, more specifically, in the checks and balances provided to ensure more meaningful data subject choice and the requirement to conduct a data protection impact assessment (DPIA) in Article 35 of the GDPR in particular.

E-AI again provides an excellent case study to demonstrate the challenges associated with ensuring that controllers comply with the Regulation in a meaningful manner. Similarly to other computational systems, E-AI presents clear risks of unfair or biased outcomes.[46] In addition, however, there are also well-documented accuracy concerns with E-AI, with critics questioning the methodological foundations of the technology and arguing that this fails to capture the richness of emotional experiences.[47] The traditionally dominant approach

[45] See on this Damian Clifford, Inge Graef, and Peggy Valcke, 'Pre-Formulated Declarations of Data Subject Consent—Citizen-Consumer Empowerment and the Alignment of Data, Consumer and Competition Law Protections' (2019) 20 German Law Journal 679. For an analysis posing a similar question, see I van Ooijen and Helena U Vrabec, 'Does the GDPR Enhance Consumers' Control over Personal Data? An Analysis from a Behavioural Perspective' (2019) 42 Journal of Consumer Policy 91.

[46] Indeed, here reference can be made to the fact that an awareness of this problem has resulted in the growth of 'discrimination-aware data mining' or 'fair machine learning' research, which aims to counteract the negative impact of machine learning. Reuben Binns, 'Fairness in Machine Learning: Lessons from Political Philosophy' [2018] Journal of Machine Learning Research 1, 1. Such research aims to embed fairness into the very design of machine learning techniques to reduce the occurrence of unfair outcomes. In other words, the 'learning processes' are designed so that the outcome matches what has been pre-defined as 'fair'. The debates so far have therefore largely focused on the potential for bias, the need for increased transparency of automated decision-making systems, and indeed the challenges of effectively facilitating this transparency both technically and legally (ie the opacity of neural networks and trade secrecy and intellectual property protections).

[47] Lisa Feldman Barrett, 'Are Emotions Natural Kinds?' (2006) 1 Perspectives on Psychological Science 28, as cited by Robin Markwica, *Emotional Choices: How the Logic of Affect Shapes Coercive Diplomacy* (OUP 2018) 72.

for detecting emotions—especially in relation to Facial Action Coding Systems (FACS), ie emotion detection through facial movements—namely, the categorical approach and its reliance on research into 'basic emotions' as introduced by Ekman and colleagues, has been repeatedly criticized.[48] The research of Ekman and his colleagues suggests that there are six basic emotions which can be recognized universally: happiness, sadness, surprise, fear, anger, and disgust.[49] However, alternative lines of research have arguably demonstrated that a single label or basic emotion does not accurately reflect the complex contextual, social, and cultural factors that speak to the nature of an affective state, with some scholars referring to FACS as mere pseudoscience.[50] The inaccuracy of E-AI certainly poses significant risks. But can the GDPR not be construed as the ready-made answer to the challenges posed by the emergence of E-AI, given that controllers are required to conduct a DPIA for 'high risk' data processing?

This section will explore this question in detail. The first subsection will (1) examine the role of fairness in EU data protection law and then analyse how the fairness checks and balances aim to bolster the role of choice. In the second subsection, the analysis will (2) explore the role for impact assessments and design requirements as another example of the checks and balances and examine the contention that compliance is driven by minds and not hearts. In doing so, the analysis will also highlight how the GDPR arguably obliges more meaningful engagement with the requirements in the GDPR than is suggested by its critics. The subsection will also consider how other areas of law may intersect with the GDPR in order to mitigate the more societal/collective risks of harm that arguably pose challenges to data protection law's effectiveness.

1. Fairness checks and balances

Fairness is a 'core' data protection principle.[51] It is included in both Article 8(2) of the Charter of Fundamental Rights of the EU[52] and Article 5(1)(a) of

[48] As discussed by Hatice Gunes and Maja Pantic, 'Automatic, Dimensional and Continuous Emotion Recognition' (2010) 1 International Journal of Synthetic Emotions 68.

[49] Although subsequent research has suggested additional and/or alternative universal emotions, and has elaborated the theory, the central premise of there being universally recognizable emotions has remained a constant. See ibid.

[50] See *AI Now Report 2018* (AI Now Institute, New York University 2018) 14 <https://ainowinstitute.org/publication/ai-now-2018-report-2> accessed 4 October 2023; Andrew McStay, 'Empathic Media and Advertising: Industry, Policy, Legal and Citizen Perspectives (the Case for Intimacy)' (2016) 3 Big Data & Society 1, 3–6.

[51] European Data Protection Supervisor, 'Opinion on Coherent Enforcement of Fundamental Rights in the Age of Big Data' (EDPS 2016) Opinion 8/2016 8—where it is noted that 'fairness of personal data processing is a core principle alongside lawfulness and transparency'.

[52] Charter of Fundamental Rights of the European Union OJ C326, 391–407.

Table 5.1 EU data protection law and fairness

Such data must be **processed fairly** for specified purposes and on the basis of the consent of the person concerned or some other legitimate basis laid down by law. Everyone has the right of access to data which has been collected concerning him or her, and the right to have it rectified.	Art 8 (2) Charter
Personal data shall be processed lawfully, **fairly**, and in a transparent manner in relation to the data subject ('lawfulness, **fairness** and transparency');	Art 5 (1)(a) GDPR

the GDPR (see Table 5.1). Fairness is understood by many as the cornerstone upon which the other data protection principles are built.[53] The principle reflects the desire to protect against any negative consequences stemming from personal data processing, even in the absence of an intent to deceive by the controller, and requires controllers to take the data subject's interests and reasonable expectations into account.[54] However, fairness remains a rather nebulous concept in EU data protection law. In this subsection I will delineate the different roles played by fairness in EU law by analysing the role of fairness in the EU Charter of Fundamental Rights and its relationship with the fairness principle provided in the Regulation, before then analysing the manifestations of the fairness principle in the checks and balances provided by the GDPR.

(a) Delineating the role(s) of fairness

The adoption of the Lisbon Treaty gave the EU Charter of Fundamental Rights binding force. This was a significant moment in the development of EU data protection law as the right to data protection was recognized as a right for the first time in EU law in Article 8 of the Charter. As is evident from Table 5.1, Article 8(2) states amongst other things that personal data 'must be processed fairly'. However, despite the obvious significance of fairness, and in part due to its specific inclusion in Article 8(2), precisely mapping the role of fairness is challenging. As I have previously argued, determining how fairness in Article 8(2) of the Charter has an impact on the substance of the right to data protection provided in Article 8 and on the relationship and potential overlaps

[53] eg Bygrave notes that 'it embraces and generates the other core principles of data protection laws'. Bygrave (n 9) 58.

[54] Damian Clifford, 'The Data Protection Fairness Principle and the GDPR' in Michèle Finck (ed), *Oxford Encyclopedia of EU Law* (OUP 2022) para 3.

with fairness as provided as a principle in Article 5(1)(a) of the GDPR remains uncertain.[55]

Authors such as Hijmans have argued that the right to data protection is best characterized as a right to 'fairness checks and balances'.[56] This interpretation is far from universally accepted, however, with some scholars suggesting that fairness is just one of the elements derived from Article 8(2)–(3) of the Charter, which should be understood as being encompassed within the substantive content of the right to data protection.[57] A third, and rather popular, alternative positions information self-determination at the centre of the right to data protection.[58] Although a more thorough analysis of the merits of these (and other) alternatives and how they relate to the discussion of the essence of data protection law is beyond the scope of this chapter, they demonstrate a potentially important role for fairness as the key, or at least one of the core, element(s) of the right to data protection.

However, the uncertainties do not stop there when it comes to the potential roles for fairness in EU data protection law. Indeed, notwithstanding the debates regarding the exact nature of the right, there is also a significant overlap with Article 52(1) of the Charter and the case law relating to the need to 'fairly balance' competing rights and interests in the implementation of EU law.[59] Indeed, in its case law on the application of Article 52(1), the Court of Justice has referred to the legislator's duty to strike a fair balance between fundamental rights in the adoption of EU secondary law.[60] A failure to meet this requirement has resulted in the invalidating of certain legislative instruments[61] and, therefore, in addition to the potential role for fairness in the right to data protection, the GDPR as a secondary EU law manifests the legislator's aim of fairly

[55] ibid 6.

[56] Hielke Hijmans, *The European Union as Guardian of Internet Privacy: The Story of Art 16 TFEU* (Reprint of the original 1st edn 2016, Springer 2018) 54–62.

[57] See also Lorenzo Dalla Corte, 'A Right to a Rule: On the Essence and Rationale of the Fundamental Right to Personal Data Protection' in Rosamunde van Brakel and others (eds), *Data Protection and Democracy* (Hart 2020).

[58] See here: Jef Ausloos, *The Right to Erasure in EU Data Protection Law* (OUP 2020) 60–69.

[59] Clifford (n 54) para 8.

[60] See on this Clifford and Ausloos (n 40); Ausloos (n 58) 280–89.

[61] To illustrate, one can refer here to Joined Cases C–293/12 and 594/12 *Digital Rights Ireland Ltd v Minister for Communications, Marine and Natural Resources and Kärntner Landesregierung, Requests for a preliminary ruling from the High Court (Ireland) and the Verfassungsgerichtshof*, ECLI:EU:C:2014:238, which annulled Council Directive 2006/24/EC of 15 March 2006 on the retention of data generated or processed in connection with the provision of publicly available electronic communications services or of public communications networks and amending, and the *Schrems* cases (Case C–362/14 *Maximillian Schrems v Data Protection Commissioner*, ECLI:EU:C:2015:650; Case C–311/18 *Data Protection Commissioner v Facebook Ireland Ltd, Maximillian Schrems*, ECLI:EU:C:2020:559), which invalidated the Safe Harbour and Privacy Shield agreements for data transfers between the EU and the US, respectively.

balancing competing rights and interests.[62] Through this role of fairness, the key to determining what amounts to fair personal data processing requires the application of the GDPR's provisions.[63]

The Regulation can be understood, therefore, as a system of fairness checks and balances with the fairness principle (along with the other rights, obligations, and supervisory monitoring) part of the balance struck. This aim can be seen in Article 1(2) of the GDPR which essentially states that the Regulation protects fundamental rights and freedoms and in particular the right to data protection where a data subject's personal data are processed.[64] Accordingly, there are potentially three overlapping roles for fairness in EU data protection law: (1) fairness as a key part of the right to data protection, (2) the GDPR as a legislative 'fair balance', and (3) the fairness principle as part of that balance in Article 5(1)(a).

There is also a clear overlap between fairness and proportionality,[65] and given its various manifestations and rather uncertain meaning, it can be difficult to determine where the principle begins and ends. The simple separation between the three potential roles for fairness is arguably somewhat misleading, however, as all three seem rooted in the same need to fairly balance rights and interests. Arguably, the fairness principle provided in Article 5(1)(a) simply provides a mechanism and places a responsibility on the shoulders of controllers to take such matters into account.[66] In essence, there is an obligation to consider fairness in the operation of the legislative rights and responsibilities evident in the Regulation and this reflects the role of the fairness principle contained in Article 5(1)(a). There is, therefore, a need to examine how fairness can be better understood and broken down when it is seen as part of the fair balance struck by the legislator in the GDPR.

(b) Fair processing and fair choices

Although the fairness principle is key to the other data protection principles provided in the GDPR, in that it is hard to see a violation of another principle

[62] Indeed, irrespective of the complex EU constitutional law debates, it is clear from the Court of Justice case law that the legislator was required to 'fairly balance' the competing rights and interests when adopting the Regulation (see also European Commission, 'Communication from the Commission, Strategy for the Effective Implementation of the Charter of Fundamental Rights by the European Union' (COM (2010) 573/4)).

[63] For a more elaborate discussion of the relationship between the Charter and the GDPR, see Ausloos (n 58) 289–330; Clifford and Ausloos (n 40).

[64] See Ausloos (n 58) 69–81; Clifford and Ausloos (n 40).

[65] For a discussion of proportionality in EU data protection law case law, see Lorenzo Dalla Corte, 'On Proportionality in the Data Protection Jurisprudence of the CJEU' (2022) 12 International Data Privacy Law 259.

[66] Clifford (n 54) para 13.

not also being unfair, when viewing Article 5(1)(a) in isolation it is unclear whether this provision was intended as one principle (ie the 'lawfulness, fairness and transparency' principle), two principles (ie lawfulness and transparency to be viewed through the lens of the notion of fairness), or indeed, three distinct principles.[67] As argued elsewhere, this is particularly so when Article 5(1)(a) is viewed alongside the other principles in Article 5 (ie purpose limitation (Article 5(1)(b)), data minimization (Article 5(1)(c)), accuracy (Article 5(1)(d)), storage limitation (Article 5(1)I), integrity and confidentiality (Article 5(1)(f)), and accountability (Article 5(2)).[68] Although from a detailed reading of the Regulation it appears uncontroversial to state that Article 5(1)(a) stipulates three distinct (albeit interwoven) principles, such uncertainties reflect the ambiguous nature of the principle. The subtle separation between lawfulness, fairness, and transparency, however, requires careful consideration. The explicit and implicit references to this core principle (as revealed by guidance and case law) can be mapped in order to differentiate it from those of lawfulness and transparency.[69]

Understanding the role of the fairness principle is also important to appreciate fully the role of choice in the GDPR as part of the fairness checks and balances provided. The application of the fairness principle manifests itself in two ways, namely (1) procedural fairness or a more process-orientated notion of fairness, and (2) fair balancing or a more outcome/effects-orientated one.[70] Both of these manifestations effectively run concurrently and interdependently in the context of any given processing operation.[71] The first of these is strongly connected to the transparency principle in that there are explicit references to the requirement for fair and transparent processing in the Regulation. Articles 13 and 14 of the GDPR deal with the information to be provided to the data subject and include a reference to the need to provide information regarding the exercising of data subject rights 'to ensure fair and transparent processing in respect of the data subject'.[72] The fairness of personal data processing has therefore been strongly linked with the effective implementation of the transparency principle, thereby reflecting the reliance on the capacity of data subjects to make decisions relating to their personal data. Indeed, as noted by Bygrave, in this sense fairness aims not only to

[67] ibid 14.

[68] ibid 15.

[69] See Clifford and Ausloos (n 40).

[70] ibid. Interestingly, Malgieri observes that this dualist understanding of the role/manifestation of the fairness principle seems to have also been established in the modernized Council of Europe Convention 108. This manifests itself in art 5 of the Convention through the references to the need to process 'fairly and in a transparent manner' and strike a 'fair balance'. Malgieri (n 35) 158.

[71] See Clifford and Ausloos (n 40).

[72] Arts 13(2) and 14(2).

tackle the collection and further processing of personal data, but also deception as to the nature and purposes of the processing operations.[73] The application of Article 22 of the GDPR, the provision restricting automated decision-making including profiling, and connected provisions provide another excellent illustration of this focus on *ex ante* fair and transparent information in the Regulation. This provision provides that a data subject has the right not to be subject to an automated individual decision and, as such, does not specifically regulate the decisions themselves or how they are reached.

Despite the strong connection between the principles, however, transparency and fairness are not synonymous. Importantly, fairness in the GDPR extends beyond the assessment of the decision-making capacity of an individual to the fairness of processing operations more generally. Hence, although a controller may be open and thus entirely transparent about their intended data processing, this does not negate the fact that the inherent asymmetries may inhibit the data subject from exercising their informed autonomous choice in practice, thereby rendering the processing unfair.[74] The fairness principle thus plays an important role in the balancing of rights and interests across the framework despite this remaining somewhat implicit from a purely textual analysis of the Regulation. This represents the second manifestation of the fairness principle mentioned (i.e. fair balancing or the more outcome/effects-orientated manifestation) which seems to align with the idea that fairness, at its core, refers to the need to prevent adverse effects through the balancing of conflicting rights and interests.[75] Implicitly, there has thus been a recognition of the need for a 'fair balance' of competing fundamental rights and interests, which appears to be manifested through the explicit references to 'fair and lawful' processing in the Regulation. Here reference can also be made to various guidance documents demonstrating the link between the fairness principle and non-discrimination as an example of this fair balancing.[76]

This link between fairness and discrimination is connected to what Malgieri categorizes as the more effects-based understanding of fairness.[77] Discriminatory effects can be seen as just one form that an unfair or

[73] Bygrave (n 9) 58–59.

[74] ibid 58.

[75] Malgieri (n 35) 156.

[76] eg in its opinion on automated decision-making, the Article 29 Working Party observes, inter alia, that '[p]rofiling may be unfair and create discrimination, for example denying people access to employment opportunities, credit or insurance, or targeting them with excessively risky or costly financial products'. Article 29 Working Party, 'Guidelines on automated individual decision-making and profiling for the purposes of Regulation 2016/679' (2018) WP 251.

[77] Malgieri (n 35). See Information Commissioner's Office, 'Big Data, Artificial Intelligence, Machine Learning and Data Protection' (2017) 20170904 Version: 2.2 19–22 <https://ico.org.uk/media/

unbalanced outcome may take, however, with the prejudicial outcome not proportionate or necessary to whatever goal is being pursued.[78] Thus, although non-discrimination could be understood as one interpretation of the fairness principle, it is arguable that it is more the case that discriminatory effects are an important example of an unfair outcome. This seems to align with viewing fairness as a principle designed to counteract asymmetry.[79] The need to provide weight to the data subject's interests and expectations is also apparent in case law. More specifically, in its references to fairness the Court of Justice seemingly acknowledges that the principle implies a level of protection given the inherent asymmetric data subject–controller relationships and hence, the potential for negative consequences for data subjects stemming from personal data processing even in the absence of an intent to deceive by a controller.[80] The fairness principle thus requires controllers to take the rights and interests of data subjects into account while also requiring controllers to ensure that data subjects are informed and capable of making choices.

Fair balancing is therefore strongly connected to the lawfulness principle and thus the application of the conditions for lawful processing in Article 6(1), but this connection is also demonstrated in the exercising of data subject control rights in Articles 15–22 of the Regulation. From a systematic analysis of the GDPR, the 'lawfulness' principle can be traced directly to Article 6 of the Regulation which stipulates the conditions for lawful processing.[81] This seemingly indicates that compliance with the lawfulness principle is largely dependent on the application of one of the conditions in Article 6(1).[82] As described in the previous chapter, each of the conditions for lawful processing provided for plays a distinct and delineated role, and in the context of E-AI the nature of the specific deployment (and, indeed, if sensitive personal data

for-organisations/documents/2013559/big-data-ai-ml-and-data-protection.pdf> accessed 4 October 2023; Commission Nationale Informatique & Libertés (CNIL), 'How Can Humans Keep the Upper Hand? The Ethical Matters Raised by Algorithms and Artificial Intelligence' (2017) <www.cnil.fr/sites/cnil/files/atoms/files/cnil_rapport_ai_gb_web.pdf> accessed 4 October 2023; CNIL, *Algorithms and Artificial Intelligence* (Report on Ethical Issues, 2018) <www.cnil.fr/en/algorithms-and-artificial-intelligence-cnils-report-ethical-issues > accessed 4 October 2023.

[78] Clifford (n 54) para 21.

[79] Clifford and Ausloos (n 40) 141.

[80] eg in relation to the exercising of the data subject right to access and the fair balance to be struck between the controller and the data subject, see Case C–553/07 *College van burgemeester en wethouders van Rotterdam v MEE Rijkeboer*, ECLI:EU:C:2009:293 and Case C–486/12 *X*, ECLI:EU:C:2013:836; in relation to the balancing of different fundamental rights, see Case C–275/06 *Productores de Música de España (Promusicae) v Telefónica de España*, ECLI:EU:C:2008:54; *Google Spain SL and Google Inc v Agencia Española de Protección de Datos* (n 13) 12.

[81] See Clifford and Ausloos (n 40).

[82] See generally ibid. eg one can refer to Recitals 49, 83, 116, and Arts 4(12), 5(1)(f), 17, 18, 23(2)(d), and 32(2).

are processed and Article 9 is triggered) will determine how these conditions apply in practice. This defined role for the lawfulness principle does not mean however that fairness plays no part in the operation of the conditions for lawful processing in Article 6(1) of the Regulation. The fairness principle is in fact arguably central to the application of the conditions for lawful processing as is evident in their operation but also in the determination of which condition is appropriate in the specific circumstances.[83] A failure to validly obtain consent, for instance, or to rely on public or legitimate interests instead of consent would clearly violate not only the lawfulness principle but also fairness. Hence, I believe that assessment of the fairness of relying on a specific condition for lawful processing may result in the conclusion that another is more suitable.

Consent is an obvious example of the role of data subject choice in the fairness checks and balances provided by the legislature and is thus a good example to demonstrate the role fairness plays in the application of the conditions. Consent is defined in Article 4(11) of the GDPR as 'any freely given, specific, informed and unambiguous indication of the data subject's wishes by which he or she, by a statement or by a clear affirmative action, signifies agreement to the processing of personal data relating to him or her'. This definition is then further specified in the conditions for consent in Article 7 of the GDPR, as noted in Chapter 4.[84] More specifically, Article 7 appears to establish a burden of care on controllers regarding their responsibility to ensure that data subjects have been informed and that they have understood the information provided. The controller is also required to be able to demonstrate consent (Article 7(1)) keeping in mind that, in assessing the 'freely given' definitional condition, rendering access to the service conditional on consent may invalidate the reliance on consent (Article 7(4)). In short, consent is required to be presented in a manner which is clearly distinguishable from other matters if given in the context of a written declaration (Article 7(2)) and must represent a meaningful choice as evidenced by the ability to withdraw consent (Article 7(3)).

Given the clear significance of providing fair and transparent information to exercise choice through consent but also in the fair balancing of the rights and interests at stake in determining, for instance, whether consent is in fact freely given, there is obviously an important role for the fairness principle. Fairness

[83] As observed by Malgieri, this role for fairness in determining the appropriateness of a specific condition for lawful processing is clear in the Article 29 Working Party opinion on consent. Malgieri (n 35) 157.

[84] For a discussion of each of these, see Article 29 Working Party, 'Guidelines on consent under Regulation 2016/679' (2017) WP 259.

and lawfulness are therefore strongly linked. However, similarly to transparency, fairness is not synonymous with lawfulness. Indeed, processing which is lawful under the conditions for lawful processing as outlined in Article 6(1) may still violate the broader notion of fairness in the GDPR. To clarify, although the fairness principle in the application of the relevant condition for lawful processing may be satisfied in certain circumstances, data subject rights offer an *ex post* fair balancing exercise on a more individualized basis, which may render any future processing unfair and unlawful.[85] In its references to fairness, the Court of Justice seemingly acknowledges that the principle provides a level of protection, given the inherent asymmetric data subject–controller relationships in the operation of data subject rights.[86]

Previous literature has demonstrated how the right of access and the right to data portability are versatile in the sense that they allow for the repurposing of data and facilitate transparency.[87] The right of access in particular is understood as an enabling right in that the Court of Justice has interpreted it as a prerequisite for the 'rectification, erasure or blocking of data'.[88] Certainly, data subjects first have to know what data a controller has before they can make an informed choice to invoke another control right.[89] The other rights provided focus on data (rectification and erasure) or processing operations (restriction, object, and automated decision-making) and thus seemingly have a more specific focus.[90] The control rights provided for in Articles 15–22 of the GDPR thus act as mechanisms through which individuals can exercise choice, even in circumstances where the initial processing of their personal data may have been legitimized without their exercising any preference. For example, if we take as an illustration the right to object provided in Article 21, it is clear that even if the right were successfully invoked, the lawfulness of the processing established *ex ante* would not be affected. Any further/future processing would

[85] Clifford and Ausloos (n 40).

[86] eg in relation to the exercising of the data subject's right to access and the fair balance to be struck between the controller and the data subject, see *College van burgemeester en wethouders van Rotterdam* (n 80); *Productores de Música de España (Promusicae) v Telefónica de España* (n 80); *Google Spain SL and Google Inc v Agencia Española de Protección de Datos* (n 13).

[87] Alexandra Giannopoulou and others, 'Intermediating Data Rights Exercises: The Role of Legal Mandates' (2022) 12 International Data Privacy Law 316, 320.

[88] Case C–434/16 *Peter Nowak v Data Protection Commissioner*, ECLI:EU:C:2017:994, para 54; *College van burgemeester en wethouders van Rotterdam* (n 80) 51.

[89] Jef Ausloos, Réne Mahieu, and Michael Veale, 'Getting Data Subject Rights Right A Submission to the European Data Protection Board from International Data Rights Academics, to Inform Regulatory Guidance' (2020) 10 Journal of Intellectual Property, Information Technology and Electronic Commerce Law 3 <www.jipitec.eu/issues/jipitec-10-3-2019/5031> accessed 4 October 2023.

[90] Giannopoulou and others (n 87) 320–21.

be unlawful if the right to object was successfully invoked.[91] This points to the role played by the fairness principle in the operation of data subject rights, in that these inevitably involve a balancing of interests in practice in order to determine whether they can be successfully invoked.[92]

The role of the fairness principle in the operation of data subject rights is evident in the Court of Justice's decision in the *Rijkeboer* case.[93] In this case, Mr Rijkeboer had requested access to the details of third parties who had been sent information relating to him held by the Rotterdam Municipality. In its judgment, the Court noted that although time limits may be imposed on the retention of the metadata, any such limit requires 'a fair balance between, on the one hand, the interest of the data subject in protecting his privacy, in particular by way of his rights to object and to bring legal proceedings and, on the other, the burden which the obligation to store that information represents for the controller'.[94] Similar statements regarding the need to fairly balance rights and interests are also evident in the Court's analysis of other data subject rights.[95] In the context of E-AI, this reflects the need to fairly balance interests and thus, is indicative of the examples given in Chapter 4 regarding the challenges of effectively invoking these rights in practice.

The discussion of the failure to apply the conditions for lawful processing and, indeed, the data subject rights provided in the Regulation can also be seen as a failure to comply with the fairness principle. Indeed, even leaving aside how the fairness checks and balances aim to bolster the role of choice, we can also link the discussion regarding compliance with the challenges of effectively implementing the principles for lawful processing, as discussed above in Section B and in Chapter 2 (in particular, purpose limitation, data

91 To illustrate this point further, one can refer to art 21(3) in particular. This provision stipulates that, '[w]here the data subject objects to processing for direct marketing purposes, the personal data shall no longer be processed for such purposes'. Hence, when personal data processing is based on legitimate interests as a condition for lawful processing for such purposes, the data subject has the right to object and, if invoked successfully, controllers will no longer be able to process the data subject's personal data for such purposes even if successfully invoking the right to object in such circumstances does not render any prior processing unlawful.

92 For a discussion, see also Ausloos (n 58) 70–73.

93 *College van burgemeester en wethouders van Rotterdam* (n 80).

94 ibid 54.

95 eg as explained by the Court in its *Google 2* judgment, art 17(3)(a) is 'an expression of the fact that the right to protection of personal data is not an absolute right but [...] must be considered in relation to its function in society and be balanced against other fundamental rights, in accordance with the principle of proportionality'. Case C–136/17 *GC v Commission nationale de l'informatique et des libertés (CNIL)*, ECLI:EU:C:2019:773, para 57. This provision 'expressly lays down the requirement to strike a balance between the fundamental rights to privacy and protection of personal data guaranteed by Articles 7 and 8 of the Charter, on the one hand, and the fundamental right of freedom of information guaranteed by Article 11 of the Charter, on the other'. *College van burgemeester en wethouders van Rotterdam* (n 80) 59.

minimization, and security). Compliance with these principles also raises important issues regarding the appropriate implementation of the fairness principle. The fairness principle certainly extends beyond the assessment of the decision-making capacity of an individual to the fairness of processing operations more generally. The fairness and accountability principles thus go hand in hand in this regard, with the controller being responsible for the fair balancing of rights and interests when processing personal data. In this regard, it is interesting to refer to Hijmans and Raab, who see fairness as an element of the accountability principle.[96] Although it is suggested that such an understanding mistakenly relegates fairness to being a mere component of the accountability as opposed to a distinct principle, there is an important overlap between these principles. The importance of this overlap becomes more evident when we consider the role of fairness in the operation of the key accountability mechanisms provided in the Regulation.

2. Embedding (un)fairness

Although risk has always been important in EU data protection law, the GDPR is an example of a risk-based legislative framework in that it places risk at its operative centre, affecting the interpretation of all rights and obligations contained therein.[97] The Regulation explicitly introduced the principles of accountability and transparency, the notion of data protection by design and by default, and moved towards a risk-based approach.[98] There is therefore a clear emphasis on controller accountability and a flexible decentred regulatory approach framed in terms of 'coordinating, steering, influencing and balancing interactions between actors'.[99] This is illustrative of (1) the focus on risk and responsiveness,[100] and (2) the enhanced focus on accountability and the auditing

[96] Hijmans and Raab (n 1) 11.

[97] Article 29 Working Party, 'Statement on the role of a risk-based approach in data protection legal frameworks' (2014) WP 218; Claudia Quelle, 'The "Risk Revolution" in EU Data Protection Law: We Can't Have Our Cake and Eat It, Too' in Ronald Leenes and others (eds), *Data Protection and Privacy: The Age of Intelligent Machines* (1st edn, Hart 2017) 33.

[98] Although both the accountability and transparency principles had implicitly played a role in Directive 95/46/EC, this is the first time that these principles have been expressly provided for in an EU data protection legislative text.

[99] Julia Black, 'Decentring Regulation: Understanding the Role of Regulation and Self-Regulation in a "Post-Regulatory" World' (2001) 54 Current Legal Problems 103.

[100] Julia Black and Robert Baldwin, 'Really Responsive Risk-Based Regulation' (2010) 32 Law & Policy 181, 186–87; Robert Baldwin and Julia Black, 'Really Responsive Regulation' (2008) 71 Modern Law Review 59, 62.

of performance,[101] features that are clearly evident in the GDPR's approach.[102] The GDPR places controllers in charge of how they comply with the Regulation and thus how they balance fundamental rights and interests fairly when personal data are processed.[103] Fairness plays an important role in the accountability mechanisms provided for in the Regulation, such as the requirement to conduct an impact assessment and also the requirement for data protection by default and by design. As noted in Section B, at least in part these regulatory mechanisms aim to foster meaningful compliance and embed the values of data protection law to ensure *fair* personal data processing in the operation of its requirements.[104]

(a) Impact assessments and design

The risk-based approach in the GDPR shapes (and indeed is shaped by) the interaction between the fairness and accountability principles. There is a strong connection between the 'riskiness' (and indeed the role of risk more generally) and the fairness principle in effectively balancing the potential risk to rights with the purposes of the processing. In this manner, the requirement to conduct a DPIA and a preliminary assessment to determine whether a DPIA is required can be understood as examples of *ex ante* regulatory mechanisms and 'early warning systems' that aim to identify the impact of potential risks and fairly balance and mitigate the potential risks with a clear connection to the accountability principle.[105] In an *ex post* sense, the requirement to conduct a DPIA is also an important means of demonstrating compliance.[106] Indeed, according to Recital 84, '[t]he outcome of the assessment should be taken into account when determining the appropriate measures to be taken in order to demonstrate that the processing of personal data complies with this Regulation.' Therefore, these requirements are legislative instruments designed as part of the GDPR's fairness check and balances.

There has been an ongoing discussion regarding the application of data protection law as a means of counteracting the negative impacts of algorithmic

[101] This oversight remains a challenge: see Colin Scott, 'Evaluating the Performance and Accountability of Regulators Berle V: Capital Markets, the Corporation, and the Asian Century: Governance, Accountability, and the Future of Corporate Law: The Fifth Annual Symposium of the Adolf A. Berle, Jr. Center on Corporations, Law & Society' (2013) 37 Seattle University Law Review 353, 373.

[102] See Clifford and Ausloos (n 40).

[103] ibid.

[104] Yeung and Bygrave (n 39) 141–42.

[105] Eleni Kosta, 'Article 35. Data Protection Impact Assessment' in Christopher Kuner and others (eds), *The EU General Data Protection Regulation (GDPR): A Commentary* (OUP 2020) 669.

[106] Lorenzo Dalla Corte and Rosamunde Elise Van Brakel, *Data Protection Impact Assessment Methods for the Urban Environment* (Tilburg Institute for Law, Technology and Society 2022) 2.

decision-making. Authors such as Hacker have pointed to the GDPR and the flexibility of the fairness principle provided for in Article 5(1)(a) of the Regulation, and the obligation contained in Article 35 to conduct DPIAs, as means of mitigating these undesirable effects.[107] A DPIA thus assesses the 'likelihood and severity of the high risk, taking into account the nature, scope, context and purposes of the processing and the sources of the risk'.[108] To better understand the operative function of this instrument as a manifestation of this positioning of fairness, reference can be made to literature on the role, application, and manner in which a DPIA should be conducted.[109] Although an in-depth analysis of the extensive number of DPIA methodologies employed is beyond the scope of this chapter, it should be noted that these vary considerably in content and quality, with a range of public and private organizations (including standards organizations) playing a role in trying to formalize the requirement.[110]

A simple overview of some of the key guidance documents, however, reveals that such mechanisms are partly a systematized way in which the Regulation's requirements can be grouped and understood.[111] The requirements surrounding the obligation to conduct a DPIA are hence highly procedural, thereby leaving the role for fairness implicit.[112] Despite referring to the need to assess the necessity and proportionality and the risks to the rights and freedoms of data subjects as integral parts of a DPIA, there is often no explicit cross-reference to the fairness principle in the key guidance documents. For example, there is no reference to the fairness principle in the Article 29 Working Party guidance on the requirement to conduct a DPIA, the recent European Data Protection Supervisor (EDPS) Survey Report on the DPIAs conducted by the EU institutions,[113] the Commission nationale de l'informatique et des libertés (CNIL) and the Irish Data Protection Commissioner's general guidance on the obligation to conduct a DPIA, or, indeed, in the CNIL's privacy

[107] Philipp Hacker, 'Teaching Fairness to Artificial Intelligence: Existing and Novel Strategies against Algorithmic Discrimination under EU Law' (2018) 55 Common Market Law Review 1143 <https://kluwerlawonline.com/journalarticle/Common+Market+Law+Review/55.4/COLA2018095> accessed 8 October 2020.

[108] Recital 90 of the GDPR.

[109] See Dalla Corte and Van Brakel (n 106).

[110] ibid.

[111] ibid.

[112] Reference here can be made to the Article 29 Working Party opinion on DPIAs that stipulates the criteria for an acceptable DPIA. Article 29 Working Party, 'Guidelines on Data Protection Impact Assessment (DPIA) and determining whether processing is "likely to result in a high risk" for the purposes of Regulation 2016/679' (2017) WP 248 rev.01.

[113] European Data Protection Supervisor, 'EDPS Survey on Data Protection Impact Assessments under Article 39 of the Regulation' (case 2020-0066) <https://edps.europa.eu/sites/edp/files/publication/20-07-06_edps_dpias_survey_en.pdf> accessed 4 October 2023.

impact assessment methodology or the DPIA template of the Information Commissioner's Office (ICO).[114] This is interesting, since less nebulous principles such as purpose limitation, data minimization, and storage limitation are all generally referred to expressly. Importantly, however, although the key to determining what 'fairly balanced' personal data processing amounts to is the application of the checks and balances in the GDPR, this does not eliminate the need to interpret what is 'fair' (or indeed unfair) in the operation of the requirements through the lens of the fairness principle in Article 5(1)(a) of the Regulation. Indeed, despite the lack of a specific reference to the fairness principle in this DPIA documentation, there is clearly a role for the fairness principle in the DPIA process and outcome.

More specifically, there are at least three places in which one can view a role for the fairness principle provided for in Article 5(1)(a) of the Regulation. First, in the determination of what is meant by 'high risk' in Article 35(1). Secondly, in the interpretation of the situations identified as being specific cases of high risk in Article 35(3). Thirdly, in Article 35(7), which specifies the content of a DPIA. Regarding the first of these, very simply, a failure to conduct a DPIA properly (or indeed at all) would be unfair. Article 35(1) obliges controllers to perform a DPIA when a data processing operation (or set of similar operations) 'is likely to result in a high risk to the rights and freedoms of natural persons', and in particular if this operation makes use of new technologies. Article 35(3) of the Regulation non-exclusively lists three specific cases when a DPIA is required, and Article 35(4) mandates DPAs to publish a list of processing operations that are subject to the requirement to conduct a DPIA. The European Data Protection Board (EDPB) has highlighted that the national DPAs should include an explicit statement that the lists are non-exhaustive and that they build upon and complement the Article 29 Working Party DPIA guidelines.[115] Interestingly, the Article 29 Working Party has suggested that when it is not clear whether the processing operation(s) will result in a 'high risk' (or a low/medium risk), it is advisable to conduct the DPIA in any case.[116] In addition, as noted by Kosta, 'although DPIAs are not mandatory for all data processing operations, in practice, controllers must always carry out a preliminary assessment in order to identify whether the processing is likely to result in a high risk and thus require a DPIA'.[117] This reflects the obligation on the appointed data

[114] Information Commissioner's Office, 'Sample DPIA Template' 20180209 v0.3 <https://ico.org.uk/media/about-the-ico/consultations/2258461/dpia-template-v04-post-comms-review-20180308.pdf> accessed 4 October 2023.
[115] Kosta (n 105) 676.
[116] Article 29 Working Party, 'Guidelines on Data Protection Impact Assessment' (n 112).
[117] Kosta (n 105) 671.

protection officer (where required, see Article 37 of the GDPR) generally to 'inform and advise' and 'monitor compliance' as per Article 39(1)(a), in addition to the more specific obligations to provide advice and monitor pursuant to the obligation to conduct a DPIA in Article 35.

As the starting point for the requirement to conduct a DPIA is strongly linked to the accountability principle, it is arguable that this has led to silence on the role of fairness. In addition, this process-orientated approach may also be explained by the fact that there is an apparent inconsistency in the wording of Article 35: although Article 35(1) refers to the 'risks to the rights and freedoms of natural persons' (thereby implying that the risks referred to are not just privacy and/or data protection risks), if this risk is high controllers are required to assess the impact 'on the protection of personal data' and thus not on fundamental rights and freedoms more generally.[118] Fairness is omitted from these discussions despite the fact that fairness in Article 5(1)(a) must operate implicitly, both in terms of the procedural and fair balancing manifestations, due to the fact that it represents the need to fairly weigh the respective rights and interests at stake. The omission is also perhaps linked to the fact that a DPIA examines planned/future processing of personal data as opposed to ongoing processing operations (leaving the obligation to review to one side). In this vein, a failure to properly conduct a DPIA is more a failure in terms of accountability that may in turn result in a breach of the fairness principle. That said, in order to fulfil the obligations laid down in Article 35, one surely has to assess the potential impact on the fairness principle. Despite the fact that discussion of the fairness principle is often missing in this DPIA documentation, however, I believe that there is clearly a role for the fairness principle in the DPIA process.[119] It would be counterintuitive and seemingly bizarre to disregard this 'core' principle in what is effectively an accountability and legitimacy check for future processing operations. Indeed, as the DPIA must take place

[118] See Raphaël Gellert, 'Understanding the Notion of Risk in the General Data Protection Regulation' (2018) 34 Computer Law & Security Review 279.

[119] This significant role for the fairness principle is better reflected in the EDPS guidance. Indeed, although the guidance remains at a high level in the 'assessment of proportionality and necessity' step, it provides a far more nuanced breakdown of how the data protection principles interact with the DPIA process and the specific steps they identify by providing a series of guiding questions for the respective principles including fairness. Importantly, although the EDPS guidance refers to the requirement to conduct a DPIA in Regulation (EU) 2018/1725 of the European Parliament and the Council of 23 October 2018 on the protection of natural persons with regard to the processing of personal data by the Union institutions, bodies, offices, and agencies and on the free movement of such data, and repealing Regulation (EC) No 45/2001 and Decision No 1247/2002/EC, L295/39 (ie as it applies to the EU institutions), given the similarity of the obligations and therefore the insights it can provide, it is still relevant here. European Data Protection Supervisor, 'Accountability on the Ground Part II: Data Protection Impact Assessments & Prior Consultation' (2019) <https://edps.europa.eu/sites/edp/files/publication/19-07-17_accountability_on_the_ground_part_ii_en.pdf> accessed 4 October 2023.

prior to the high-risk processing in question, it is important to take it into account during the design stage, even if the requirement is iterative/continuous in nature.[120] Fairness therefore plays an integral role in the DPIA process as it is essentially an assessment of the fairness of a future personal data processing operation(s).

The omission of the fairness principle from these discussions arguably demonstrates the difficulties of drawing hard lines around the fairness principle in practice given its expansiveness. Indeed, in reviewing the literature, in addition to lawfulness and transparency, fairness is also often mentioned alongside the reasonable expectations of the data subject,[121] the proportionality and necessity of the processing,[122] the need to counteract the inherent imbalance or asymmetries evident in the ecosystem,[123] and the need to mitigate potentially harmful and or discriminatory effects.[124] As such, fairness seems embedded in all areas of the GDPR and, in this regard, reference can again be made to the EDPB guidance on Data Protection by Design and by Default in which specific design elements are proposed as a means of considering the implementation of the fairness principle.[125] These are represented below in Table 5.2 along with the explanation provided. This list aligns well with viewing fairness as a principle intended to counteract asymmetry and thus as a protection against negative consequences stemming from personal data processing even in the absence of an intent to deceive by the controller.

Indeed, some items appear to be abstract examples of elements that are unfair (non-discrimination, non-exploitation, consumer choice, power balance, no risk transfer, no deception, and truthful) whereas others seem to relate to specific process-orientated counter-measures that may be used to prevent unfair outcomes (interaction, human intervention, and fair algorithms). The rest appear to reflect important underlying rights and values (autonomy, expectation, respect rights, and ethical) and, thus, it seems uncontroversial to suggest that fairness is therefore inherently linked with balancing competing rights and interest in an ecosystem dictated by power and information asymmetries.

[120] For a discussion on how the DPIA process may be used iteratively and in a more representative manner, see Rachelle Bosua, Damian Clifford, and Megan Richardson, 'Contact-Tracing Technologies and the Problem of Trust—Framing a Right of Social Dialogue for an Impact Assessment Process in Pandemic Times' (2023) 5 Law, Technology and Humans 193.

[121] See Bygrave (n 9) 350; European Data Protection Board, 'Guidelines 4/2019 on Article 25 Data Protection by Design and by Default' (2020) 18.

[122] European Data Protection Board (n 121) 23.

[123] ibid 64.

[124] Malgieri (n 35) 154.

[125] European Data Protection Board (n 121) 65.

Table 5.2 EDPB guidance on fairness

Design Element	EDPB Explanation
Autonomy	Data subjects should be granted the highest degree of autonomy possible to determine the use made of their personal data, as well as over the scope and conditions of that use or processing.
Interaction	Data subjects must be able to communicate and exercise their rights in respect of the personal data processed by the controller.
Expectation	Processing should correspond with data subjects' expectations.
Non-discrimination	The controller shall not unfairly discriminate against data subjects.
Non-exploitation	The controller shall not exploit the needs or vulnerabilities of data subjects.
Consumer choice	The controller should not 'lock in' their users in an unfair manner. Whenever a service processing personal data is proprietary, it may create a lock-in to the service, which may not be fair, if it impairs the data subjects' possibility to exercise their right of data portability in accordance with Article 20.
Power balance	Power balance should be a key objective of the controller-data subject relationship. Power imbalances should be avoided. When this is not possible, they should be recognised and accounted for with suitable countermeasures.
No risk transfer	Controllers should not transfer the risks of the enterprise to the data subjects.
No deception	Data processing information and options should be provided in an objective and neutral way, avoiding any deceptive or manipulative language or design.
Respect rights	The controller must respect the fundamental rights of data subjects and implement appropriate measures and safeguards and not impinge on those rights unless expressly justified by law.
Ethical	The controller should see the processing's wider impact on individuals' rights and dignity.
Truthful	The controller must make available information about how they process personal data, they should act as they declare they will and not mislead the data subjects.
Human intervention	The controller must incorporate qualified human intervention that is capable of uncovering biases that machines may create in accordance with the right to not be subject to automated individual decision making in Article 22.
Fair algorithms	Regularly assess whether algorithms are functioning in line with the purposes and adjust the algorithms to mitigate uncovered biases and ensure fairness in the processing. Data subjects should be informed about the functioning of the processing of personal data based on algorithms that analyse or make predictions about them, such as work performance, economic situation, health, personal preferences, reliability or behaviour, location or movements.

Source: Data from European Data Protection Board, 'Guidelines 4/2019 on Article 25 Data Protection by Design and by Default' (2020).

Determining what is fair therefore seems couched in terms of balancing and an analysis of the necessity and proportionality of the processing which feeds into the amorphous and context-dependent nature of what might be deemed a fair outcome. Fairness thus seems imbedded in any interpretation of the other principles, be that, for example, in the form of the more concrete spelling out of the transparency requirements in Articles 12–14 of the GDPR or in the assessment of whether latterly defined purposes are compatible with the original one(s) identified in compliance with the purpose limitation principle. There is therefore a need to think more deeply about the relationship between fairness as a 'core' principle of the GDPR and the methodological approach to a DPIA for a better understanding of the relationship between the principles provided for in Article 5 but also the various meanings attributed to fairness. Indeed, it is important to clarify that explaining the separation between the manifestations of fairness does not fill in the ambiguities that are left in the interpretation of the framework within which the fairness principle in Article 5(1)(a) plays a key role.

Moreover, although determining what is fair *in abstracto* is a rather fruitless exercise, delineating the indicative elements to be considered when analysing the fairness of a (potential future) processing operation may provide some grounding to understand and differentiate a fair from an unfair outcome. Indeed, in this regard we can refer to many of the sticky interpretative issues which go to the very core of the operation of the Regulation. Reference can be made, for example, to the interpretation of the conditions for consent in Article 7 and in particular the meaning of the 'freely given' stipulation, assessing the scope of what is included in 'necessary' processing in Article 6(1)(b)–(f) as discussed in Chapter 4 as an indicative example.[126] Due to the role of the fairness principle, therefore, it is difficult to extract a concrete and actionable framework to assess fairness and inform a controller on how to undertake a balancing exercise given the complex context-dependent nature of the principle. All the practical uncertainties of fairness in Article 5(1)(a) (in terms of the substantive outcome of a balancing exercise) effectively mean that, for a controller, the aspect that can really be *entirely* controlled is the conformity with the accountability-based requirements designed by the legislator to strike a fair balance.

Performing the DPIA process in a thorough fashion may therefore constitute a large part of doing what is 'fair' practically speaking, given that defining what

[126] See here eg Clifford, Graef, and Valcke (n 45).

is fair in terms of a substantive outcome is context-dependent. Reference here can be made to Article 35(4)–(6) and (8)–(11) and in particular Article 35(9) relating to the inclusion of the views of data subjects or their representatives where appropriate in that, although the inclusion of broader interests may lead to better outcomes,[127] the requirements do not speak to the balance that should be struck in terms of how these perspectives should be taken into account in a final decision to move forward with the personal data processing or not. This point is indicative of the fact that a controller's purposes for processing may run counter to certain interpretations as to how the fairness principle plays a role in the interpretation of key rights and requirements and thus the categorization of certain processing operations as unfair and unlawful. There are of course certainly clear instances where a processing operation will be unfair. In practice, however, the lines to be drawn are far more blurred, as what is fair is open to interpretation until there is a Court ruling or a specific legislative provision specifying its unfairness. The manner in which controllers responded to the notice and consent regime for the use of cookies and other similar devices discussed in Chapter 4 is a clear example of this point. Put simply, it is difficult to argue that the current approach to operationalizing consent in cookie banners as an example reflects an approach that is grounded in the rationale and logic of the Regulation (which explains the challenges against the IAB Europe cookie consent standard framework).[128]

The point, therefore, is that controllers are arguably incentivized to focus on compliance in a formal sense. This may reflect the point that meaningful compliance may be counter to (or more extremely, completely at odds with) their business model. Although fairness is certainly concerned with the mitigation of unfair balances, as manifested through the interpretation of the rights and requirements provided for in the Regulation, the more positive aspect of the principle may sometimes be absent, arguably reflecting the historical roots of data protection law but also the push towards managerialism and outsourcing.

(b) Risking lawfulness and legitimacy

Although substantial compliance with the fairness principle would seemingly demonstrate what Koops refers to as the 'attitude, vision and mindset'

[127] For a discussion of this point, see Bosua, Clifford, and Richardson (n 120).

[128] See 'The BE DPA to Restore Order to the Online Advertising Industry: IAB Europe Held Responsible for a Mechanism That Infringes the GDPR | Autorité de Protection des Données/Gegevensbeschermingsautoriteit' <www.dataprotectionauthority.be/citizen/iab-europe-held-responsible-for-a-mechanism-that-infringes-the-gdpr> accessed 23 September 2023.

necessary to move beyond mere compliance in terms of process[129] to compliance in substance, fairness is (1) undefined and complicated, and (2) context-dependent and hence open to interpretation in terms of its precise application in a given set of circumstances. These features mean that the substantive effect of the principle may arguably be undermined to the point where the 'attitude, vision and mindset' necessary to achieve meaningful engagement with the framework becomes lost in mere fair process/procedure.[130] The utility of relying on the fair balancing of interests is thus arguably undercut by the fact that it is the controller who is holding the scales. The very design of the GDPR further exacerbates this issue, as the framework seems to assume the legitimacy of personal data processing purposes and fails to give a clear meaning to fairness. The deployment of an obviously inaccurate system would surely be considered unfair but arguably only where controllers have misled the data subject as to its capacity. To demonstrate this (perhaps controversial) point, we can apply the negative (focus on unfairness) and positive (focus on fairness) manifestations of the fairness principle to an entirely inaccurate deployment of E-AI deployed in the hypothetical example of Ruth's home relied on in the previous chapters of this book to demonstrate the contrasting impacts.

Taking our focus on avoiding unfairness first: here we can imagine a controller focused on compliance accounting for all possibilities in the terms and conditions and privacy policy. There is thus likely to be a clear focus on the provision of fair and transparent information, at least in a formal sense, which covers the bases and does not mislead data subjects in an unfair manner by including statements waiving any liability for inaccuracy. Moreover, although much of the personal data processing in this context may be thought of as necessary for the performance of the service offered through the device, as it may be that sensitive personal data are processed, it is likely that the explicit consent of the data subject will be sought. Other than this formal requirement and other important considerations such as how to operationalize data subject rights, however, it is likely that this will (at least generally speaking) encapsulate the compliance efforts. Without some push by a DPA, it is hard to imagine a controller considering whether the deployment of the technology represents a proportionate balancing of the rights and interests at stake.[131]

[129] Koops, 'The Trouble with European Data Protection Law' (n 2) 255.
[130] ibid.
[131] For the challenges associated with implementing DPIAs in practice, see Dalla Corte and Van Brakel (n 106).

Alternatively, viewing this example through the lens of a positive duty to act fairly, one could argue that an obviously inaccurate computational system would lead to an unfair outcome, as it would simply represent a disproportionate interference with the right to data protection. There is certainly support for this view in statements from regulators—for example, in 2022 the UK's Information Commissioner's Office warned against the use of E-AI due to the immaturity of the technology and indicated that they would be monitoring the market closely. However, given (1) the malleable nature of the fairness principle, and (2) the general focus of the GDPR on the risks of personal data processing, as opposed to the applications for which the data are used, it is unclear how far such statements reach—especially when one considers the number of inaccurate consumer devices freely available on the market. To be clear, I am not advocating for a narrow process-orientated approach but instead I am merely arguing that a constrained interpretation is a potential outcome of a controller's compliance efforts without regulatory supervision, pressure, and a perceived risk of penalties due to an infringement. This is particularly the case where it may be difficult to legitimize the use of the technology without a more permissive/narrow approach. E-AI is an excellent example in this regard: due to obvious accuracy issues it is hard to see how its use could be proportionate (and thus fair) in many contexts.

On the other hand, however, the grey areas that are left in the operation of the GDPR and more specifically the fair balancing of rights and interests required through the operation of Article 5(1)(a) provide a role for broader debates within the operation of the fairness principle in a particular context to determine the risks of a specific technology and the legality of a processing operation. In simple terms, in this manner fairness becomes the avenue through which such debates could be filtered into the Regulation. As noted by Butterworth,[132] this appears, for example, to map the UK ICO's approach in its guidance on 'Big data, artificial intelligence, machine learning and data protection'.[133] Reference here can also be again made to the EDPB guidance on Data Protection by Design and by Default and the specific design elements that are proposed.[134] However, Butterworth argues that this approach seems to stretch the GDPR and its fair processing requirement to address the challenges brought about by AI, such as collective harms, and that there may be a need for 'legislation defining socially acceptable limits and controls on the

132 Butterworth (n 40) 267.
133 Information Commissioner's Office, 'Big Data' (n 77).
134 European Data Protection Board (n 121) 65.

application of artificial intelligence, and providing effective rights of redress for individuals and groups that may suffer harm'.[135] There are certainly challenges affecting the capacity of the Regulation to have a meaningful impact on the mitigation of the negative impacts associated with the inaccuracy of E-AI, for instance. Indeed, as analysed in Chapter 3, the provisions defining the material scope of the GDPR illustrate that a context-dependent assessment is necessary to determine whether personal data (or indeed sensitive personal data) are processed.[136]

Therefore, the use of E-AI in a smart home, such as in the hypothetical example of Ruth already discussed in Chapters 3 and 4, and, for instance, the deployment of similar sensors in a smart advertising panel in a public place are not comparable situations in every respect. Taking this public display advertising example as a starting point, one must then wonder how to interpret the application of the GDPR and its limits/limitations if it is questionable whether personal data are in fact processed. In other words, what if the specific application of E-AI does not aim to single out a natural person by design? Does this mean that all the risks are catered for? To illustrate this point we can refer again to the testing of the emotion-sensitive public advertising in 2015 developed by *M & C Saatchi*, as discussed in Chapter 3, which raised important questions regarding the application of the GDPR.[137] The use of E-AI may therefore encroach on a variety of human rights, including our rights to freedom of expression;[138] freedom of assembly and association;[139] equality and non-discrimination;[140] freedom of thought, conscience, and religion;[141] privacy;[142] and data protection[143] in addition to underlying key notions of autonomy and human dignity.[144] Such monitoring can also have an impact on an individual's ability to *self-present*, referring to the ability of individuals to

[135] Butterworth (n 40) 267.

[136] Paul M Schwartz and Daniel J Solove, 'Reconciling Personal Information in the United States and European Union' [2013] SSRN Electronic Journal 886 <www.ssrn.com/abstract=2271442> accessed 14 September 2018.

[137] John Still, 'Is Artificial Intelligence the next Step in Advertising?' *The Guardian* (27 July 2015) <www.theguardian.com/media-network/2015/jul/27/artificial-intelligence-future-advertising-saatchi-clearchannel> accessed 26 November 2018.

[138] Art 10 ECHR; art 10 CFREU.

[139] Art 11 ECRH; art 12 CFREU.

[140] Art 14 ECHR; arts 20–21 CFREU.

[141] Art 9 ECHR; art 10 CFREU.

[142] Art 8 ECHR; art 7 CFREU.

[143] Art 8 CFREU.

[144] See Peggy Valcke, Damian Clifford, and Viltė Kristina Dessers, 'Constitutional Challenges in the Emotional AI Era' in Hans-W Micklitz and others (eds), *Constitutional Challenges in the Algorithmic Society* (CUP 2021).

present multifaceted versions of themselves,[145] and thus behave differently depending on the circumstances.[146] Indeed, as described in Chapter 3, E-AI arguably adds a layer of intimacy-invasion via the perceived capacity to not only detect emotions as *expressed*, but also those emotions that are being deliberately *disguised*, thereby potentially eroding this capacity entirely. This may be an issue irrespective of the accuracy of E-AI (ie the mere observation or perception of surveillance can have a chilling effect on behaviour).[147]

E-AI therefore presents a range of risks and, put simply, data processing risks range far beyond the specific threats associated with confidentiality or the protection of information but encompass broader societal concerns associated with freedom of action, self-determination, and autonomy.[148] These risks may or may not be addressed by data protection law depending in part on whether personal data are processed, but also because data protection law does not address the substantive fairness of the outcomes of computational systems in practice given that it focuses predominantly on processing risk and not the substantial parts of the profiling applications.[149] The GDPR is thus arguably simply not capable of regulating all the risks associated with any and every deployment of technology as some may require a more sector-specific analysis to take into account the specific risks, rights, and interests at stake. At the same time, however, the GDPR is only one framework amongst many in EU law and the intersecting areas of the national law of the Member States. There are important points of analysis at these fringes, therefore, in terms of the difference between, for example, fairness and lawfulness as they are understood within the boundaries of data protection law and how it intersects with other regulatory frameworks.

To illustrate this point three important examples are worth highlighting. First, the future role of the AI Act[150] in terms of its intersections with data protection given the move to ban the use of E-AI in certain sectors. Secondly, the role of consumer and national contract law in the analysis of data protection

[145] Richard Warner and Robert H Sloan, 'Self, Privacy, and Power: Is It All Over?' (2014) 17 Tulane Journal of Technical & Intellectual Property 61.

[146] James Rachels, 'Why Privacy Is Important' (1975) 4 Philosophy & Public Affairs 323.

[147] Ryan Calo, 'The Boundaries of Privacy Harm' (2011) 86 Indiana Law Journal 1142–43.

[148] As noted by Calo, '[e]ven where we know intellectually that we are interacting with an image or a machine, our brains are hardwired to respond as though a person were actually there', ibid 1147.

[149] Bert-Jaap Koops, 'On Decision Transparency, or How to Enhance Data Protection after the Computational Turn' in Mireille Hildebrandt and Katja de Vries (eds), *Privacy, Due Process and the Computational Turn: The Philosophy of Law Meets the Philosophy of Technology* (Routledge 2013).

[150] Proposal of the European Parliament and of the Council Laying Down Harmonised Rules on Artificial Intelligence (Artificial Intelligence Act) and Amending Certain Union Legislative Acts (COM (2021) 206 final).

law demonstrates intersections linked to both the data gathering and the data use side of the problems discussed.[151] And, thirdly, the role of competition law in the analysis of data protection law illustrates how market power can play a role in the concurrent and complementary application of different areas of law.[152] These examples are excellent illustrations of how the alignment of different areas of EU law addresses different aspects of the regulatory issues posed by digital technologies. For example, the application of the Unfair Terms Directive and the Unfair Commercial Practices Directive to data subjects' decisions to give up data, the content of privacy policies, and the unilateral imposition of changes are significant. In addition, the recent ruling from the Court of Justice in the *Meta Platforms* case discussed in Chapter 4 is an excellent illustration of how a breach of the GDPR may lead to a breach of competition law.[153] Therefore, although the GDPR is not the solution to all problems associated with the deployment of computational systems it is an important cog in the regulatory wheel. Criticisms of data protection must thus account for the fact that through a broad notion of fairness and key accountability mechanisms, controllers are encouraged (and arguably compelled) to counteract the negative societal impacts, and I therefore believe that the criticisms should be tempered accordingly to account for the more nuanced reality.

D. Limits of the Challenge

There is a danger of understanding a data protection law 'compliant' deployment as unquestionably desirable as compliance efforts may speak to fair process/procedure and not to whether the specific deployment represents a proportionate balancing of rights and interests and accounts for risks appropriately.[154] The affective feature of the challenge posed by the key role played by

[151] See Damian Clifford and Jeannie Marie Paterson, 'Data Rights and Contract Law: Formation, Incorporation and Vitiating Factors' in Damian Clifford, Jeannie Marie Paterson, and Kwan Ho Lau (eds), *Data and Private Law* (Hart 2023); Damian Clifford and Jeannie Paterson, 'Consumer Privacy and Consent: Reform in the Light of Contract and Consumer Protection Law' (2020) 94 Australian Law Journal 741.

[152] See Clifford, Graef, and Valcke (n 45); Inge Graef, Damian Clifford, and Peggy Valcke, 'Fairness and Enforcement: Bridging Competition, Data Protection, and Consumer Law' (2018) 8 International Data Privacy Law 200; Inge Graef, *EU Competition Law, Data Protection and Online Platforms: Data as Essential Facility* (Kluwer Law International 2016); Francisco Costa-Cabral and Orla Lynskey, 'Family Ties: The Intersection between Data Protection and Competition in EU Law' (2017) 54 Common Market Law Review 11.

[153] Case C–252/21 *Meta Platforms v Bundeskartellamt*, ECLI:EU:C:2023:537.

[154] Lynskey reaches a similar conclusion: Orla Lynskey, 'Complete and Effective Data Protection' (2023) 76 Current Legal Problems 297 <http://eprints.lse.ac.uk/120212/> accessed 25 September 2023.

those processing personal data is that compliance requires their hearts and not just minds and the law arguably fails to take this into account. Although there is merit to this challenge, in practice, however, data protection laws such as the GDPR do aim to instil fairness in the design of computational systems through the role of the fairness and accountability principles and legislative mechanisms such as the requirement to conduct an impact assessment and by design obligations. Undoubtedly, controllers have their subjective reasons for acting in specific ways. This may reflect their business model, but it also may reflect the risk-based manner in which the problems of complying with data protection law is approached.

Arguably, there is an inherent tension in the way in which the language of risk is deployed in the context of fundamental rights protection, given that risk assessments are normally concerned with tangible harms that are mathematically quantifiable, thus seemingly implying that rights violations occur on a scale and can be ranked.[155] The choice of language may therefore be a factor in encouraging more process-orientated approaches. More generally, however, it must also be acknowledged that this assessment is certainly shaped by fundamental rights and therefore outside of jurisdictions similar to the EU that have a similarly framed constitutional foundation to data protection, fairness may have a far more tempered meaning and, thus, effect. This is a point that will be explored in more detail in the next chapter. Even leaving aside these differences, however, it must also be considered whether data protection law asks too much of those processing personal data by embedding a broader role for fairness and thus whether the expectations for data protection's impact are set too high by data protection enthusiasts. In addition, it might also be wondered whether the criticisms outlined are actually features of data protection law, and indeed the law in general, as opposed to examples of the affective features of the challenge identified.

My point is that I believe there are few (if any) areas of law that reach 'the hearts and minds' of those regulated. There are a whole host of industries and examples where compliance is approached in a managerialized fashion, and here we consider the requirement to conduct a DPIA as an example. In the private sector, this could be understood as part of the duty of the company officers, given their mandate to protect the interests of the shareholders. I believe, therefore, that there are elements of a '[p]rocedure followed, problem solved' approach to legal requirements generally, and that there are plenty of scandals

[155] Yeung and Bygrave (n 39) 146.

to demonstrate that even in highly regulated industries procedures may not be followed.[156] For example, the requirement to conduct a DPIA was originally inspired by the requirement in environmental law to conduct an impact assessment—but we can hardly point to this area of law as an example that reached the hearts of all of those regulated. It is difficult to know how the 'attitude, vision and mindset' necessary to achieve meaningful compliance could actually be fostered through the framework when legislative developments such as the GDPR seem to have been inspired (at least in part) by the need to regulate digital platforms, but these platforms' business models appear (at least in some respects) to run counter to meaningful compliance.

Therefore, there are limits to the challenge to data protection law. In addition, the pieces are still in motion and the GDPR as a specific example is arguably only now hitting its stride as a range of significant cases are being decided by the Court of Justice. Enforcement is certainly key to the effective implementation of data protection law, and, in this regard, it is important to note that there is significant variation in the enforcement mechanisms relied upon, the levels of fines that can be issued by regulatory bodies, and the existence and/or nature of individual causes of action that are provided for in different jurisdictions. Indeed, in tracking the adoption of data protection laws globally, Greenleaf notes that to determine whether something can be classified as a data protection law, it is necessary to analyse whether it (1) contains almost all the principles provided in the OECD Guidelines and Convention 108, and (2) is not merely self-regulatory and has some form of 'officially-backed enforcement'.[157] The second of these characteristics is easy to identify but is one of the aspects of these laws which demonstrates the most significant variation. In essence, it means that authors such as Greenleaf do not consider mechanisms such as the soft law manifestation of the FIPPs regulating the private sector at the federal level in the US to be examples of data protection laws. Although this classification system may itself warrant further analysis and, as there has been a clear pattern of hard laws being adopted (even in the US), the point may be increasingly a moot one, it does demonstrate the significance of robust enforcement, in both the form of individual rights of action and the need for a DPA.

[156] There are seemingly endless examples here. To name but a few we can think of the financial crisis and the banks, pharmaceuticals and oxycontin, Volkswagen and 'diesel gate', etc. On what regulators from different areas can learn from such failures, see Julia Black, 'Learning from Regulatory Disasters' (2014) 10 Policy Quarterly 3 <https://ojs.victoria.ac.nz/pq/article/view/4504> accessed 23 September 2023.

[157] See on this how Greenleaf describes his method for including a framework as a data protection laws, in Graham Greenleaf, 'Sheherezade and the 101 Data Privacy Laws: Origins, Significance and Global Trajectories' (2014) 23 Journal of Law, Information and Science 4.

There is an obvious connection here between controller compliance and the potential violation of trust, as trust implies a degree of risk-taking on behalf of the data subject in that these laws clearly have a performative function of ensuring that data subjects feel that they trust the digital environment sufficiently to actively engage in the market.[158] However, put simply, trust cannot coexist with guarantees[159]—it is the absence of such guarantees that creates risks.[160] Data subjects, for example, trust controllers with their personal data (at least in effect) even though controllers cannot make any absolute guarantees regarding the security of that data. Risk can be understood as being comprised of (1) negative/positive forecasting of events, and (2) the taking of decisions on this basis.[161] It can be approached both from the perspective of the entity's assessment of the potential risks associated with a deployment of a computational system, for instance, but also the perception of risk associated with engaging with such technologies on behalf of the individual. Trust is inherently associated with both these aspects, as an individual may be hesitant to use a technology if they perceive a risk (whether genuine or not) and, to enhance trust, an entity will aim to illustrate how they have mitigated any potential risks through, for example, a fair and accountability-driven deployment of their technology.

Trust, however, is inevitably imperfect in that there is always some degree of risk as to whether trust is misdirected.[162] In her analysis of this notion O'Neill clarifies the fickle nature of trust with reference to two sides of the same problem, or, in the author's words, 'misplaced trust' and 'misplaced mistrust'.[163] Trust is therefore clearly a subjective notion that can only be defined in context, from the definer's own particular perspective.[164] It goes to the heart of why, for instance, we may or may not feel comfortable with the risks associated with

[158] In analysing the notion of trust, Vandezande extracts interdisciplinary insights from philosophy, psychology, sociology, economics, computer science, and law and concludes that, '[w]hile there are certainly clear divergences between how the different scientific disciplines [...] view the concept of trust, there are also a number of common elements to be distinguished. Overall, the abstract notion of trust can be characterised as an attribute to interpersonal relationships that serves as a bet for future possibilities and that constitutes a degree of risk-taking.' In saying this the author goes on to note that although trust is evident in law, it manifests itself in diffuse and divergent forms. Niels Vandezande, *Virtual Currencies A Legal Framework* (Intersentia 2018) 109–10.

[159] Helen Nissenbaum, 'Can Trust Be Secured Online? A Theoretical' [1999] Etica e Politica 15.

[160] See Josh Boyd, 'The Rhetorical Construction of Trust Online' (2003) 13 Communication Theory 392.

[161] Gellert (n 118) 280, with reference to Bertrand Zuindeau, 'O. Godard, C. Henry, P. Lagadec, E. Michel-Kerjan, 2002, Traité des nouveaux risques, éditions Gallimard, collection folio-actuel' [2003] Développement durable et territoires <https://journals.openedition.org/developpementdurable/1320> accessed 20 December 2023; Peter L Bernstein, *Against the Gods: The Remarkable Story of Risk* (Wiley 1996).

[162] Onora O'Neill, *Autonomy and Trust in Bioethics* (1st edn repr, CUP 2002) 141.

[163] ibid.

[164] See Boyd (n 160).

being exposed to tracking in digital environments. There is also an important link between trust and transparency but also opacity and the maintaining of individual ignorance[165]—an unfair distribution of risks and benefits between individuals and those processing their personal data may lead to data subject outrage.[166] Trust therefore has an important emotional element that can be fostered by those processing data through deliberate strategies that may promise practices quite different from the reality provided.[167] Those processing personal data also have a clear incentive to suppress negative emotional reactions to incidences such a data breaches.[168] It has been questioned whether companies, for instance, are in fact more concerned about managing public feelings and regulatory pressure about the protection of personal data than focusing on security.[169]

Too much trust can therefore be unhelpful and, in the digital environment, the pervasive nature of personal data processing certainly gives rise to concerns and perhaps a more pessimistic view of controllers' willingness to engage meaningfully with data protection law. This presents clear issues not only in terms of the effective operation of key accountability mechanisms, such as the requirement to conduct a data protection/privacy impact assessment (DP/PIA), but also in terms of how the data subject can effectively engage actively to protect their own personal data. This is particularly the case as trust may also be the target of design and, indeed, manipulative design practices.[170] However, these points, at least in my opinion, do not mean that data protection law is necessarily useless. Compliance will always be a moving target, particularly when the technology is changing so rapidly.

In saying that, however, I believe that the difficulty in understanding the logic and rationale of the GDPR specifically, and the key yet undefined role played by the fairness principle (and its connection to, and the unclear nature

[165] Luke Stark, 'The Emotional Context of Information Privacy' (2016) 32 The Information Society 14, 22.

[166] Sabine Roeser, 'The Role of Emotions in Judging the Moral Acceptability of Risks' (2006) 44 Safety Science 689, 696.

[167] Stark (n 165) 22.

[168] In this vein, one is reminded of the fallout from the *Cambridge Analytica* scandal and Facebook's public relations management efforts to mitigate the impact of the breach. Indeed, it is also interesting to point out Facebook's initial response to the scandal and its insistence that it was not caused by a data breach, as its users had in fact 'consented' to Cambridge Analytica's processing of their personal data. However, users still felt a violation of trust which resulted in a very noticeable Facebook marketing campaign via mainstream media and public display advertising. See 'The Cambridge Analytica Files' *The Guardian* <www.theguardian.com/news/series/cambridge-analytica-files> accessed 4 October 2023.

[169] Stark (n 165) 22.

[170] Ari Ezra Waldman, 'Cognitive Biases, Dark Patterns, and the "Privacy Paradox"' (2020) 31 Current Opinion in Psychology 105, 107–08.

of, the right to data protection), is an important limitation and perhaps gives pause to policymakers in other jurisdictions (see Chapter 6 for more on this). Complying with the fairness principle in the GDPR is a challenge in part due to the fact that what is fair is a malleable notion dependent on the context but also due to the regulatory environment and the allocation of responsibilities. The GDPR provides the principle, and the general consensus is that fairness is core to data protection. Despite this however, the Regulation does not provide a definition of fairness. Two warning shots are perhaps warranted in a more overarching sense to demonstrate potential issues associated with its significance.

First, the GDPR has been the golden-haired child of the EU legal order. In this regard, one can refer to expanding interpretations of key definitions, and thus it is interesting to consider how the expansionist interpretation of the GDPR leads to the question of how far 'not right' may be from 'not legal' given the role of the fairness principle in the GDPR. This points to the flexibility associated with fair balancing exercises and therefore to the fact that, although understandings of what may be unethical or unfair are difficult to delineate, the degree to which such debates need to be considered may vary from what is necessary in order to be deemed legal. And, secondly, due to the vagueness of the GDPR provisions and the room for fair balancing throughout the Regulation, there is arguably a need to further specify the legality of computational systems such as E-AI through the further alignment of different areas of law rather than leaving such matters merely to ethical debates.[171] This partly relates to the fact that (1) there are limits to what can be expected of those processing personal data—even those which strive for the fullest implementation of the fairness principle, but also the fact that (2) the Regulation, for example, is designed to apply in a range of contexts across both the public and private sectors. Hence, the assessment of the legitimacy of a purpose can be determined by areas of law outside the operation of data protection law. This is a feature of the framework not a weakness. I think it is arguably necessary then to look to the alignment of other areas of law such as the EU's AI Act but also for instance, consumer and competition law, to fill data protection's gaps and not to its wholesale change or abandonment.

[171] Paul Nemitz, 'Constitutional Democracy and Technology in the Age of Artificial Intelligence' (2018) 376 Philosophical Transactions of the Royal Society A: Mathematical, Physical and Engineering Sciences 20180089, 8.

E. Conclusion

The analysis in this chapter has shown that data protection law arguably fails to appropriately account for how the interests of those processing personal data shape the application of the framework. I demonstrated that the fairness principle, as an open-textured key tenet of such frameworks, affords this flexibility and that, in practice, the GDPR as an example may be applied in a manner aimed at avoiding unfairness as opposed to instilling fairness in the design and deployment of computational systems such as E-AI. This may in fact reflect the historical roots of the notion of fairness in data protection law. The case study revealed that even in the context of obvious inaccuracy issues, such as the highly publicized inaccuracy of E-AI, the GDPR as the high-water-mark example of such frameworks may arguably struggle to be the regulatory solution to the problem presented.

The open-textured nature of the fairness principle in the Regulation combined with the key positioning of controllers plays an important role in the effectiveness of the framework. The weakness of data protection law therefore seem obvious. However, I also believe that the framework plays an important role. In some ways, certain of the criticisms presented speak more to the limits of data protection law as a solution to specific regulatory problems as opposed to its limitations as one such regulatory framework. I also question whether similar critiques may be made against many other areas of law. The next chapter will explore these points in detail and argue for data protection law's normative value despite the challenges linked to the effectiveness of the instrumental role played by mechanisms of individual control.

6

The Limits of Data Protection Law

A. Introduction

Data protection law is easy to criticize. There are some core features of data protection law that are challenged by technological developments and the realities of human behaviour. The previous chapters have demonstrated these weaknesses. The question, therefore, is what value a focus on individual control over personal data adds despite these criticisms. In this chapter, I explore the conceptual value of control as distinct from its instrumental role. In so doing, I analyse the uncertain foundations of data protection law by describing control as one such underpinning value with potentially different meanings and, arguably, even an uncertain relationship with data protection law—depending on the jurisdiction. I believe that in order to assess the effectiveness of data protection law we need a better understanding of its underlying values and the potential differences between jurisdictions to appreciate the significance of critiques and value of comparative insights.[1] I explore how control, as a conceptual value, points to the significance of the capacity to make subjective choices given its instrumental link to the subjective control rights evident in data protection law.

However, although data protection law affords us subjective rights so that we can make our own choices, it also assumes our objective rational capacity to make them and then fails to account for the role of emotion in decision-making (see Chapters 4 and 5). This false dichotomy between rationality and emotions arguably undermines the instrumental role played by control. Therefore, in this chapter, I argue that a conceptualization of rationality that understands emotion as one of its constituent components may be required in order to preserve control's conceptual value. In addition, even leaving aside its potential conceptual value, I also suggest that instrumentalizing control has practical value. This approach recognizes that the assumed rational capacity of data subjects may be the lesser of two evils compared with ceding control to

[1] I have developed this argument based on a similar one made in the context of administrative law, see Peter Cane and others, *Principles of Administrative Law* (3rd edn, OUP 2018) 346–64.

Data Protection Law and Emotion. Damian Clifford, Oxford University Press. © Damian Clifford 2024.
DOI: 10.1093/oso/9780192845863.003.0006

controllers or some third party. We need to frame our discussion of the challenges associated with data protection law more appropriately. I suggest that we need to differentiate between data protection law's limitations as a regulatory instrument and its limits as one legislative framework amongst many others and the general law, and to look to a more transversal analysis of the issues posed by intensive personal data processing.

In Section B, I analyse the affective value of individual control by looking at its conceptual value as opposed to its instrumental role, while also questioning whether other conceptual values may be at play. In Section C, I analyse the assumption in data protection law that we, as data subjects, have the objective rational capacity to make choices, and hence the failure to account for the role of our emotions in decision-making. In Section D, I analyse the expressive role of data protection law and explore how differentiating between data protection's limitations as a regulatory response and limits as one framework amongst many can allow us to focus on ensuring its effectiveness and its role in the development of an effective regulatory environment that expresses the need to protect/balance important societal values.

B. Affective Value of Control

Data protection law and its focus on the control of personal data through subjective rights has its limitations. Some scholars suggest, for example, that the law should instead focus on mitigating the harms associated with the uses of personal data, as the harms remain too abstract when the focus is on such a broad category of information.[2] It has also been suggested that the common law privacy torts, for instance, offer a more normatively coherent protection of the right to privacy, given that they focus on the narrower category of private information and the proportionality of interferences.[3] And, from an instrumentalist perspective, there are scholars who are very critical of relying too heavily on our personal data and our empowerment as the target and approach of regulatory interventions.[4] Each of these critiques challenges the legitimacy

[2] See eg Daniel J Solove, 'Data Is What Data Does: Regulating Based on Harm and Risk Instead of Sensitive Data' (11 January 2023) <https://papers.ssrn.com/abstract=4322198> accessed 29 June 2023; Lucas Bergkamp, 'EU Data Protection Policy: The Privacy Fallacy: Adverse Effects of Europe's Data Protection Policy in an Information-Driven Economy' (2002) 18 Computer Law & Security Review 31.

[3] See Jelena Gligorijevic, 'Tort-Based Protections for Data Privacy' in Damian Clifford, Jeannie Marie Paterson, and Kwan Ho Lau (eds), *Data and Private Law* (Hart 2023).

[4] See eg Ari Waldman, 'Privacy's Rights Trap' [2022] Northwestern University Law Review Online <https://scholarlycommons.law.northwestern.edu/nulr_online/327> accessed 4 October 2023; Daniel Solove, 'The Limitations of Privacy Rights' (2023) 98 Notre Dame Law Review 975; Julie E Cohen, 'How

of data protection laws. I believe that the risk of harm posed by intensive personal data processing means that it is not a question of whether we need these frameworks, but rather a question of what form they should take. In addition, data protection law serves a different function from privacy torts, given that they are seemingly concerned with the *fairness* of processing irrespective of whether there may be an impact on privacy.

In this chapter, then, we are concerned with the critiques of the instrumental role played by control. At the centre of the instrumentalist critiques is the idea that we are not able to act in our own interests—that, amongst other things, the rational data subject at the centre of a control rights-orientated approach to data protection fails to conform to the reality. In describing the expressive value of law and how it sets norms, Waldman argues that the focus on control in data protection law sends two problematic messages that are ill-suited to tackle the risk of harms posed: (1) privacy is an individual right against others and that it is our individual responsibility, and (2) that it is our responsibility to manage the data extracted from our social behaviours.[5] There are certainly features of the digital environment, and the ways in which individuals and those processing personal data engage with it, which render a focus on the individual control of personal data challenging, if not impossible, to achieve in practice. As Kaminski observes, control is a term that many 'scholars now love to hate'.[6]

1. Control's conceptual value

The analysis in the earlier chapters of this book has arguably contributed more fodder to this hate fire. In Chapter 3, I described our emotional disengagement from the risks of harm associated with personal data processing due to the blurring boundaries between the personal data and sensitive personal data categories protected in data protection law. In Chapter 4, I explored the emotional disconnect between how data subjects behave, and the risks of harm associated with personal data processing. And, finally, in Chapter 5, I described how there has arguably been compliance in process and not in substance, thereby undermining the effectiveness of frameworks such as the General Data

(Not) to Write a Privacy Law' (2021) 21 Knight First Amendment Institute <https://knightcolumbia.org/content/how-not-to-write-a-privacy-law> accessed 4 October 2023.

5 Waldman, 'Privacy's Rights Trap' (n 4) 98.

6 Margot Kaminski, 'The Case for Data Privacy Rights (Or "Please, a Little Optimism")' (2022) 97 Notre Dame Law Review Reflection 385, 391.

Protection Regulation (GDPR) and exposing individuals to risks of harm. But what about the non-instrumentalist or conceptual role for the notion of control? In essence, what I am questioning is whether striving towards providing individuals with control over their personal data has some conceptual value even if this may never be fully realized in practice in an instrumentalist sense.

In her analysis of the notion of control in EU data protection law, Lynskey draws this distinction between the conceptual and instrumental roles that control may play in the GDPR.[7] From an instrumental perspective, she explains the manifestation of the subjective control rights, and consent in particular, to describe how this notion of control manifests itself in the Regulation. Conceptually, Lynskey explains that an important question is whether control *should* play a role in data protection law and that this question is crucial to establishing data protection law's legitimacy.[8] In short, I believe that the question of what data protection law achieves can only be effectively answered after we first address the question of what it is for[9]—and, as will be demonstrated in this subsection, there are many challenges linked to answering this question appropriately.

(a) Control, risk, and harm

Certainly, the feeling that we have lost control over our personal data has motivated the adoption of data protection law frameworks. The fear, shock, anger, and indignation associated with the violation of what is understood as a social norm and individual right, and the associated risks of harm (or perceived risks thereof), and hence the feeling that our personal data is out of our control, have at least partly motivated (and continue to motivate) their development.[10] Hence, control seems inherently connected with the notion of harm. There are a range of potential harms that may stem from personal data processing. Public awareness of the potentially harmful effects of computational systems has also steadily increased. I have discussed these harms throughout this book, in particular through my use of hypothetical examples, but generally these include physical or economic harm, social or political harm, and spiritual harm.[11] As has been demonstrated through the Emotional Artificial Intelligence (E-AI) case study, applications of AI potentially lead both to individual harms (eg invasions of privacy or reduced autonomy resulting in economic loss), and to

[7] Orla Lynskey, *The Foundations of EU Data Protection Law* (OUP 2015) 177–228.

[8] ibid 194.

[9] Cane and colleagues make a similar argument in the context of the values unpinning administrative law; see Cane and others (n 1) 346–64.

[10] Kaminski (n 6) 394.

[11] See also Damian Clifford, Megan Richardson, and Normann Witzleb, 'Artificial Intelligence and Sensitive Inferences: New Challenges for Data Protection Laws' in Mark Findlay and others (eds), *Regulatory Insights on Artificial Intelligence: Research for Policy* (Edward Elgar 2022).

societal or group harms (eg discriminatory/biased algorithmic outcomes, the proliferation of hate speech and fake news, and the undermining of democratic values). Consequently, a data subject's ability to exercise control over their personal data is generally closely imbricated with the prevention of such harms and, therefore, human identity and flourishing—thereby seemingly justifying the protections in data protection laws.[12] This link to values such as identity and privacy thus featured strongly in the historical origins of data protection law. As described by Bygrave in his account of the various conceptual values unpinning data protection laws, there are also a range of values and interests that are associated with the notion of privacy, such as individuality, autonomy, dignity, integrity, and emotional release, for example, in the form of the capacity to take refuge from having to conform to social expectations.[13] A focus on harm alleviation, therefore, would appear to legitimize an approach that aims to mitigate risks by giving data subjects 'control' over their personal data. This view is reflected in the non-binding recitals of the GDPR.[14]

Indeed, the recitals of the GDPR seem to provide that preventing a 'loss of control' is a target of the Regulation in itself, even aside from the mitigation of harms such as those linked to identity theft or fraud, discrimination, loss of confidentiality etc—listed as examples in recital 85. This focus on control is of particular interest when we consider that harm is not a *conditio sine qua non* for the application of the framework even if it may be relevant in the assessment of damages.[15] Indeed, reference here can also be made to the United Kingdom (UK) Supreme Court's rulings interpreting the UK's implementation of the old Data Protection Directive 95/46/EC regarding the need to prove harm to obtain compensation, with the mere violation of the legislation (or loss of control of personal data) deemed insufficient.[16] We can thus point to the challenges this poses for the effectiveness of data protection law and also highlight the significance of the role of the regulators and administrative fines in the mitigation of collective harms that may not result in cognizable harms to individuals.[17] Similar arguments could be made about data protection laws more generally

[12] ibid.

[13] Lee A Bygrave, *Data Protection Law: Approaching Its Rationale, Logic and Limits* (Kluwer Law International 2002) 133–36.

[14] More specifically, recital 7 states that '[n]atural persons should have control of their own personal data' with three further references to the importance of ensuring individual control over personal data in recitals 68, 75, and 85—with 'loss of control' over personal data mentioned as a form of 'physical, material or non-material harm' in recital 85 in particular.

[15] Lynskey, *The Foundations of EU Data Protection Law* (n 7) 195.

[16] See *Lloyd v Google LLC* [2019] EWCA Civ 1599, [2020] QB 747.

[17] See Kwan Ho Lau, 'Data Rights Incursions: Two Hurdles in the Pursuit of Damages' in Clifford, Paterson, and Lau (eds) (n 3).

given the prevalence of such rights even in the more market-orientated versions of these instruments.[18]

The focus of data protection law, then, is on the fair processing of personal data even if no legally cognizable harm is risked in specific circumstances, and there is thus an apparent value to affording control that is not necessarily directly linked to harm alleviation. In her analysis of these issues, Lynskey suggests that it could be claimed that control in data protection is an objective 'pursued for liberal aims'.[19] Certainly, data protection laws appear to be based on a set of liberal assumptions seemingly reflecting their value in individualistic terms.[20] In this sense, therefore, control has an affective value—it allows data subjects the capacity to make their own subjective choices. I believe that this manifests a general interest in affording individuals some power to control their personal data even in the absence of a defined list of tangible or intangible harms laid out in the law.[21] Arguably, this is an important manifestation of the values underlying the notion of privacy discussed by Bygrave and referred to in this subsection. In fact, this role for subjective choice may also reflect the conceptual uncertainties regarding the nature of the privacy interests at stake.

(b) Control and autonomy

Recognizing a role for control represents an appreciation of the value in allowing individuals to make their own choices, including the value in being left to make mistakes and arguably also as a positive standard to encourage people to strive to be 'rational',[22] but also because the experience of privacy is itself subjective.[23] It illustrates the value in individuals bringing their own

[18] We can refer here to the OECD Guidelines and the APEC Privacy Framework but also the various state consumer privacy laws that have developed in the US. See The Guidelines on the Protection of Privacy and Transborder Flows of Personal Data (OECD) 1980; Asia-Pacific Economic Cooperation (APEC) Privacy Framework <www.apec.org/docs/default-source/Publications/2017/8/APEC-Privacy-Framework-(2015)/217_ECSG_2015-APEC-Privacy-Framework.pdf > accessed 4 October 2023; California Consumer Privacy Act of 2018, Virginia Consumer Data Protection Act (2021), Utah Consumer Privacy Act (2022), Texas Data Privacy and Security Act (2023), Tennessee Information Protection Act (2023), Montana Consumer Data Privacy Act (2023), Iowa Consumer Data Protection Act (2023), Indiana Consumer Data Protection Act (2023), Connecticut Data Privacy Act (2022), and Colorado Privacy Act (2021).

[19] Lynskey, *The Foundations of EU Data Protection Law* (n 7) 196.

[20] See Colin J Bennett and Charles D Raab, *The Governance of Privacy: Policy Instruments in Global Perspective* (Taylor & Francis Group 2003) 13–31.

[21] Lynskey, *The Foundations of EU Data Protection Law* (n 7) 195–96.

[22] See Gillian K Hadfield, 'The Second Wave of Law and Economics' (1996) 46 The University of Toronto Law Journal 181.

[23] In outlining her behavioural understanding of privacy, which draws on social interaction theory to look at the way in which privacy is experienced, Hughes suggests that this struggle relates to the fact that the experience of privacy is often subjective. See Kirsty Hughes, 'A Behavioural Understanding of Privacy and Its Implications for Privacy Law' (2012) 75 The Modern Law Review 806.

actions in defence of their interests (even if this is not possible in certain jurisdictions) and this demonstrates clear overlaps with the discussion of the right to privacy and its link to autonomy. More specifically, in her discussion of the right to privacy, Ziegler highlights its two strands, namely (1) privacy as seclusion or intimacy (which is often spatially defined or, alternatively, in terms of substance vis-à-vis what is considered private); and (2) privacy as freedom of action, self-determination, and autonomy—with both strands necessary for the development of one's personality.[24] The second of these relates to Article 8 of the European Convention on Human Rights (ECHR) case law on autonomy,[25] whereas the first refers more explicitly, for example, to state-led invasions of privacy most aptly characterized recently by the European Court of Human Rights (ECtHR) case law on mass surveillance.[26] The operation of privacy is thus context-dependent, and despite the various attempts to define and/or '*taxonomize*' privacy, it largely remains an elusive notion.[27] This is despite the voluminous literature theorizing it. For example, Feldman conceptualizes privacy as being 'conditioned by the nature of social life', with individuals existing in several different 'social spheres, which interlock, and in each of which they have different responsibilities, and have to work with people in relationships of varying degrees of intimacy'.[28] This approach seems to share a common thread with Nissenbaum's theory of contextual privacy and

[24] Katja S Ziegler, 'Introduction: Human Rights and Private Law—Privacy as Autonomy' in Katja S Ziegler (ed), *Human Rights and Private Law: Privacy as Autonomy* (1st edn, Hart 2007) 1.

[25] eg in *Pretty v United Kingdom* App no 2346/02 (ECtHR, 29 April 2002) 423. The ECtHR found that art 8 ECHR included the ability to refuse medical treatment and that the imposition of treatment on a patient who has not consented 'would quite clearly interfere with a person's physical integrity in a manner capable of engaging the rights protected under art 8(1) of the Convention'. The link between the right to privacy and autonomy is thus strong. This connection has been repeatedly illustrated in the ECtHR jurisprudence dealing with individuals' fundamental life choices including, inter alia, in relation to sexual preferences/orientation, and personal and social life (including a person's interpersonal relationships). Reference to such cases illustrates the role played by the right to privacy in the development of one's personality through self-realization and autonomy (construed broadly). Here it is also interesting to refer to the notion of 'intellectual privacy' in US literature as developed by Neil Richards, *Intellectual Privacy: Rethinking Civil Liberties in the Digital Age* (OUP 2015); and for a similar line of argumentation, see Eric Barendt, 'Privacy and Freedom of Speech' in Andrew T Kenyon and Megan Richardson (eds), *New Dimensions in Privacy Law: International and Comparative Perspectives* (CUP 2006) 11–31.

[26] See Eleni Kosta, 'Surveilling Masses and Unveiling Human Rights—Uneasy Choices for the Strasbourg Court' [2018] Tilburg Law School Research Paper.

[27] Despite the extensive attempts to do so: see egDaniel J Solove, 'A Taxonomy of Privacy' (2006) 154 University of Pennsylvania Law Review 477.

[28] Feldman notes that there are four dimensions within each of these social spheres that need to be considered, namely space, time, action, and information, with the privacy-related rights being claimed therein dependent on the circumstances and, thus, which of the dimensions is at stake. David Feldman, 'Secrecy, Dignity, or Autonomy? Views of Privacy as a Civil Liberty' (1994) 47 Current Legal Problems 41, 52.

the conceptualization of privacy in terms of appropriate (or indeed inappropriate) information flows.[29]

In weighing the circumstances in light of the relevant dimension, Feldman further observes that there are certain values that will fluctuate in importance depending on the context, such as, inter alia, secrecy (better conceptualized as selective disclosure), dignity, and autonomy.[30] Such an approach aligns well with the ECtHR case law on Article 8 of the ECHR in that, although there is much discussion of 'secrecy' (ie the autonomous control of information), the right to privacy also encompasses a conceptualization of privacy defined in terms of intimacy or seclusion but, importantly, also as freedom of action, self-determination, and autonomy. It also seems to align with the United Nations (UN) Human Rights Committee's conceptualization of the right to privacy in Article 17 of the International Covenant on Civil and Political Rights (ICCPR).[31] Feldman argues that there is a strong link with controlling the boundaries of social spheres within the traditional conception of liberal individualism and, with this, the notion of autonomy.[32]

Although Feldman's approach is just one account, his conceptualization seems to share some overlaps with others. For example, Moreham understands privacy in the common law 'as the state of desired inaccess'[33] and the seminal article by Warren and Brandeis argued for the 'right to be let alone' and essentially the right be secluded from the invasions of the press.[34] Writing through a 'law and emotion' lens, Taslitz sees privacy as the solution to the fear of being misjudged, given that it deals with the creation of boundaries and protects us from being mis-defined and judged out of context or, in other words, our way of expressing our need for 'individualized justice: for being judged for who we really are'.[35] There is also a significant overlap with discussions of informational privacy in the United States (US), which, as noted by Bennett, is broadly

[29] Helen Nissenbaum, *Privacy in Context: Technology, Policy, and the Integrity of Social Life* (Stanford University Press 2009); Helen F Nissenbaum, 'Privacy as Contextual Integrity' (2004) 79 Washington Law Review 119.

[30] Feldman (n 28) 53–59.

[31] See *Coeriel & Aurik v the Netherlands* Comm 453/1991 (1994) [10.2]. 'The Committee observes that article 17 provides, inter alia, that no one shall be subjected to arbitrary or unlawful interference with his privacy, family, home or correspondence. The Committee considers that the notion of privacy refers to the sphere of a person's life in which he or she can freely express his or her identity, be it by entering into relationships with others or alone.'

[32] Feldman (n 28) 53–59.

[33] Nicole A Moreham, 'Privacy in the Common Law: A Doctrinal and Theoretical Analysis' (2005) 121 Law Quarterly Review 628, 636.

[34] Samuel D Warren and Louis D Brandeis, 'The Right to Privacy' (1890) 4 Harvard Law Review 193.

[35] See Andrew E Taslitz, 'The Fourth Amendment in the Twenty-First Century: Technology, Privacy, and Human Emotions' (2002) 65 Law and Contemporary Problems 125.

analogous to data protection.[36] The classic definition of informational privacy is provided by Westin, who described it as 'the claim of individuals, groups or institutions to determine for themselves when, how and to what extent information about them is communicated to others'.[37] This individual rights-based understanding of privacy has certainly significantly influenced understandings of privacy.

(c) Recognizing differences

A focus on control has, therefore, transcended borders and although it seems closely imbricated with harm there is also an important connection between control, autonomy, and the liberal objective of the legislation. However, as Bygrave notes, 'the grip of that paradigm varies from country to country and culture to culture' in that there is also a recognition in Europe that data protection has a more collective dimension since it is necessary for active participation in public life.[38] The importance of these collective/societal values is also a potential significant part of data protection laws. In analysing the different ideologies underpinning the European and US approaches, Lindsay describes the difference as 'deep-seated':

> On the one hand, the American approach takes autonomous individuals as given, and conceives the role of the law as one of setting limits on government in order to secure pre-existing individual autonomy. On the other hand, the European approach regards individual autonomy as being only fully realised in society, and conceives an important role for the law in creating the conditions for autonomous individuals as participating members of a community.[39]

It is important to note, therefore, that despite the analysis of the merits of control in jurisdictions such as the US, it is sometimes difficult to translate insights directly between jurisdictions, given the significantly diverging substantive provisions in the laws of each jurisdiction but also conceptually in terms of their respective underpinnings.[40]

[36] Colin J Bennett, *Regulating Privacy: Data Protection and Public Policy in Europe and the United States* (Cornell University Press 1992) 14.

[37] Alan F Westin, *Privacy and Freedom* (Atheneum 1967) 7. This has been repeatedly linked to the discussion on the 'ownership' of personal data, a rhetoric which repeatedly emerges in policy.

[38] Lee A Bygrave, 'Privacy and Data Protection in an International Perspective' [2010] Scandinavian Studies in Law 172.

[39] David Lindsay, 'An Exploration of the Conceptual Basis of Privacy and the Implications for the Future of Australian Privacy Law' (2005) 29 Melbourne University Law Review 131, 169.

[40] Lynskey, *The Foundations of EU Data Protection Law* (n 7) 178.

More specifically, it could be that the critiques of control speak well to the US circumstances but do not reflect the position elsewhere, such as in Europe. As mentioned in Chapter 2, in the US, informational privacy has historically been dealt with by a patchwork of statutes and, although there have been significant developments in the adoption of GDPR-style statutory protections at the state level, this has yet to manifest itself in federal legislation in the regulation of the private sector or in the form of a federal constitutional right to data privacy/protection. Similarly, in Australia, although there is the Privacy Act 1988 (Cth) at the federal level, there are significant divergences in the standards of protection afforded between this and international comparators such as the GDPR. Furthermore, and, more conceptually, despite preambular references to the right to privacy in Article 17 of the ICCPR and the obvious aim of protecting it, or at least, balancing it with the public interests associated with personal data use, there is no constitutional right to privacy or data privacy/protection recognized in Australian federal law. This further reflects the point that although the ICCPR is potentially of significance, its impact on the application of national data protection laws in reality may be limited.

2. Privacy or data protection?

It is therefore unclear what this focus on privacy means for data protection law and the conceptual value of control in these jurisdictions and how they compare. This lack of clarity is impacted by the uncertainty surrounding the notion of privacy itself. Indeed, although I provided only a smattering of the different conceptualizations of privacy in the previous subsection, it is sufficient to make the simple point that scholars have struggled to identify the interests that should be protected by privacy laws, even if there are some commonalities shared in several of these theories regarding the need to respect boundaries.[41] This perhaps explains why privacy and its related interests are never defined in data protection laws. However, this potentially detracts from their capacity for prescriptive guidance, thereby perpetuating the uncertainty regarding their conceptual basis.[42] To confuse matters further, privacy is clearly not the only interest at stake in data protection law, with the economic or market-making driver also playing a significant role as described in Chapter 2. However, there

[41] See Hughes (n 23).
[42] Lee A Bygrave, *Data Privacy Law: An International Perspective* (OUP 2014) 119.

are also interests beyond these examples. For instance, Article 1 of Convention 108 + states:

> The purpose of this Convention is to protect every individual, whatever his or her nationality or residence, with regard to the processing of their personal data, thereby contributing to respect for his or her human rights and fundamental freedoms, and in particular the right to privacy.[43]

This extremely broad statement of the Convention's object and purpose therefore leaves open a huge range of interests upon which the conceptual basis may be grounded.[44] A similar statement is contained in Article 1(2) of the GDPR, but the uncertainty is made even more complicated in the European Union (EU), given the distinct right to data protection in Article 8 of the EU Charter of Fundamental Rights (Charter). Indeed, in the EU it can be argued that the focus on control or informational self-determination is directly linked to the right to data protection provided for in Article 8 of the Charter and thus not to privacy. More specifically, the draft versions of the Charter made specific reference to self-determination and, despite its deletion, as mentioned in Chapter 5, it is argued by some that the right is still very much driven by this notion and thus strongly linked with the concept and with the ability to develop one's personality.[45] Through such a conceptualization, data protection's underlying rationales of autonomy and informational self-determination pursue the tackling of (informational) power asymmetries that are particularly prevalent today, hastened by technological progress and market forces.[46] A focus on control, however, does not automatically render us entirely and solely responsible for what happens to our personal data, and recognizing control rights in statute does not exclude the capacity for paternalistic interventions. The simple fact that we have data protection law as a statutory intervention in many

[43] Modernized Convention for the Protection of Individuals with Regard to the Processing of Personal Data (Convention 108 +), art 1.

[44] This argument is based on the same one made by Bygrave in relation to the old Convention 108. See Bygrave, *Data Privacy Law* (n 42) 119.

[45] This link between the notion of informational self-determination and data protection owes its foundations to the German Federal Constitutional Court (*Bundesverfassungsgericht*) and the 1983 Population Census case *Volkszählungsurteil* [1983] BVerfGE BvR 209/83, with some scholars suggesting that this case has been very influential in the development of EU data protection law, see Jef Ausloos, *The Right to Erasure in EU Data Protection Law* (OUP 2020) 60–69.

[46] Antoinette Rouvroy and Yves Poullet, 'The Right to Informational Self-Determination and the Value of Self-Development: Reassessing the Importance of Privacy for Democracy' in Serge Gutwirth and others (eds), *Reinventing Data Protection?* (Springer Netherlands 2009) 68–69 <http://link.springer.com/10.1007/978-1-4020-9498-9> accessed 16 January 2015; Serge Gutwirth, *Privacy and the Information Age* (Raf Casert tr, Rowman & Littlefield 2002) 86.

jurisdictions designed to constrain the behaviour of those processing personal data is clear evidence of this point.

Accordingly, there is potentially a conceptual difference in the starting points of different jurisdictions, and although the GDPR is often singled out as a fundamental rights-based regime in contrast to others, its focus on safeguarding the distinct EU right also represents a fundamental difference. The right to data protection, however, has been positioned in a variety of ways in the respective constitutional traditions of the Member States of the EU[47] and therefore, at least to some extent, is itself an unknown quantity with uncertain overlaps with the right to respect for private life protected in Article 7 of the Charter and Article 8 of the ECHR. Despite the fact that both the rights undoubtedly protect information or data privacy/protection, it has been repeatedly argued that the right to data protection serves objectives beyond the protection of privacy and likewise that privacy incorporates aspects which remain out of focus for the protection of personal data.[48]

More specifically, the right to privacy encompasses matters extending well beyond those which fall within the right to data protection in that, although the right to privacy includes data or informational privacy matters (at least at first glance) in line with the right to data protection, it also encompasses protections which do not hang on the informational component. Indeed, de Hert and Gutwirth observe that 'few direct manifestations of intimacy-oriented conceptions of privacy can be found in the provisions of data protection laws and, conversely, broader privacy concepts are not of a nature to explain data protection principles such as purpose limitation, data quality or security'.[49] In support of the authors' contention one can also refer to Lynskey, who notes

[47] eg Fuster categorizes the approaches into five groups, namely where (1) the protection of personal data is linked to another right such as the right to data protection (such as the right to privacy); (2) the protection of personal data is connected to a *sui generis* fundamental right in the constitution or as a norm with constitutional status (by providing a right to data protection); (3) there is a specific mandate to legislate for the protection of personal data; (4) the constitution does not explicitly address the protection of personal data but the constitutional court has established a *sui generis* right with similar content (eg informational self-determination in Germany); and (5) there is no clear linkage between fundamental rights and personal data protection. Gloria González Fuster, *The Emergence of Personal Data Protection as a Fundamental Right of the EU* (1st edn, Springer 2014) 175.

[48] See eg Gloria González Fuster and Raphaël Gellert, 'The Fundamental Right of Data Protection in the European Union: In Search of an Uncharted Right' (2012) 26 International Review of Law, Computers & Technology 73; Maria Tzanou, 'Data Protection as a Fundamental Right next to Privacy? "Reconstructing" a Not so New Right' (2013) 3 International Data Privacy Law 88; Juliane Kokott and Christoph Sobotta, 'The Distinction between Privacy and Data Protection in the Jurisprudence of the CJEU and the ECtHR' (2013) 3 International Data Privacy Law 222; Paul De Hert and Serge Gutwirth, 'Data Protection in the Case Law of Strasbourg and Luxemburg: Constitutionalisation in Action' in Serge Gutwirth and others (eds) (n 46); Lynskey, *The Foundations of EU Data Protection Law* (n 7) 103–04.

[49] De Hert and Gutwirth (n 48) 8.

that the positioning of data protection as a distinct right is appealing, in that it explains why privacy law does not cover all aspects of data protection and also that it respects the diverging constitutional traditions of the Member States.[50]

A good illustration of the differences in scope between the right to data protection and the right to privacy is evident in the fact that data protection applies to personal data in the public domain, whereas for privacy and private information this is context-specific.[51] This difficulty, which is evident in privacy theory, is also manifested in the case law of the ECtHR on Article 8 of the ECHR.[52] Indeed, the ECtHR decisions have dealt with the dissemination of publicly available information and thus an infringement of privacy by publication as opposed to the initial collection of the information.[53] Although reference can be made to the dictum from *Rotaru v Romania* that 'public information can fall within the scope of private life where it is systematically collected and stored', some conceptual challenges remain.[54]

In her analysis of the rights to data protection and privacy, Lynskey delineates the rights on the basis of their substantive scope of application with reference to ECtHR case law on Article 8 of the ECHR and Court of Justice of the European Union (Court of Justice) case law on Article 8 of the Charter, respectively.[55] In particular, she highlights that the right to data protection covers a broader range of data and data-related actions. More specifically, Lynskey refers to the fact that (1) the concept of personal data is not context-dependent relative to the notion of 'privacy interference'; (2) the definition of personal data includes data relating to an unidentified yet 'identifiable' natural person; and (3) data protection offers a broader range of rights for individuals than privacy.[56] Hence, despite acknowledging that there is a large degree of overlap between the respective rights, the author argues that the right to

[50] Lynskey, *The Foundations of EU Data Protection Law* (n 7) 104.

[51] Here reference can be made to the traditional conceptual difficulties associated with defining when the right to privacy applies in public as such a claim seems almost paradoxical at first sight. See Helen Nissenbaum, 'Protecting Privacy in an Information Age: The Problem of Privacy in Public' (1998) 17 Law and Philosophy 559, 567.

[52] The leading case here is *Von Hannover v Germany* App no 59320/00 (ECtHR, 24 June 2004) 294. Reference can also be made to *Peck v the United Kingdom* App no 44647/98 (ECtHR, 28 January 2003) 44. And also the more recent decision in *Satakunnan Markkinapörssi OY and Satamedia OY v Finland* App no 931/13 (ECtHR, 27 June 2017) 607.

[53] Therefore, as noted by Edwards and Urquhart, '[w]hat remains less clear is if (or when) Article 8 interprets as an infringement recording, processing and storage of private material disclosed in public, rather than its actual dissemination'. See Lilian Edwards and Lachlan Urquhart, 'Privacy in Public Spaces: What Expectations of Privacy Do We Have in Social Media Intelligence?' (2016) 24 International Journal of Law and Information Technology 279, 300.

[54] *Rotaru v Romania* App no 28341/95 (ECtHR, 4 May 2000) 192 [43].

[55] Orla Lynskey, 'Deconstructing Data Protection: The "Added-Value" of a Right to Data Protection in the EU Legal Order' (2014) 63 International & Comparative Law Quarterly 569.

[56] ibid 581–86.

data protection can arguably be understood as offering individuals more control over their data relative to the right to privacy and that this separation is driven by (1) the desire to promote informational self-determination which flows from an individual's right to personality, and (2) the connected point of aiming to alleviate power and information asymmetries between individuals and those that process personal data.[57] Therefore scholars point to important differences between the rights even if the analysis of one leads us to cross over into the other and there is uncertainty as to the precise meaning of the right to data protection.

Moreover, as described in Chapter 5, even leaving aside the uncertain overlaps between the rights to data protection and privacy, there are those who construe the right to data protection, for instance, as a system of (fairness) checks and balances or, alternatively, as a right to a rule.[58] Consequently, it seems that understanding the right to data protection as linked to informational self-determination may be controversial, as it is not a construct familiar to all EU Member States.[59] However, even if we conceptualize the right to data protection alternatively as being about fairness checks and balances, for instance, it still seems to indicate that it is important to establish a framework for the protection of personal data and to provide rights, given the explicit reference to consent and the right to access in Article 8(2) of the Charter. In addition, these checks and balances could still require defaults to be set in favour of the individual even where data subject choice does not play a role. Undoubtedly, such a conceptualization nevertheless recognizes the inevitability and benefits of data processing, but at the same time seeks to prevent disproportionate impacts on the individual and society irrespective of how one construes the right.[60] In this regard, it is interesting to note some of the other values linked to the emergence of data protection laws outlined by Bygrave and, in particular, those associated with data quality and notions such as the importance of context.[61] These were

[57] ibid 587–97.

[58] See generally Hielke Hijmans, *The European Union as Guardian of Internet Privacy: The Story of Art 16 TFEU* (Softcover reprint of original 1st edn of 2016 edn, Springer 2018); Lorenzo Dalla Corte, 'A Right to a Rule: On the Essence and Rationale of the Fundamental Right to Personal Data Protection' in Rosamunde van Brakel and others (eds), *Data Protection and Democracy* (Hart 2020).

[59] Lynskey, *The Foundations of EU Data Protection Law* (n 7) 178–79. Indeed, it should be recognized that the EU is a *sui generis* legal order in itself, and that the proper interpreter of the Charter provisions is the Court of Justice, albeit with reference to the national constitutional traditions of the Member States and international fundamental rights mechanisms. Therefore, although it may be incorrect to transplant informational self-determination from the German constitutional tradition, this does not exempt the potential for the Court of Justice to develop its own approach.

[60] See generally Federico Ferretti, 'Data Protection and the Legitimate Interest of Data Controllers: Much Ado about Nothing or the Winter of Rights?' (2014) 51 Common Market Law Review 843, 849.

[61] Bygrave, *Data Protection Law: Approaching Its Rationale, Logic and Limits* (n 13) 136–37.

also significant in the adoption of some of the earlier national data protection laws and they certainly appear to point to considerations well beyond those encapsulated by what can be regarded as privacy concerns.[62]

Therefore, although the significance of the more apparent privacy focus in certain jurisdictions (even where no such right may exist) compared to that evident in the GDPR is something of an 'unknown quantity', control is certainly not the only value protected in data protection laws. We have to be mindful, therefore, that data protection legislation serves different objectives. For example, even viewing data protection as a distinct right covering a broader scope of information, the GDPR can be positioned as a legislative instrument designed *in part* to be a more effective mechanism for informational self-determination and personal development by fostering increased data subject control over their personal data through a variety of checks and balances in order (*as to the remaining part*) to ensure the better functioning of the internal market.[63] Indeed, we must not forget that data protection laws have dualist goals—protecting data protection/privacy and market-making/facilitation. These statutory frameworks are hence not just about control and not just about the right to data protection/privacy—data protection laws establish a system of checks and balances often based on a set of principles. There may be other competing values. For instance, Bygrave refers to operational efficiency as a potential example of a value on the side of those processing personal data.[64]

Understanding the values behind the legislation is thus of significant importance and, I would argue, far from clear. There are uncertainties linked to the scope of—and interests protected by—the right to privacy but also the right to data protection and its connection to and differences from privacy. The development of data protection law in many other jurisdictions is also a factor here given that, at its outset, data protection developed mostly in liberal democracies in North America, Europe, Australia and New Zealand.[65] Indeed, this also reflects the potential for the efficiency-orientated values to take the reins, as demonstrated by instruments at the international level, such as the Asia-Pacific Economic Cooperation (APEC) Privacy Framework, but also at the national level. In the Singaporean Personal Data Protection Act, for example, there is no explicit reference to the right to privacy—or any such constitutional right for that matter—demonstrating an obvious disconnect from the approach evident

[62] Bygrave, *Data Privacy Law* (n 42) 3.

[63] See Damian Clifford and Jef Ausloos, 'Data Protection and the Role of Fairness' [2018] Yearbook of European Law 1.

[64] Bygrave, *Data Protection Law: Approaching Its Rationale, Logic and Limits* (n 13) 160–64.

[65] ibid 125–64.

in other jurisdictions. Hence, although legislators can be motivated by the desire to mitigate the fears of individuals due, inter alia, to their own concerns regarding data processing and a desire to embed a notion of control, this might not represent the full picture.

It is difficult to differentiate the genuine emotional concerns of legislators from the ordinary demands of politics—sometimes laws can be purely expressive or symbolic in nature.[66] Thus, it could be argued that data protection law aims to change how people feel about risks of harm through a system of checks and balances with a mere symbolic appearance of control and that this is the very point of the legislation in terms of the economic/(in)efficiency fears discussed in Chapter 2.[67] In fact, there is certain evidence to suggest that having a sense of control can impact a data subject's decision to provide personal data and, thus, lead to over-disclosure,[68] and the fact that we have increasingly robust frameworks but an apparent erosion of our data protection and privacy is seemingly paradoxical.[69] Emotions certainly affect our judgements about risk. The exact role of emotion in risk perception, however, is disputed. In his foreword to the edited collection *Emotions and Risky Technologies*, Robert Solomon discusses how someone with a fear of flying may objectively be aware of just how low the risk of an accident is without this knowledge having any effect on their subjective fear.[70] Fear appears to blur the objective appraisal of the risk. Solomon explains how such examples have been used to argue for a dichotomy between emotion and reason, with the actions of individuals then presented as paradoxes. This reflects the dominant understanding of the nature of emotion in the perception of risk, with a range of scholarship describing emotion as an irrational heuristic bias.[71] In other words, this literature argues that emotion biases our quantitative assessment of risk. When they lack the empirical evidence, or the capacity to understand evidence, it suggests that ordinary people rely on emotional reactions to inform their risk perceptions.

[66] Carol Sanger, 'Legislating with Affect: Emotion and Legislative Law Making' (2013) 53 Nomos 38, 42.

[67] This is a point adapted from an argument made by Sanger, see ibid 40.

[68] Alessandro Acquisti, Laura Brandimarte, and George Loewenstein, 'Privacy and Behavioral Economics' in Bart P Knijnenburg and others (eds), *Modern Socio-Technical Perspectives on Privacy* (Springer International 2022) 71–72 <https://doi.org/10.1007/978-3-030-82786-1_4> accessed 12 September 2023.

[69] Lee A Bygrave, 'The Future of Privacy Law Scholarship: Some Brief Reflections' (2016) 2 European Data Protection Law Review 459, 459.

[70] Robert C Solomon, 'Foreword: "Acceptable Risk"—On the Rationality (and Irrationality) of Emotional Evaluations of Risk' in Sabine Roeser (ed), *Emotions and Risky Technologies*, vol 5 (Springer Netherlands 2010) <http://link.springer.com/10.1007/978-90-481-8647-1> accessed 17 August 2017.

[71] Roeser's edited collection demonstrates the difference between the dominant approach and the alternative by having contributions from both sides of the debate, see Sabine Roeser (ed), Emotions and Risky Technologies (n 70).

As described in the previous chapters, however, emotions play a role in all decision-making. This has led scholars to suggest that emotions are far more complex in risk assessments than mere reactions, in that they are anticipatory and involve some uncertainty as to what course of action to take.[72] However, much of the existing literature on risk and emotions maintains the separation between rationality and emotions. Emotions are understood in this literature as irrational influences, in line with Kahneman's separation between System 1 and 2 reasoning discussed in Chapter 4.[73] There is an established body of empirical research exploring this heuristic role for emotion in the analysis of personal and societal risks. This research suggests that people often make snap judgements based on emotional reactions to the perceived riskiness of the activity in question. Although this research acknowledges some merit to these 'emotional' decisions, the conventional view is that these judgements are not nearly as effective as slow reflective ones.[74] The literature describes how emotionally driven risk appraisals can lead people and, importantly, also legislators, to take positions that seem counter to society's best interest and is illustrative of these points.[75]

Emotions are certainly significant in the perception of risk and the outcome of decision-making. However, as the analysis in the previous chapter tells us, emotions are not only an irrational influence—they pervade decision-making including in our perceptions and decisions regarding risk. Solomon has argued, for instance, that emotions are not opposed to reason but rather are its constituents.[76] It is argued in this alternative literature that the dominant approach neglects complexity by understanding risk perception in technocratic terms, thereby failing to explicitly reflect on the values that are relevant to risk perception.[77] On the basis of such an understanding, the role of emotion in risk assessment is more complicated than theories that simply dichotomize reason and emotion would suggest. Despite the disagreement regarding the exact role of emotion in risk perception, however, there is still a lot of common ground between these accounts—emotions such as fear certainly play an important role in policymaking, whether you see this as an irrational bias or one of the

[72] See Solomon (n 70).

[73] Daniel Kahneman, 'Maps of Bounded Rationality: Psychology for Behavioral Economics' (2003) 93 The American Economic Review 1449, 1451.

[74] ibid.

[75] Cass Sunstein, *Laws of Fear: Beyond the Precautionary Principle* (CUP 2009).

[76] Solomon (n 70); Dan M Kahan, 'Two Conceptions of Emotion in Risk Regulation' (2008) 156 University of Pennsylvania Law Review 740; Dan M Kahan, 'Emotion in Risk Regulation: Competing Theories' in Roeser (ed), Emotions and Risky Technologies (n 70); Sabine Roeser, 'Emotional Reflections About Risks' in ibid.

[77] See Kahan, 'Emotion in Risk Regulation: Competing Theories' (n 76).

constituents of reason. There may be a whole range of reasons for feeling a particular way—some of which may be gut reactions but the majority involving some deliberative evaluation of a specific situation. This line of scholarship therefore argues that emotions can act in conjunction with rationality. Thus, an alternative to the conventional understanding is that emotions play a role in terms of both good and bad decisions about risk—whatever this might mean.

Leaving aside the uncertainties, however, and focusing purely on the effects of data protection law in terms of its capacity to affect behaviour and outcomes neglects a discussion of the values these laws aim to promote (and whether control is in fact one of them). The point to take away, then, is that those who are critical of data protection law are often more focused on control's instrumental value, meaning that they miss the uncertainty regarding its precise conceptual value. Data protection scholarship also often seems to fail to account for the fact that control is just one of data protection law's potential underlying conceptual values. We certainly have to be mindful of economic objectives of these frameworks. Although I appreciate the challenges to the instrumental role of control, I believe that such critiques do not fully account for its potential conceptual value and what this might mean in light of the other potential values such as efficiency and, for example, the facilitation of personal data transfers.

Without a clearer understanding of data protection law's conceptual values, the more critical instrumentalist literature may also be making assumptions when judging the success or failure of data protection law.[78] A failure to engage with the non-instrumentalist values of data protection thus needs to be taken into account when assessing the significance of the critics' conclusions. To clarify, it may be that data protection law, at least in certain jurisdictions, is more aptly described as being grounded in the need for fair personal data processing rather than control. Or, alternatively, perhaps we should take into account arguments in favour of property rights in personal data and that data protection law should promote this stricter understanding of control as a value. Although I am far from convinced by the second of these options, for reasons eloquently outlined by Weatherall, it should be noted more generally that with a more accurate understanding of data protection law's conceptual values we would be able to argue more convincingly that the instrumentalist critiques of data protection law are (or indeed are not) fatal.[79]

[78] Building on a point made by Cane and colleagues in an administrative law context, see Cane and others (n 1) 346–64.

[79] See Kimberley Weatherall, 'IP and Data, IP in Data, IP as Data' in Clifford, Paterson, and Lau (eds) (n 3).

C. Affective Challenge to Rationality and Reform

The analysis of the potential conceptual value of control in the previous section does not account for the instrumental challenges of accounting for it in practice. Interestingly, a law and emotion analysis arguably complements this instrumentalist critique. Although data protection law provides subjective control rights so that we can make our own choices, as described in Chapter 4 it assumes our objective rational capacity to make them and fails to account for the role of our emotions in decision-making, understanding it as merely the by-product of a choice or as a bias negatively impacting our capacity to make a 'rational' one. This false dichotomy between rationality and emotions arguably undermines the instrumental role played by control. In this section, I will argue that we should be wary of removing the room for subjective rights in data protection, as the control-orientated approach to data protection law may be expressing society's cultural values; instead, therefore, I will look at ways in which these subjective aspects could be better catered for in the regulatory framework.

1. Emotion and by design processes

Accounting for the role of emotion will enhance the effectiveness of the legal protections provided in data protection law but it also explains their significance. There is arguably an important value in the protection of personal data as being linked to the safeguarding of individuals from harm but also our autonomous capacity to choose. This does not mean that we should never consider limiting or even removing the role of the individual. Data protection has its limitations, but I believe the solution is not to replace data protection law or remove the data subject as a key actor from the framework. Instead, I think we should supplement data protection law and in some cases reform it. Thinking more normatively, there may also be a case for a broader shift. Indeed, as explained in Chapter 4, seeing emotion as part of rationality as a normative construct is consistent with the conceptual starting point that emotions are typically based on a belief or judgement[80] and thus that emotion should be

[80] See eg Martha C Nussbaum, *Upheavals of Thought: The Intelligence of Emotions* (CUP 2003); Jon Elster, *Alchemies of the Mind: Rationality and the Emotions* (Digital printing, CUP 2003); Martha C Nussbaum, '"Secret Sewers of Vice": Disgust, Bodies, and the Law' in Susan Bandes (ed), *The Passions of Law* (New York University Press 2001); Dan M Kahan and Martha C Nussbaum, 'Two Conceptions of Emotion in Criminal Law' (1996) 96 Columbia Law Review 269.

included in the conceptualization of rationality.[81] As emotion plays a key role in all decision-making, a natural question is how emotion may be harnessed to safeguard autonomous decision-making capacity.

In this vein, more attention needs to be given to the emotional context of data protection. Stark refers to this process as '"data visceralization"—making the tie between our feelings and our data visible, tangible, and emotionally appreciable'.[82] Underlying this approach is the fact that emotions play a key role in the appreciation of risk and, therefore, there is a need to explore how insights into emotions could be harnessed to bolster risk perceptions.[83] Embedding a cognitive theory of emotion in data protection law could help individuals focus on salient aspects.[84] One can point here to the potential role for human–computer interaction and user interface (UI) and user experience (UX) designers[85] to reflect the needs of users in technology design to respond to the regulatory challenges in a more contextually aware manner.[86] It is well established in technology law that design plays an important role in the regulation (construed broadly) of human behaviour.[87] There is therefore room for further analysis exploring how such an aim could be practically realized, and this also points to the need for further interdisciplinary research to embed such insights within human–computer interactions.[88] Designers are increasingly required to

[81] Sabine Roeser, 'The Role of Emotions in Judging the Moral Acceptability of Risks' (2006) 44 Safety Science 689, 695.

[82] Luke Stark, 'The Emotional Context of Information Privacy' (2016) 32 The Information Society 14, 23. For a similar proposal in relation to privacy policies, see Ryan Calo, 'Against Notice Skepticism in Privacy (and Elsewhere)' (2012) 87 Notre Dame Law Review 1027.

[83] See Kahan, 'Emotion in Risk Regulation: Competing Theories' (n 76).

[84] Roeser, 'Emotional Reflections About Risks' (n 76) 238.

[85] To clarify:

> [t]he fact of telling the user what they can and cannot do falls within the user interface design (or UI) which strives to build a coherent visual language. It is built through the design of interactions or IxD, i.e. how the interface interacts between the system and the user, to enable it to achieve its objectives. The concept of user experience (or UX) has recently emerged; it includes an expanded version of the design of interaction focusing on the user journey as a whole, focusing on the emotional quality of experience and the commitment between a service and its users.

Régis Chatellier and others, 'Shaping Choices in the Digital World From Dark Patterns to Data Protection: The Influence of Ux/Ui Design on User Empowerment' (Commission nationale de l'informatique et des libertés 2019) IP Reports Innovation and Foresight N°06 8.

[86] Lachlan Urquhart, 'Ethical Dimensions of User Centric Regulation' (2018) 47 SIGCAS Computers & Society 81, 84.

[87] See eg Lawrence Lessig, 'The Law of the Horse: What Cyber Law Might Teach' (1999) 113 Harvard Law Review 501; Lawrence Lessig, *Code: And Other Laws of Cyberspace* (Basic Books 1999); Lawrence Lessig, *Code: Version 2.0* (Basic Books 2006).

[88] See Lachlan Urquhart and Tom Rodden, 'New Directions in Information Technology Law: Learning from Human–Computer Interaction' (2017) 31 International Review of Law, Computers & Technology 150.

take ethical decisions beyond what is strictly provided for within legal frameworks, and thus design decisions are not neutral.[89]

More collaborative research between human–computer interaction designers, philosophers, legal scholars, etc is hence needed to translate such abstract debates into practical outcomes and to prevent any potential 'moral overload' in relation to the difficult decisions requiring complicated trade-offs and reflection.[90] Although such research is necessary to map the potential in this area, from a legal perspective some might argue that it remains too abstract and future-orientated (at least for now). Admittedly, even though broad requirements such as data protection/privacy by default and by design could be construed as fostering the need for controllers to explore such means of harnessing data subject engagement to empower individuals, this may be wishful thinking in light of the process-orientated approach to compliance (see Chapter 5). This may also be the case given that, as noted by Solove, the abstract nature of the harms linked to choices regarding personal data makes them more difficult to translate into visceral terms.[91]

Even leaving aside this very valid point, we may in any case have to wait until design practices are incorporated more fully into the corpus of information technology (IT) regulation strategies to find out.[92] Certainly, commercial interests run counter to these developments, with certain commercial operators in fact having been shown to deploy deceptive design strategies such as dark patterns to deceive/manipulate data subjects (see Chapter 4). A more pragmatic regulatory enforcement approach without a more fundamental shift might then be to focus instead on what is clearly unfair, at least until such time as the law more actively embraces the regulation of design practices.[93] As Waldman notes, '[r]ights of control still require individuals to overcome every trick designed into platforms that encourage inertia or inaction or disclosure',[94] and thus there is plenty of room for further regulatory action in this regard. There have been moves to ban dark patterns, for example, in some of the state consumer data privacy laws being adopted in the

89 Here reference can for instance be made to the report issued by the Institute of Electrical and Electronic Engineers (IEEE) on ethically aligned design which will play an important role in determining the high-level principles for the IEEE community.'Ethically Aligned Design: A Vision for Prioritising Human Well-Being with Autonomous and Intelligent Systems' (Institute of Electrical and Electronic Engineers (IEEE) 2019) 082-02–19.

90 Urquhart (n 86) 89.

91 Daniel J Solove, 'Introduction: Privacy Self-Management and the Consent Dilemma' (2013) 126 Harvard Law Review 1880, 1885.

92 Urquhart (n 86) 84. See Chatellier and others (n 85) calling for further research in this area.

93 This does not undermine the need for such research.

94 Ari Ezra Waldman, *Industry Unbound: The Inside Story of Privacy, Data, and Corporate Power* (CUP 2021) 107.

US[95] and in the EU in the Digital Services Act,[96] and there has also been significant enforcement action in both these jurisdictions as examples.[97]

Such moves toward legislating also speak to how we regulate the design of such technologies in order to enhance public trust and thus the broader potential of impact assessments in this regard.[98] It is established in the technology law literature that design plays an important role in regulating human behaviour.[99] Such developments are important as they clarify the potentially significant role of the notion of data protection by design and default (or *by design* obligations more generally[100]) and impact assessments but also the acceptable limits of what is permissible under data protection law as discussed in Chapter 5. Underlying design decisions are the threats posed to human rights such as privacy, freedom of expression, equality, and individual autonomy, with the law and policy analysis providing insights into (1) the mitigation of the undesired effects of AI; (2) the need for regulation; and (3) the form that any changes should take.[101] I believe that the regulation of design and, indeed, the design process must therefore extend beyond the confines of data protection law frameworks and gain a more detailed appreciation of the risk of harm

[95] Virginia Consumer Data Protection Act (2021), Utah Consumer Privacy Act (2022), Texas Data Privacy and Security Act (2023), Tennessee Information Protection Act (2023), Montana Consumer Data Privacy Act (2023), Iowa Consumer Data Protection Act (2023), Indiana Consumer Data Protection Act (2023), Connecticut Data Privacy Act (2022), Colorado Privacy Act (2021), and California Consumer Privacy Act of 2018.

[96] Regulation (EU) 2022/2065 of the European Parliament and of the Council of 19 October 2022 on a Single Market For Digital Services and amending Directive 2000/31/EC (Digital Services Act) (Text with EEA relevance) [2022] OJ L277/1–102.

[97] 'FTC Report Shows Rise in Sophisticated Dark Patterns Designed to Trick and Trap Consumers | Federal Trade Commission' (15 September 2022) <www.ftc.gov/news-events/news/press-releases/2022/09/ftc-report-shows-rise-sophisticated-dark-patterns-designed-trick-trap-consumers> accessed 23 September 2023; 'Data Protection Commission' (*Data Protection Commission*, 15 September 2023) <www.dataprotection.ie/news-media/press-releases/DPC-announces-345-million-euro-fine-of-TikTok> accessed 23 September 2023; Forbrukerrådet (Norwegian Consumer Council), 'Deceived by Design: How Tech Companies Use Dark Patterns to Discourage Us from Exercising Our Rights to Privacy' (*Forbrukerrådet (Norwegian Consumer Council)*, 2018) <https://fil.forbrukerradet.no/wp-content/uploads/2018/06/2018-06-27-deceived-by-design-final.pdf> accessed 25 April 2019; Chatellier and others (n 85).

[98] See Rachelle Bosua, Damian Clifford, and Megan Richardson, 'Contact-Tracing Technologies and the Problem of Trust—Framing a Right of Social Dialogue for an Impact Assessment Process in Pandemic Times' (2023) 5 Law, Technology and Humans 193.

[99] See generally, for some examples of notable works discussing design and regulation, Ian Brown and Christopher T Marsden, *Regulating Code: Good Governance and Better Regulation in the Information Age* (The MIT Press 2013); Lessig, *Code* (n 87).

[100] See Lee A Bygrave, 'Security by Design: Aspirations and Realities in a Regulatory Context' (23 May 2022) <https://papers.ssrn.com/abstract=4117110> accessed 11 June 2023.

[101] For a discussion of the regulatory challenges posed by AI and ML, see Julia Black and Andrew Douglas Murray, 'Regulating AI and Machine Learning: Setting the Regulatory Agenda' (2019) 10 European Journal of Law and Technology <www.ejlt.org/index.php/ejlt/article/view/722> accessed 29 June 2023.

linked to the uses of technologies such as E-AI, as opposed to the mere processing of personal data.[102]

The Articial Intelligence Act (AI Act) in the EU is arguably a significant example of where this is already occurring, which is certainly an important development.[103] This is particularly the case as these harms are often the consequence of (poor) design choices rather than bugs in the code/system. We can refer to the discussion in Chapter 5 of E-AI and Facial Action Coding (FACS) as an excellent example. Comparisons can be made with the moves to regulate risk-sensitive consumer products, such as pharmaceuticals, from the 1960s and 1970s onwards and the development of product liability rules and regulatory oversight mechanisms to mitigate the disparate harms linked to badly designed products. There is a need, therefore, to continue exploring how both (1) bad or technically flawed design choices, and (2) design choices that work as intended but lead to unforeseen negative outcomes should be addressed in the regulation of design practices and the design process and the circumstances in which practices or technologies can be banned. The designers of these technologies, then, are risk creators: these potential harms are the consequence of design choices.[104] Certainly, the EU is ahead in terms of some of this thinking, but generally such developments demonstrate that a more deliberate focus on design is needed to gain more robust protections, as designers are increasingly required to take ethical decisions beyond what is strictly provided for within legal frameworks. Focusing only on the regulation of the effects of AI and the collection of seemingly innocuous personal data ostensibly disconnected at the point of collection from potential harms results in opacity around the design process and cedes too much power to designers. There is therefore a need for continued socio-legal research and policymaking to focus on the design of technologies, such as E-AI, underpinned by machine learning (ML).

Data protection law, however, is still important. I believe that it has institutionalized significant changes that are positive—this is often missed in criticisms of individual control and its effectiveness. At the same time, I acknowledge that there is a difference between discussing the role of rational decision-makers generally in the law and discussing them in the context of data

[102] For a discussion of the role of impact assessment to consider broader values, see Alessandro Mantelero, *Beyond Data: Human Rights, Ethical and Social Impact Assessment in AI* (Springer Nature 2022).

[103] Proposal of the European Parliament and of the Council Laying Down Harmonised Rules on Artificial Intelligence (Artificial Intelligence Act) and Amending Certain Union Legislative Acts COM (2021) 206 final).

[104] See Lorna Woods, 'The Duty of Care in the Online Harms White Paper' (2019) 11 Journal of Media Law 6, 13.

protection law specifically. In other words, although the more theoretical law and emotion arguments, such as the one made by Arkush questioning whether objective approaches that assume our rational capacity should simply be replaced (see Chapter 4), should be approached cautiously, this does not exclude the capacity for more paternalistic interventions being adopted as alternatives/supplements to data protection law specifically. Indeed, there are those who suggest that data protection law should not be about individual control rights and our rational capacity to protect our interests but instead about power and the facilitating of social interactions.[105]

Waldman, for instance, argues that we should be less concerned with how people feel their personal data should be protected and more worried about how the law could be framed to achieve 'the collective goal of democratic governance'.[106] This line of argumentation then leads us to an important question, namely: rather than playing around the fringes and trying to develop a better rationality construct, should we instead look to alternative regulatory interventions? This question is important given that there are countless examples of where data subjects fail to exercise control. Scholars have argued, for instance, that a focus on individual control is not just insufficient to counteract the harms associated with the information economy, but is actually counterproductive and will exacerbate them.[107] Others see control rights as a necessary component of data protection law but think that regulatory frameworks often rely too heavily on them and merely create an illusion of protection.[108] However, there is a potential difference between the reasons we have individual control in data protection law and the reasons why it fails. We arguably have individual control embedded in data protection law as we recognize a value in people being free to choose and that this has moral force even if there is no real certainty on the conceptual values underpinning data protection law. The manifestations of individual control in data protection law have clear limitations in an instrumental sense because, for reasons seemingly connected to the aim of achieving fairness and justice (but also for practical reasons), the operation of these manifestations is constructed to be assessed objectively.

The analysis in Chapters 3–5 revealed that there is no simple solution to the problems presented even if I believe the situation is not as dire as the critics

[105] See Daniel J Solove, 'Privacy and Power: Computer Databases and Metaphors for Information Privacy' (2001) 53 Stanford Law Review 1393; Julie E Cohen, *Between Truth and Power: The Legal Constructions of Informational Capitalism* (OUP 2019); Waldman, *Industry Unbound* (n 94).

[106] Waldman, 'Privacy's Rights Trap' (n 4) 99.

[107] See Waldman, 'Privacy's Rights Trap' (n 4).

[108] Solove, 'The Limitations of Privacy Rights' (n 4) 993.

present. My more theoretical point here is that a move away from control would eliminate the conceptual value it arguably aims to instil—ie affording each of us the opportunity to make subjective choices. I believe there is certainly value in control rights and thus data protection law as we know it. We should also keep in mind that proposed alternatives (1) will come with their own issues, and (2) will not necessarily stand in opposition to data protection law as we know it to the point where we will have a binary choice between one or the other. Abandoning control would effectively require a more top-down approach and further objectify regulatory interventions. As noted by Kaminski, it would mean a 'one-size-fits-most' approach.[109] It is therefore unclear whether the adoption of such regulatory interventions would actually further advantage those being regulated. Admittedly, this is very far from the idealistic aims that critics of control would hope for in a regulatory framework, but I cannot help but be sceptical. Although it may be possible to conceive of a regulatory framework that gets everything right, I believe there is just no political or indeed public appetite for such a paternalistic approach as it would run counter to the prevailing interests of the large technology platforms, for example, and also arguably legislators, meaning that some half-way house is more likely.

2. Control's practical value

Any half-way house that eliminates control or even dilutes its significance by, for example, weakening consent and/or its role could therefore, in effect, objectify the framework further. Indeed, Solove, a proponent of playing down the utility of control rights, has noted specifically in relation to the role of consent that it is both troubling but also necessary—what he refers to as the 'consent dilemma'.[110] As further noted by the author in a subsequent article, because there are those who want to trade in their personal data, want their location tracked, those who are willing to accept the business model of websites but also those who want none of these things, 'autonomy demands at least some freedom to choose even when people's choices are not in their best interests or are made under troublesome circumstances'.[111] Arguably, this also highlights the significance of *ex ante* individual choice (eg consent) but also the *ex post* opportunity

[109] Kaminski (n 6) 398.
[110] Solove, 'Introduction' (n 91).
[111] Daniel J Solove, 'Murky Consent: An Approach to the Fictions of Consent in Privacy Law' (22 January 2023) 6 <https://papers.ssrn.com/abstract=4333743> accessed 11 June 2023.

to change our minds in certain circumstances (eg consent withdrawal and data subject rights) analysed in Chapter 4.

In terms of the public appetite for regulatory protections, reference can be made to the contributions of cultural cognition theory, a conception of the cultural theory of risk and, in particular, the work of Kahan.[112] In defining the theory, Kahan describes it as a model of human rationality that sees 'emotions as constituents of reason' with individuals concerned with expressing the values that define their identities.[113] The theory therefore suggests that when confronted with risks, and debates regarding how to regulate them (if at all), we are not weighing (rationally or irrationally) the risks but are instead assessing 'the *social meaning* of that activity'[114] in order to express the values that define our identity. It operates by considering people's values along two dimensions: (1) Group: how individualistic or communitarian-orientated people are, and (2) Grid: if they prefer hierarchal structures based and clear rankings and roles or are more egalitarian in their views.[115] The theory in its essence argues that these dispositions will render people more likely to respond to risks in specific ways and that people gravitate towards the perceptions of risk depending on their worldviews.

It is thus, arguably, our worldviews that lead to expressively rational stances towards risks. Cultural cognition theory would suggest that the fears discussed in Chapter 2 are in fact expressive of certain values that have motivated emotive responses. For example, people who are more individualistic and hierarchal in their views may express fears associated with a loss of control over personal data, but they may be mindful of the impact on industry or government uses of personal data, as they perceive unconsciously that such fears will result in regulatory restrictions.[116] In fact, the fears may be more aligned with the impact of data subject mistrust or distrust in relation to the processing of personal data. In contrast, people who are more communitarian and egalitarian in their views may already be suspicious and therefore may be more open to stronger regulatory interventions. These people may be concerned by the potential for disparate impacts on more vulnerable members of the community and concerned

[112] Kahan, 'Two Conceptions of Emotion in Risk Regulation' (n 76) 108–09.
[113] ibid.
[114] ibid.
[115] See Dan M Kahan and Donald Braman, 'Cultural Cognition and Public Policy' (2006) 24 Yale Law & Policy Review 149; Dan M Kahan, 'Cultural Cognition as a Conception of the Cultural Theory of Risk' in Sabine Roeser and others (eds), *Handbook of Risk Theory: Epistemology, Decision Theory, Ethics, and Social Implications of Risk* (Springer Netherlands 2012) <https://doi.org/10.1007/978-94-007-1433-5_28> accessed 28 June 2023.
[116] These examples have been adapted from those given by Kahan and others. See Kahan and Braman (n 115); Kahan, 'Cultural Cognition as a Conception of the Cultural Theory of Risk' (n 115).

with the asymmetries in power and the effects of surveillance. They may also be more open to data sharing for communitarian purposes such as genetic research. My point is that data protection law appeals to all these groups in a way by seemingly leaving room for individual choice. It is hard to know what would happen, therefore, if control rights were removed as choices would have to be baked in.

This is an area requiring further exploration but if control rights are abandoned the outcome may seem to fly in the face of the reasons why scholars point to the need for alternatives to data protection law as we know it in the first place, thereby demonstrating a subjective assessment of what amounts to harm worthy of diluting the interests of individuals. We therefore need to consider the full extent of what removing the role of the individual from data protection law might mean in reality. Are we saying that we would have no data subject rights such as those in the GDPR? No right to object to specific uses of our data? No right to request the erasure of our information and potentially no direct right of action to bring our own claims in the protection of our interests? The road to the recognition of a broader array of rights (or indeed, their very recognition in hard law in certain jurisdictions)[117] has been a long one. It seems foolish to me to walk back from them just as data protection law is starting to grow teeth. Even if I am more optimistic as to the capacity of control rights in light of their successes, as discussed in Chapter 4, I tend nevertheless to agree with Solove that they are far from a panacea and should still sit alongside what he refers to as mechanisms to bring 'the collection, processing, and transfer of personal data under control'.[118]

Doing away with the role of the rational data subject would undermine the potential conceptual role for control as linked to the roots of liberal autonomy and effectively lead to a far more paternalistic form of governance whereby the state would decide how individuals' welfare and preferences should be formulated in the context of the processing of their personal data. Put simply, I am extremely sceptical of whether such an approach would be at all desirable and wonder if pursuing this option would result in an outcome that flies directly in the face of what the critics of control want in an alternative. As Sanger notes, '[a]lmost any subject of regulation stirs emotions in those who care about the issue at hand',[119] and those processing personal data (in particular the large technology platforms) care deeply. It seems counterintuitive to me for scholars

[117] Kaminski makes this point in the US context: see Kaminski (n 6).
[118] Solove, 'The Limitations of Privacy Rights' (n 4) 979.
[119] Sanger (n 66) 40.

to criticize control and question enforcement and the influence of big technology companies without reflecting on what their influence might result in if there were no room for data subjects to exercise subjective rights in data protection laws.

Indeed, in this regard it is arguable whether the criticisms presented by the US scholars in particular follow in the footsteps of Critical Legal Studies (CLS) in general and thus suffer from some of the same weaknesses. In essence, CLS literature, which often focuses on common law contract law, criticizes legal formalism (ie the idea that the law is a value-free set of abstract rules that can be applied to any situation with predictable outcomes) and aims to expose how judges make political decisions that serve the agenda of maintaining the existing economic and social order with a preference for form over substance.[120] In doing so, this agenda suppresses communitarian values and collective interests in favour of individualistic and market-orientated assumptions with the few examples of altruism then perceived as merely means of pre-empting more meaningful reform.[121] CLS is a broad and significant body of scholarship, but some criticisms have been made including: (1) the failure of the literature to propose genuine alternatives that account for a reality beyond a communitarian ideal;[122] (2) the overstating of certain weaknesses, including with regard to the effects of the ambiguity or indeterminacy of certain rules/principles;[123] and (3) failing to recognize that these same ambiguities can be used to generate social change.[124] These criticisms are arguably also relevant to the critiques of data protection law, a point that needs further exploration in future research. There may therefore be a more pragmatic value to instrumentalist notions of control.

The impacts of the criticisms of control have already been felt in some jurisdictions. For instance, in the debates regarding the reform of the Australian Privacy Act 1988 (Cth), the legitimacy of relying on consent has led to the proposal that individuals should have an option to opt out from the use of their information for the purposes of targeted advertising rather than requiring an

[120] eg see this argument made in the context of contract law: Roberto Mangabeira Unger, 'The Critical Legal Studies Movement' (1983) 96 Harvard Law Review 561; Duncan Kennedy, 'Form and Substance in Private Law Adjudication' (1976) 89 Harvard Law Review 1685; Robert Hillman, 'The Crisis in Modern Contract Theory' [1988] Cornell Law Faculty Publications <https://scholarship.law.cornell.edu/facpub/566> accessed 4 October 2023.

[121] eg see this argument made in the context of contract law: Unger (n 120); Kennedy (n 120); Hillman (n 120).

[122] eg see this argument made in the context of contract law (albeit in stronger terms): John Murray, Jr, 'Contract Theories and the Rise of Neoformalism' (2002) 71 Fordham Law Review 869.

[123] See eg this argument made in the context of contract law: Hillman (n 120).

[124] See eg this argument made in the context of contract law: ibid.

opt-in. Another alternative is the approach to consent adopted in Singapore where, in the Personal Data Protection Act 2012 (PDPA),[125] the legislator has adopted the notion of 'deemed consent' as a separate notion from the more substantive as opposed to formal notion of consent generally required under the Act. Deemed consent arises under the Act when (1) an individual 'voluntarily provides' personal data to an organization for a purpose provided it is reasonable;[126] (2) it is necessary for the formation or conclusion of a contract;[127] or (3) notice is given and the individual does not opt out of the collection, use, and disclosure of their personal data.[128] Although such approaches potentially increase the value of consent when it is required (eg for the trading of their information to data brokers and when sensitive personal information are used), there are clear controversies with seemingly legitimizing such business models which seem to cut to the core of the critiques of the instrumentalist value of control presented by US scholars in particular. In addition, although they are far from the wholesale abandonment of control (they are arguably just a weaker manifestation), they do demonstrate how criticisms of consent in particular can potentially lead to the further legitimization of controversial business models that the critics of the instrumental role of control use as the basis for their critique (behavioural advertising and other data extractive business models). My point is therefore simple: our choice of legislation is not one that can be neatly divided in two between control/rights-based regulatory interventions and those which prioritize notions such as trust and relationships, bans, or some other form of more paternalistic regulatory intervention.

Furthermore, although Waldman, for example, points to the need for the aggressive enforcement of competition law in the US to ensure the availability of choices for consumers and the quality of algorithmic decision-making, these are arguably not replacements for data protection law but rather complementary regimes that again have been discussed in many other jurisdictions as supplements for some time[129] and are now, finally, being applied in a complementary manner, for instance by the EU Court of Justice.[130] Even Waldman's call for bans in his sketch of a more radical alternative to data protection law as we know it[131] is certainly not prevented by the adoption of data protection legislation. For example, we can refer to the circumstances in which a decision

125 Personal Data Protection Act 2012.
126 ibid s 15(1).
127 ibid s 15(3).
128 ibid s 15A.
129 Waldman, 'Privacy's Rights Trap' (n 4) 104.
130 Case C-252/21 *Meta Platforms v Bundeskartellamt*, ECLI:EU:C:2023:537.
131 Waldman, 'Privacy's Rights Trap' (n 4) 105.

to give up some personal data may result in the formation of a valid consumer contract and how the protections afforded in consumer law (and indeed national contract law) may play a role in the regulation of market behaviour[132] or notably the EU's AI Act for example.[133] There are obvious synergies that demonstrate the importance of moving towards a transversal analysis and how different areas of law can apply together for collective aims in the regulation of the information economy. In other words, data protection law does not exist in a vacuum as is evident through the increasing alignment between different regulatory bodies.[134]

Even with the adoption of a top-down approach as a replacement for rights-based approaches, however, there is likely to be still some level of designation, meaning that the interests of individuals are likely to be further diluted through compliance-orientated thinking if we see them as a replacement instead of a supplement to data protection law. This is potentially problematic in itself. Simply put, technology-neutral regimes that apply across a range of contexts cannot provide rules for everything.[135] I believe that this points to a fundamental critique of at least some of the criticisms of control that are presented and alternatives that are suggested: they are often explicitly or implicitly focused on the private sector despite the fact that data protection regimes often apply to both public and private uses of personal data.[136] They certainly regulate the private platforms, but data protection laws are often not limited to this and thus apply to both private and public law contexts. Even where data protection laws are focused only on private organizations, however, I believe that there are still just too many contextual variables

[132] See Damian Clifford and Jeannie Marie Paterson, 'Data Rights and Contract Law: Formation, Incorporation and Vitiating Factors' in Clifford, Paterson, and Lau (eds) (n 3); Damian Clifford and Jeannie Paterson, 'Consumer Privacy and Consent: Reform in the Light of Contract and Consumer Protection Law' (2020) 94 Australian Law Journal 741.

[133] Proposal of the European Parliament and of the Council Laying Down Harmonised Rules on Artificial Intelligence (n 103).

[134] For an excellent example, see the UK Digital Regulation Cooperation Forum. DRCF, 'Home' (*DRCF*, 27 April 2023) <www.drcf.org.uk/home> accessed 23 September 2023.

[135] Kaminski (n 6) 398.

[136] eg in outlining alternative approaches in his analysis of the adoption of data protection/privacy legislation in the US, Waldman provides a brief sketch of two—which he terms a moderate approach and a more radical one—but his conceptualization of the problems is rooted in his understanding of the private sector uses of personal data. This is despite the fact that he is critical of control-orientated approaches generally. His moderate approach looks to the possibility of the Federal Trade Commission (FTC) conducting regular audits to ensure the accuracy of data in databases, the robust enforcement of the data minimization principle, and, for instance, a significant boost to the FTC's budget to create and enforce regulations. The author's sketch of the radical alternative, put simply, calls for bans—a ban on behavioural targeting and location tracking and the subsidizing of not-for-profit intermediaries that would offer alternatives—and for structural changes in terms of how the law is implemented and a move away from the 'managerial information economy'. But it is arguable that this demonstrates a very narrow understanding of these legislative frameworks. Waldman, 'Privacy's Rights Trap' (n 4) 104–05.

to account for all possibilities in a prescriptive manner within one data protection law. However, I also think that this reveals an important point, in that there is a real need to consider whether we should, for example, look to alternatives to consent as a condition for lawful processing *in certain circumstances* as, arguably, relying on it too heavily for high-risk processing contexts dilutes its value practically.

As described in Chapter 4 in particular, I think the example of the regulation of the use of cookies is a prime example of where things should have been done better. This is the quintessential example of what critics see as the failings of such frameworks and the GDPR in particular (even if the requirement is actually mandated in the EU by the *lex specialis* provisions in the ePrivacy Directive). This requirement for consent, however, is ineffective and, as I argued in Chapter 4, devalues the notion of consent or what Schermer and colleagues have referred to as a recipe for 'consent desensitisation'.[137] There have been discussions of better ways in which to regulate the consent to cookies for over fifteen years and these are a significant example of a regulatory failure to develop an approach in the interests of data subjects.[138] As noted in Chapter 4, Apple's ATT consent framing is an excellent counterexample to these failings, arguably demonstrating how this can work in practice, and the slow death of cookies could be a sign of change in this regard.[139]

It is arguable that the regulation of some of these aspects is in fact the purview of other areas of law, however, and not data protection law. Certainly, recognizing a conceptual value for control does not exclude other areas of law from regulating the environment to ensure the capacity of individuals to act autonomously and in their own best interests or, indeed, paternalistically in the interests of society. And leaving aside the uncertainties regarding the exact role of control in terms of data protection law's conceptual values, it should also be noted that, pragmatically speaking, assuming the rational capacity of data subjects may be the lesser of two evils. This certainly does not exclude the possibility of ensuring the existence of an environment that may render this normative construct more effective and realistic.

[137] Bart W Schermer, Bart Custers, and Simone van der Hof, 'The Crisis of Consent: How Stronger Legal Protection May Lead to Weaker Consent in Data Protection' (2014) 16 Ethics and Information Technology 171.

[138] For a discussion, see Brown and Marsden (n 99) 56–57.

[139] See Cristobal Cheyre and others, 'The Impact of Apple's App Tracking Transparency Framework on the App Ecosystem' (19 May 2023) <https://papers.ssrn.com/abstract=4453463> accessed 22 September 2023.

D. Expressive and Effective Data Protection

Instead of throwing everything into the bucket of individual control rights-based concerns, I believe that a more nuanced approach is required. Admittedly, however, it is hard to argue with the instrumentalist critique and, more fundamentally, the law and emotion critique espoused by Arkush that 'because so much human behaviour is nonconscious, automatic, and not readily amenable to inspection, we should reevaluate areas of law that depend on proving states of mind'.[140] In this regard, then, we may need to reevaluate at least parts of data protection law and, for instance, legislate for practices that may be de facto unfair. Despite the fact that I think the rational data subject is a functional fiction that has a practical, if not also conceptual, value in the case of data protection law, I agree with the point that we may require more paternalistic interventions in the interests of individuals. This leaves me somewhere in between the optimistic and pessimistic perspectives of those frustrated with data protection law described in Chapter 2. We have to be pragmatic but also respect nuance.

At times laws can be purely expressive or symbolic in nature—there may not always be a concern with efficacy.[141] Solove, for instance, argues that although control rights have value, a legislative approach that focuses on them simply allows policymakers to 'pat themselves on the back and claim that they did something to protect privacy, but they merely [send] people on a doomed quest'.[142] Data protection law in many jurisdictions, however, is rarely just about these control rights, as demonstrated by the discussion of accountability mechanisms and the comparative analysis of the principles generally common to data protection law instruments internationally in Chapter 5. I believe, therefore, that data protection law has an expressive purpose but that it is also intended to alter the behaviour both of individual data subjects but also of those processing personal data. Admittedly, this intention to alter behaviour may differ depending on the jurisdiction—reflecting the different conceptual values which may underpin these laws, discussed above in Section B.

Data protection law certainly has its limitations, however. A more detailed discussion of what I believe to be some of the core limitations of data protection law is thus necessary. These must be taken into account to ensure more effective protection. Nevertheless, as I will argue in this section, these limitations are distinct from its limits: data protection law's limitations are the problem

[140] David J Arkush, 'Situating Emotion: A Critical Realist View of Emotion and Nonconscious Cognitive Processes for Law and Legal Theory' (2008) 5 BYU Law Review 1275, 1356.
[141] Sanger (n 66) 42.
[142] Solove, 'The Limitations of Privacy Rights' (n 4) 985.

of data protection law, while its limits, I believe, point to data protection law's potential for intersections with other areas of the regulatory landscape and the limits of law more broadly. These other areas of law may prescribe further limits on data protection law, but they may also supplement its aims and conceptual values. We need to refine our understanding of which limitations should frustrate us and how we should pragmatically understand data protection's limits to appreciate the value of a transversal analysis. Put simply, we need to focus our frustration on the right target.

1. Frustration and limitations

Legislators might be very proud of a piece of legislation that they get over the line, but this does not mean that it will be effective. My argument in this section is simple: data protection law has limitations that affect its effectiveness, but this does not mean the wholesale abandonment of data protection law as we know it. Data protection law protects our capacity to be subjective in our choices, even if it does so by creating objective standards. Although there are clear deficits with this approach, we should not throw the baby out with the bath water. The limitations of data protection law are not its features but rather poor legislative choices or ineffective enforcement. I briefly highlight in this subsection what I argue are three obvious examples of limitations that have been demonstrated through the analysis in this book. Legislators should be mindful of these points when adopting or reforming data protection law in order to avoid frustrations.

(a) Conceptual values confusion

If we want those processing personal data to move beyond compliance in process and not in substance, we need to have a better understanding of what open-textured notions such as fairness and control mean in data protection law and from whose perspective they need to be assessed. I believe that this is necessary to realize the application of data protection law.[143] At the root of this problem is the uncertain relationship between data protection laws and privacy and data protection (and, indeed, the uncertain relationship between the rights themselves). An EU scholar might tell you that data protection law is not about privacy or perhaps only partly, or not about control or only partly, or

[143] eg Lynskey makes a similar argument. See Orla Lynskey, 'Complete and Effective Data Protection' [2023] Current Legal Problems <http://eprints.lse.ac.uk/120212/> accessed 25 September 2023.

that it is about fairness and market functioning or again, only partly.[144] In the US, Australia, New Zealand, Canada, etc data protection is data/informational privacy (albeit with variations due to differences in national constitutional traditions) and seems to be informed by notions of control. However, there are also alternatives discussed in the literature based on, for example, notions of trust[145] and relations,[146] power,[147] property,[148] or context.[149]

Although some may argue that this difference amounts to little in practice, I believe it points to the conceptual values underpinning the laws and thus how they may shape the development, judicial and regulatory interpretation, and thus application of such frameworks. As I have argued, we also need an understanding of these values in order to assess what data protection law achieves or fails to achieve. It might be that data protection law is partly about all these things, but more work is required on what values these laws actually promote and those that they should promote even if they are not actually currently discussed. This may include discussions of power or trust or relations. Admittedly, however, conceptual ambiguity may also actually be a good thing from a privacy advocate's perspective as it allows them to read more into open-textured principles than would otherwise be possible. Kaminski suggests that control rights in the data protection legislation being adopted at the state level in the US may offer a 'powerful defense on the battleground of constitutional analysis'.[150] However, if we make things explicit, privacy advocates may not like the result. Despite this point, I believe we do need at least some clarity. This is significant as data protection law's values are likely to be in conflict and, thus, we may need to understand the relationship between them, as well as differences between jurisdictions when making comparisons. Frustrations arise when scholars are speaking almost the same language but with slightly different meanings attached to similar words, and legislators have to account for differences when adopting their own data protection law reforms.

[144] For an elaboration of this uncertainty through the lens of the role of the fairness principle, see Damian Clifford, 'The Data Protection Fairness Principle and the GDPR' in Michèle Finck (ed), *Oxford Encyclopedia of EU Law* (OUP 2022).

[145] Ari Ezra Waldman, *Privacy as Trust: Information Privacy for an Information Age* (CUP 2018); Neil Richards and Woodrow Hartzog, 'Taking Trust Seriously in Privacy Law' (2016) 19 Stanford Technology Law Review 431.

[146] Neil Richards and Woodrow Hartzog, 'A Relational Turn for Data Protection?' (2020) 6 European Data Protection Law Review 492; Salomé Viljoen, 'A Relational Theory of Data Governance' (2021) 131 The Yale Law Journal 573.

[147] Solove, 'Privacy and Power' (n 105); Cohen, *Between Truth and Power* (n 105); Waldman, *Industry Unbound* (n 94).

[148] Lawrence Lessig, 'Privacy as Property' (2002) 69 Social Research: An International Quarterly 247; Paul M Schwartz, 'Property, Privacy, and Personal Data' (2004) 117 Harvard Law Review 2056.

[149] Nissenbaum, 'Privacy as Contextual Integrity' (n 29).

[150] Kaminski (n 6) 395.

(b) Regulatory over/under-reach

Data protection law needs to move beyond siloed analyses and boundaries may need to be better marked out in data protection laws in order to conform to public expectations. Although I believe that a broad definition of personal data is necessary to conform to the public's expectations but also the risks as discussed in Chapter 3, other legislative choices can restrict data protection law's scope. Perhaps the most basic criticism of data protection law, as presented in Chapter 2, is that in some forms it arguably fails to conform to the expectations of the public. For instance, in my opinion, the GDPR is a clear example of regulatory overreach. The uncertainty surrounding the application and meaning of the household exemption, which states that the Regulation does not apply to the processing of personal data 'in the course of a purely personal or household activity',[151] and the expansive notion of a controller more specifically, demonstrate how, in ways, this framework may not conform to the expectations of the public. In the EU, I think there has been a tendency in some guidance and case law interpretations to view the GDPR expansively in all circumstances, as informed by fundamental rights-based teleological interpretations. However, at least in the case of the definitions of a controller (and joint controller) and the application of the household exemption, a more pragmatic approach informed by practical realities is needed.

Indeed, it has been argued that the simple dichotomy between the notions of 'controller' and 'processor' fails to account for the complexity of the relationship rendering the obligations unclear for those trying to comply and how the guidance literature actually adds complexity rather than providing clarity.[152] Indeed, this controller/processor divide has been a clear point of contention in the academic literature and case law, in particular due to the expansive manner in which the definition of a controller has been interpreted. The Court of Justice has repeatedly stated the need to interpret the definition of a controller broadly to ensure a high level of protection for data subjects. Consequently, there is a very low threshold to be considered a joint controller, but this has raised significant problems with the scholarship highlighting scenarios where compliance is effectively impossible for a joint controller.[153] More specifically,

[151] See art 2(2)(c) of the GDPR.

[152] See René Mahieu, Joris van Hoboken, and Hadi Asghari, 'Responsibility for Data Protection in a Networked World: On the Question of the Controller, "Effective and Complete Protection" and Its Application to Data Access Rights in Europe' (2019) 10 Journal of Intellectual Property, Information Technology and E-Commerce Law <www.jipitec.eu/issues/jipitec-10-1-2019/4879> accessed 4 October 2023.

[153] See ibid; Michèle Finck, 'Cobwebs of Control: The Two Imaginations of the Data Controller in EU Law' (2021) 11 International Data Privacy Law 333.

the Court has effectively established that even when you do not have access to personal data or have a very limited capacity to determine the means of the processing (eg you simply make the decision to use a particular platform), you may still be considered a joint controller if you determine the purposes of the processing.[154] Because the standard of influence over the means is low, primacy therefore appears to be given to determining 'purposes' in the definition of a controller.[155] This in turn means that as more and more data subjects also become data creators through, for example, the creation of a social media fan pages, they in turn also become joint controllers.[156] Indeed, it is clear from the definition of a controller—but also the case law—that it is certainly possible for a natural person to be a controller.[157]

However, given the role played by natural persons in data sharing in a social media or Internet of Things context, such as the use of E-AI in the hypothetical example of Ruth's smart home discussed during this book, it has been repeatedly highlighted in the literature that natural persons may be controllers even when they play no role in determining the means of the processing or do not have any access to the personal data.[158] The effects of the breadth of the definition of a controller are further exaggerated by the fact that the Court of Justice has repeatedly stated that the household exemption should be interpreted strictly and that it should not apply in situations where the personal data are made 'accessible to an unrestricted number of people'.[159] Athough at first glance the household exemption may provide a solution to the breadth of the controller definition, its strict interpretation significantly limits its impact and in fact arguably exaggerates the perceived problem. There may therefore be a complex network of actors involved in the processing of personal data even if some of the identified controllers may be natural persons with no influence at all over the means of the processing. This raises further complexities in determining the responsibilities of these respective controllers given that Article 26(3) of the GDPR affords data subjects the right to exercise their data subject rights against each of the controllers. Although the Court of Justice has stated that joint controllership does not necessarily 'imply equal responsibility',[160]

[154] Case C–2010/16 *Wirtschaftsakademie Schleswig-Holstein*, ECLI:EU:C:2018:388; Case C–25/17 *Jehovan todistajat*, ECLI:EU:C:2018:551; Case C–40/17 *Fashion ID*, ECLI:EU:C:2019:62.

[155] Finck (n 153) 335.

[156] Rebecca Wong and Joseph Savirimuthu, 'All or Nothing: This Is the Question? The Application of Article 3(2) Data Protection Directive 95/46/EC to the Internet' (2008) 25 John Marshall Journal of Computer & Information Law 241.

[157] Case C–101/01 *Bodil Lindqvist*, ECLI:EU:C:2003:596.

[158] For an excellent discussion on this point, see Finck (n 153) 338–41.

[159] See Case C–73/07 *Tietosuojavaltuutettu v Satakunnan Markkinapörssi Oy and Satamedia Oy*, ECLI:EU:C:2008:727; Case C–345/17 *Buivids*, ECLI:EU:2019:122.

[160] *Jehovan todistajat* (n 154) para 66; *Fashion ID* (n 154) para 67.

some uncertainties remain and, in effect, there is a strong argument that in certain circumstances compliance may in fact be impossible due to the manner in which these provisions have been interpreted.[161] This is significant given that, as discussed in this book, compliance itself is often already complicated.

Outside of matters of interpretation, for the legislator lessons could be learned from jurisdictions such as Australia where the Privacy Act 1988 (Cth) only applies to natural persons in the sense that they are organizations and are acting in the course of business. To be clear, I am certainly not advocating for the broad exemptions evident in the Australian Privacy Act 1988 (Cth) or the focus on consumer privacy at the state level in the US with carve-outs for small businesses. Nor am I advocating for an approach such as in the US at the federal level or in Singapore, where it is either the public sector or private sector that is legislated for respectively and not both. To my mind, these examples are problematic and in fact are examples of a regulatory gap. Finally, this is also not to say that everything has to be contained in one statute. The approach in Canada, for instance, may in fact work better.[162] Instead, I think a more modest change is needed that would better conform to the aims of data protection law and would also recognize that a variety of alternative causes of action may be available in domestic law that would cater more effectively for any gaps that were left.

Data protection law does not exist in a vacuum, and it should not be stretched to fit every problem; in some instances, the solutions to (or even the origins of) specific problems may be in other areas of law. In common law jurisdictions, we can look to privacy torts[163] or the equitable doctrine of breach of confidence,[164] which are better attuned to dealing with relationships between natural persons compared to the complex risk-based process-orientated data protection frameworks. I think that this is also reflected in the broad categories of information that are generally covered by data protection legislation. I agree with Gligorijevic that the privacy torts may offer a more normatively coherent protection of the right to privacy.[165] But I also believe that data protection law serves a different function from the privacy torts and should be clearer on this point and more attuned to its regulatory target. Indeed, if privacy can be understood as being mainly concerned with the disclosure of information, the

[161] For an analysis of this point, see Mahieu, van Hoboken, and Asghari (n 152); Lynskey, 'Complete and Effective Data Protection' (n 143).

[162] See Personal Information Protection and Electronic Documents Act (SC 2000, c 5) regulating the private sector and Privacy Act (RSC 1985, c P-21) regulating the public sector.

[163] Gligorijevic (n 3).

[164] Megan Richardson, 'Trust, Confidence and Data Rights' in Clifford, Paterson, and Lau (eds) (n 3).

[165] Gligorijevic (n 3).

expectations of the person affected, and any harm caused, data protection law may alternatively be focused on the *fairness* of personal data processing irrespective of whether there may be an impact on privacy.[166]

Data protection law will always struggle to bring about the changes to behaviour it targets (ie that of both data subjects and those processing personal data). The law on the books will always be different from the law in practice because, again, data protection law does not exist in a vacuum: it aims to regulate the behaviour of persons (both natural and legal) and, in so doing, may establish expectations of acceptable conduct. Even with the most paternalistic forms of legislative interventions in place, however, there would still be abuses. This points to the significance of remedies. Although there is certainly a significant value to an individual and representative direct right of action in data protection law, in light of the challenges of relying on a direct right of action discussed briefly in Chapter 2, I believe the key to data protection law is the enforcement authority. The role of an enforcement authority is generally not to focus on complaints between natural persons disconnected from some business/public sector purpose for processing for instance, but is instead to focus on the effects of violations of data protection law at scale and how they may affect society and hence, the most marginalized groups and interests in particular.[167]

The challenge with the GDPR, for instance, is that data protection authorities (DPAs) are required to investigate all complaints and this leads to significant questions regarding the need for more flexibility in the application of its enforcement mechanisms.[168] What we need, therefore, are properly funded enforcement authorities that are not being pulled in different directions (eg complaints between individuals versus a complaint against/investigation into a large technology platform affecting a significant number of users), cooperation between different regulators, and transparency and responsiveness in their enforcement priorities.[169] Data protection law can frustrate the public by failing to conform to their expectations; simply trying to do too much stretches capacities too thin, thereby undermining data protection law's legitimacy.[170]

[166] This point links well to the conceptual confusion points described above in Section B of this chapter in particular, but reference can also be made to the discussion of recent empirical research conducted in the Netherlands in Chapter 2 and the public's perceptions of the GDPR. See Joanna Strycharz, Jef Ausloos, and Natali Helberger, 'Data Protection or Data Frustration? Individual Perceptions and Attitudes Towards the GDPR' (2020) 6 European Data Protection Law Review 407.

[167] See Clifford and Paterson, 'Data Rights and Contract Law' (n 132).

[168] For a discussion, see Lynskey, 'Complete and Effective Data Protection' (n 143).

[169] Clifford and Paterson, 'Data Rights and Contract Law' (n 132).

[170] Lynskey, 'Complete and Effective Data Protection' (n 143).

(c) Definitional confusion

Data protection laws often struggle to define some of its core aspects appropriately. This has been made evident throughout this book, but I will mention two important examples that arguably render compliance impossible in certain circumstances. First, people have questioned the ongoing utility of providing categories of sensitive personal data in legislation such as in the GDPR, the California Consumer Privacy Act, and the Australian Privacy Act 1988 (Cth) etc, given that, amongst other things, the apparent capacity to draw sensitive inferences.[171] However, such categories continue to be included as part of these laws, which leaves question marks surrounding the legitimacy of certain practices (see Chapter 3). Secondly, scholars have criticized the definitions of a controller and a processor (and the concept of joint controllership) evident in many of these laws, given the significant challenges mentioned but also the problems they pose for compliance and the allocation of responsibility.[172] Again, however, these concepts appear to be included in emerging laws despite the fact that compliance may be extremely difficult to achieve in situations where there are a complex array of actors with different levels of involvement (see Chapter 5).

My point here is that we have to be mindful to ensure that we adopt laws where it is possible for the well-intentioned actor to comply in practice. Although a control rights-based understanding of data protection is not entirely permissive (and here we can point to the seemingly endless debate in the EU regarding the legality of programmatic advertising as an example),[173] as noted by Kirby 'to do nothing is often to make a decision'.[174] Certainly, new business models and technologies emerge and inevitably these will be questioned under data protection laws. However, when we adopt these frameworks, we have to understand the technologies and practices being regulated. Although complexity cannot be avoided in data protection law and it will (and perhaps should) always result in some degree of anxiety, a well-intentioned

[171] See Clifford, Richardson, and Witzleb (n 11); Gianclaudio Malgieri and Giovanni Comandé, 'Sensitive-by-Distance: Quasi-Health Data in the Algorithmic Era' (2017) 26 Information & Communications Technology Law 229; Paul Quinn and Gianclaudio Malgieri, 'The Difficulty of Defining Sensitive Data—The Concept of Sensitive Data in the EU Data Protection Framework' (2021) 22 German Law Journal 1583; Solove, 'Data Is What Data Does' (n 2).

[172] See Finck (n 153); Mahieu, van Hoboken, and Asghari (n 152).

[173] See Michael Veale and Frederik Zuiderveen Borgesius, 'Adtech and Real-Time Bidding under European Data Protection Law' (2022) 23 German Law Journal 226.

[174] See Michael Kirby, 'New Frontier: Regulating Technology by Law and "Code"' in Roger Brownsword and Karen Yeung (eds), *Regulating Technologies: Legal Futures, Regulatory Frames and Technological Fixes* (1st edn, Hart 2008) <www.bloomsburycollections.com/book/regulating-technologies-legal-futures-regulatory-frames-and-technological-fixes/ch17-new-frontier/> accessed 7 November 2014.

regulated entity should be able to comply.[175] To avoid frustration and to increase effectiveness, therefore, legislators need to be mindful of the impact proposed law reforms will have in order to avoid situations where compliance is practically impossible. If the legislator wishes to prohibit a particular technology or practice, I believe that this should be done expressly and not left to interpretation—at least where possible.[176]

2. Pragmatism and limits

The focus on the processing of personal data and not the substantive applications for which the data are used is a core feature of data protection law. There are those who are critical of this focus and suggest that data protection law should not be about individual control rights but instead power and the facilitating of social interactions. I believe, however, that we should understand the role of data protection law pragmatically as an important cog in the governance of computational systems while understanding, and better legislating for, its limits. My argument in this section is again simple: data protection law should not be substituted but supplemented. However, this argument is far from universally accepted. Waldman suggests that because a focus on control rights in data protection law does not deal with extractive business models, their adoption may lead policymakers to avoid more structural changes for fear of stifling innovation, '[i]f we start with individual rights, we are likely to end with them too'.[177] I think this is overly pessimistic and, in fact, actually demonstrably incorrect when we look not only at the number of jurisdictions with robust accountability requirements in data protection laws but also those that are now considering, for instance, the regulation of AI[178] and also the apparent

[175] Lynskey, 'Complete and Effective Data Protection' (n 143).

[176] eg the seemingly never-ending analysis of the legitimacy of programmatic advertising and the connected discussion regarding the lawfulness of frameworks for gathering consent might have been avoided if an explicit stance had been taken. It appears that, in effect, these practices have been made unlawful through their apparent failure to comply with the GDPR, for example. My point is that dealing more expressly with this issue would have been preferable. In saying this, however, I acknowledge (1) how difficult it would have been to reach agreement, and (2) that there is no definitive decision as to legality of these business models and thus it is at least possible (however unlikely) that the industry may develop some means of complying. In any case the point seems a moot one now, given the apparent industry moves away from real-time bidding. See Michael Veale, Midas Nouwens, and Cristiana Santos, 'Impossible Asks: Can the Transparency and Consent Framework Ever Authorise Real-Time Bidding After the Belgian DPA Decision?' [2022] Technology and Regulation 12.

[177] Waldman, 'Privacy's Rights Trap' (n 4) 103.

[178] See eg Science and Resources Department of Industry, 'Responsible AI in Australia: Have Your Say | Department of Industry, Science and Resources' <www.industry.gov.au/news/responsible-ai-australia-have-your-say> accessed 29 June 2023.

(albeit very) gradual shift in business practice following the entry into force of the GDPR. This further reflects the point that even individual rights do not exist in a subjective vacuum.[179]

Certainly, it is difficult to dispute that many of the suggestions that are presented as alternatives standing in opposition to data protection law actually have the potential to be additional or just different forms of intervention that could exist in parallel and be supplemented by and supplementary to data protection law.[180] Realizing the value of a transversal analysis can facilitate more pragmatic regulatory interventions. It is therefore necessary to align our discussion of the protections provided by each area of law and their enforcement in order to truly understand the potential gaps and adequately cater for societal risks. Indeed, in this regard it is interesting to refer to Koops, who notes that 'data protection can no longer reside in the exclusive realm of informational privacy and self-determination; rather, it must be approached from the angle of due process and fair treatment in the database age. A focus on decision transparency has good potential to achieve just that.'[181] The author proposes a dual strategy whereby upwards transparency (or data collection) is diminished through the shielding and obfuscating of data and downwards transparency (or data use) is increased via a combination of legal and technical measures. The view proffered here is that (despite the difficulties) data protection law is a response to legitimate tangible and intangible harms and has a continuing role in the protection of data subjects through the affordance of choice, but that this could be supplemented by other areas of law (both hard and soft).

Such an approach may also cater for the difficulties associated with trying to operationalize a response to the collective harms caused by personal data processing, as instead of focusing on a reconceptualization of how these may fit within a data subject rights-orientated framework, regulatory interventions may be adopted based on the collective concerns. This is consistent with the conclusion in Chapters 3, 4, and 5 that we may need to consider paternalistic protections that facilitate the conditions primed to safeguard individual data subjects and account for collective harms in statutory interventions. Indeed, as noted by Mantelero, although there may be differences of opinion regarding the precise balance to be struck between different interests in the operation of data protection

[179] Susanna Lindroos-Hovinheimo, *Private Selves: Legal Personhood in European Privacy Protection* (CUP 2021) 82.

[180] Kaminski (n 6) 390.

[181] Bert-Jaap Koops, 'On Decision Transparency, or How to Enhance Data Protection after the Computational Turn' in Mireille Hildebrandt and Katja de Vries (eds), *Privacy, Due Process and the Computational Turn: The Philosophy of Law Meets the Philosophy of Technology* (Routledge 2013) 216.

law, 'there are some collective priorities concerning privacy and data-protection that are of relevance to the general interest' which may justify intervention based on the potential harm to groups and a fundamental value of society.[182]

Precisely determining data protection law's limits is a matter to be unravelled by more inter- and intra-disciplinary research to determine, interpret, and enforce the law and its intersections with other regulatory frameworks.[183] My broader point, however, is that legislative developments such as the EU's AI Act[184] (and in the EU there are many others!)[185] but also many other areas of law, already potentially constrain uses of personal data and we can also refer to the intersections between data protection and consumer law and the application of protections such as unfair terms regulations, and unfair trading or misleading or deceptive conduct rules as specific examples of where the different areas of law have demonstrated complementary aims.[186] Targeted bans and/or other legislative interventions would allow for the further development of an environment in which consent could better function as a fiction in data protection law. This approach is better attuned to the desire to safeguard our autonomous capacity to decide for ourselves and the importance attached to this in law. I believe that this is something worth protecting even aside from the goal of alleviating the tangible and intangible harms we are protected against through these frameworks.

[182] Alessandro Mantelero, 'Personal Data for Decisional Purposes in the Age of Analytics: From an Individual to a Collective Dimension of Data Protection' (2016) 32 Computer Law & Security Review 238, 248–49.

[183] Peggy Valcke, Inge Graef, and Damian Clifford, 'iFairness—Constructing Fairness in IT (and Other Areas of) Law through Intra- and Interdisciplinarity' (2018) 34 Computer Law & Security Review 707.

[184] Proposal of the European Parliament and of the Council Laying Down Harmonised Rules on Artificial Intelligence (n 103).

[185] Regulation (EU) 2022/2065 of the European Parliament and of the Council of 19 October 2022 on a Single Market For Digital Services (n 96); Regulation (EU) 2022/1925 of the European Parliament and of the Council of 14 September 2022 on contestable and fair markets in the digital sector and amending Directives (EU) 2019/1937 and (EU) 2020/1828 (Digital Markets Act) [2022] OJ L265/1; Regulation (EU) 2019/1150 of the European Parliament and of the Council of 20 June 2019 on promoting fairness and transparency for business users of online intermediation services [2019] OJ L186/57; Directive (EU) 2019/2161 of the European Parliament and of the Council of 27 November 2019 amending Council Directive 93/13/EEC and Directives 98/6/EC, 2005/29/EC and 2011/83/EU of the European Parliament and of the Council as regards the better enforcement and modernisation of Union consumer protection rules [2019] OJ L328/7; Directive (EU) 2019/770 of the European Parliament and of the Council of 20 May 2019 on certain aspects concerning contracts for the supply of digital content and digital services [2019] OJ L136/1–27.

[186] Clifford and Paterson, 'Data Rights and Contract Law' (n 132); Damian Clifford, 'Citizen-Consumers in a Personalised Galaxy: Emotion Influenced Decision-Making, A True Path to the Dark Side?' in Lilian Edwards, Burkhard Schafer, and Edina Harbinja (eds), *Emerging Technology, Regulation and Ethics* (1st edn, Edinburgh University Press 2020); Damian Clifford, 'Data Protection and Consumer Protection: The Empowerment of the Citizen-Consumer' in Gloria González Fuster, Rosamunde van Brakel, and Paul De Hert (eds), *Research Handbook on Privacy and Data Protection Law* (Edward Elgar 2022); Clifford and Paterson, 'Consumer Privacy and Consent' (n 132).

To be clear, the instrumental role for control will never be fully aligned with our actual behaviour, as this would require individualized compliance efforts and/or a complete shift in focus to far more paternalistic interventions. However, this does not eliminate the conceptual and practical value of control that has played a role in motivating the adoption of data protection law in the first place. Indeed, in Section B of this chapter, I noted that the feeling that we have lost control over our personal data has motivated the adoption of data protection law. That the fear, shock, anger, and indignation associated with the violation of what is understood as a social norm and individual right, and associated risks of harm, stirred the public's fear. However, I would argue that it is the mix of fears (personal and efficiency-orientated) and conceptual values (individual data subjects' and of those processing personal data) that creates the environment in which these laws are adopted. It is precisely the fact that personal data processing poses a threat to different group commitments (as manifested by the different types of fear, see Chapter 2) that allows for the reaching of a consensus on what is clearly a contested issue.[187]

When we look to a more transversal analysis of the risks posed by computational systems, cultural cognition theory tells us that we should be mindful of how we communicate.[188] We need to ensure that we frame the question of risks in such a way that it '*affirms* rather than denigrates recipients' cultural identities' and 'expresses a *plurality* of social meanings' in order to reach consensus on contested risks.[189] When we look to supplement data protection laws and support more communitarian/collective and egalitarian values, we therefore need to be mindful of individual control rights and the individualistic and hierarchal views they may represent. Putting this crudely, purely focusing on the need for structural changes through paternalistic interventions is likely to run counter to individualistic and hierarchal worldviews. For some (particularly in the US) paternalism can be a dirty word.[190] However, there are many forms of paternalism and I believe that targeted interventions could in fact improve the instrumental role of individual control and thus affirm rather than denigrate differing cultural identities and allow for the finding of common ground. We need to convey the risks associated with computational systems in a way that

[187] See Kahan, 'Emotion in Risk Regulation: Competing Theories' (n 76).

[188] ibid; Kahan and Braman (n 115).

[189] Kahan, 'Emotion in Risk Regulation: Competing Theories' (n 76) 172.

[190] See Cass R Sunstein and Richard H Thaler, 'Libertarian Paternalism Is Not an Oxymoron' [2003] The University of Chicago Law Review 1159; Gregory Mitchell, 'Libertarian Paternalism Is an Oxymoron' (2005) 99 Northwestern University Law Review 1245; Claire A Hill, 'Anti-Anti-Anti Paternalism' (11 January 2007) <https://papers.ssrn.com/abstract=956153> accessed 11 June 2023.

motivates people with diverse worldviews without polarizing them.[191] This is a matter for better risk communication.[192]

Control rights certainly need to be supplemented both in data protection law through accountability mechanisms and outside it through a more transversal analysis of law and policy. However, I believe that data protection law frameworks are an important piece in the regulatory jigsaw. They are not the end or a block on future regulation but a necessary component.

E. Conclusion

This chapter has argued that, despite its flaws, data protection law and its focus on control is important. The control rights-orientated approach and the conceptual role for control aims to safeguard an important value and the subjective interests of data subjects. I believe that we create frameworks to protect our capacity to safeguard our subjective interests for a reason. Of course, there are significant issues associated with relying on objective standards to afford protections to individuals in order to allow them to make subjective choices—the previous chapters of this book have demonstrated the clear limitations of data protection law specifically. To defend the role and importance of data protection law it is necessary to specify its role and its limits. I believe that too often these are ignored both in optimistic accounts of its potential and pessimistic takes on its failings.

We need to be pragmatic and understand data protection law within (1) its historical context in terms of its connection but uncertain relationship with its privacy law roots, and (2) the dualist goals of such frameworks. However, it must also be acknowledged that there will always be a certain degree of complexity causing anxiety. We should understand the role of data protection law pragmatically as an important cog in the governance of computational systems while understanding its limits. However, accounting for the role of emotion will not only enhance the effectiveness of the legal protections provided in data protection law but also explain their significance. I have pointed to a number of ways in which a law and emotion analysis and reframing our understanding of data protection law's limitations and limits may improve its effectiveness. I believe that these are important points of reference in the development or further reform of data protection laws.

191 Kahan, 'Cultural Cognition as a Conception of the Cultural Theory of Risk' (n 115).

192 For a discussion of this and how it may be achieved, see Dan Kahan, 'Fixing the Communications Failure' (2010) 463 Nature 296.

7
Conclusion

A. Introduction

Two key conclusions emerge from the analysis in this book. First, a law and emotion analysis of data protection law allows for a clearer articulation of the problems associated with the instrumental role of control and their limits. Data protection law arguably fails to account for emotion in the moves towards individual empowerment by not recognizing that different types of data evoke different emotional responses that are context-dependent and that emotion plays a role in all decision-making. Secondly, a law and emotion analysis of data protection law allows for a clearer expression of the potential conceptual value of control and an appreciation of the need for these underlying values to be further researched. The control-rights-orientated approach and the potential conceptual value of control aim to safeguard the subjective interests of data subjects and, hence, data protection law's liberal foundations. We create data protection laws to protect our capacity to safeguard our subjective interests for a reason, and objectifying the law may arguably create more problems than changes might be able solve. I will analyse these conclusions in turn before then outlining what I see as the future for more effective data protection law.

B. Understanding the Challenges to Data Protection

This book has explored three specific challenges to the instrumental role for control through the lens of a law and emotion analysis. First, how the 'categories' approach to data protection evident in data protection frameworks such as the General Data Protection Regulation (GDPR) arguably results in emotional disengagement from the dangers associated with intensive data processing (Chapter 3). Secondly, how a more realistic understanding of the role of emotion in decision-making may challenge the part played by individual choice in the exercising of individual control rights while also somewhat paradoxically explaining the instrumental role of control in facilitating the operation of subjective rights (Chapter 4). Thirdly, in their practical application,

Data Protection Law and Emotion. Damian Clifford, Oxford University Press. © Damian Clifford 2024.
DOI: 10.1093/oso/9780192845863.003.0007

how accountability mechanisms arguably fail to consider the subjective intentions/aspirations of data subjects by affording those processing personal data significant scope and failing to recognize how compliance in process and not in substance (often through outsourced objectified methods) impacts the application of the law and the exercise of subjective control rights (Chapter 5).

As noted in the introduction, a key theme emerging from the analysis in these chapters is how the failure to account for the role of emotion in data protection law exacerbates emotional disengagement from the dangers associated with intensive data processing. The analysis in Chapter 3 explored how the pervasive processing of personal data allows for the generation of sensitive inferences and the problems this creates for the categories-based protections often found in data protection law. Through the use of Emotional Artificial Intelligence (E-AI) as a case study and using the GDPR as the high-water mark example of these laws, the analysis demonstrated how different types of E-AI with the same inherent purpose may interact with the GDPR in different ways—some may clearly involve the processing of sensitive personal data whereas others (arguably) may not. The analysis thus highlights the potential for inconsistency and the failure to account for the emotional disconnect between our feelings towards certain types of data processing and their genuine risks.

Although data protection law affords us subjective rights so that we can make our own choices (as analysed in Chapter 4), it also assumes our objective rational capacity to make them and then fails to account for the role of our emotions in decision-making. Data protection law should better account for how people actually feel about the protection of their personal data. Emotions and decision-making go hand in hand and interdisciplinary insights on the role of emotion, discussed in Chapter 4 in particular, call into question some of the regulatory choices made by the legislature. Through an elaboration of the challenges posed by a law and emotion analysis to the narrow understanding of the role of emotion in decision-making in conventional legal theory (and data protection law more specifically), I have questioned data protection law's capacity to respond appropriately to technological developments such as E-AI.

More specifically, as an example, I believe that 'consent desensitization' has resulted in emotional disengagement from the risks associated with personal data processing.[1] In this regard, the analysis in this book has demonstrated how

[1] Bart W Schermer, Bart Custers, and Simone van der Hof, 'The Crisis of Consent: How Stronger Legal Protection May Lead to Weaker Consent in Data Protection' (2014) 16 Ethics and Information Technology 171.

the failure to account for the role of emotion might have knock-on effects. For instance, the analysis in Chapter 5 in particular demonstrated how data protection law arguably fails to account for the ways in which the interests of those processing personal data shape the application of the framework appropriately. The case study analyses in Chapters 3–5 revealed that even in the context of obvious inaccuracy issues, such as the highly publicized inaccuracy of E-AI, the GDPR as the high-water mark example of such frameworks may struggle to be the regulatory solution to the problem presented. The open-textured nature of the fairness principle in the Regulation combined with the key positioning of controllers (and processors) plays a significant role in undermining the effectiveness of the framework.

The weaknesses of data protection law therefore seem obvious. There are certainly some core features of data protection law that are challenged by technological developments and the realities of human behaviour. However, in saying that, I also believe that similar critiques may be made against many other areas of law. Entities regulated by requirements laid down in principle-based statutes will always use the associated uncertainty to their advantage. We therefore need to appreciate the value that individual control arguably adds despite the criticisms of its instrumental role.

C. Conceptualizing the Values of Data Protection

Data protection law has uncertain conceptual foundations. The analysis in this book demonstrates this by describing control as one such underpinning value with potentially different meanings and arguably, depending on the jurisdiction, even an uncertain role in data protection law. In order to assess the effectiveness of data protection law, we need a better understanding of its underlying values and the potential differences between jurisdictions to appreciate the significance of critiques and the value of comparative insights. Control, as one such conceptual value, points to the significance of the capacity to make subjective choices given its link to the instrumental role of the individual control rights evident in data protection law. The false dichotomy between rationality and emotions in data protection law, however, arguably undermines the instrumental role played by control. I therefore argue that a conceptualization of rationality that understands emotion as one of its constituent components may be required to preserve control's conceptual value.

Accounting for the role of emotion will enhance the effectiveness of the legal protections provided in data protection law and this law and emotion focus also explains their significance. The book has argued that, despite its flaws, data protection law and its focus on control is important. The control-rights-orientated approach and the potential conceptual role for control aim to safeguard an important value. We create frameworks in order to protect our capacity to safeguard our subjective interests for a reason. I have pointed to a number of ways in which a law and emotion analysis, and reframing our understanding of data protection law's limitations and limits, may improve its effectiveness. I believe that these are important points of reference in the development (or, indeed, further reform) of data protection law. We need an approach that understands data protection law within (1) its historical context in terms of its connection but uncertain relationship with its privacy law roots, and (2) the dualist goals that are common in such frameworks (ie data privacy/protection and facilitating efficiency and economic gain through rules for legitimate data processing).

In addition, even leaving aside its potential conceptual value, I argue that from a practical perspective instrumentalizing control recognizes that assuming the rational capacity of data subjects may be the lesser of two evils. We may therefore need to frame our discussion of data protection's limitations more appropriately. Data protection law's complexity has caused some to question its value, to fear the consequences of its introduction, and, following its implementation, to be frustrated at its impact, or lack thereof, depending on your perspective; but these are (at least partly) manifestations of the legislative desire for a high level of protection but also flexibility/adaptability. However, it must also be acknowledged that there will always be a certain degree of complexity causing anxiety (as described in Chapter 2) and, to an extent, this may be necessary to ensure the effectiveness of data protection law. Of course, there are significant issues associated with relying on objective standards to afford protections to individuals in order to allow them to make subjective choices—Chapters 3–5 demonstrated these in detail.

To defend the role and importance of data protection law we need to delineate data protection law's limitations and its limits and to look to a more transversal analysis of the issues posed by intensive personal data processing where necessary. I believe that too often these are ignored in both the optimistic accounts of its potential and the pessimistic takes on its failings described in Chapter 2. Data protection is a response to legitimate concerns associated with the proliferation of technology and the pervasive gathering of personal data. We should understand the role of data protection law pragmatically as an important cog in the governance of computational systems while understanding its limits. Consequently, some of the criticism of the instrumental role of control speaks more to the limits of data protection law than to its limitations. Data protection law's limitations are the problem of data protection law; its limits, I believe, point to data protection law's potential for intersections with other areas of law. These other areas of law may prescribe further restrictions on data processing, but they may also supplement its aims, conceptual values, and account for data protection law's limits.

We need to refine our understanding of what should frustrate us—to use the language relied on in Chapter 2—and how we should pragmatically understand data protection law's limits to appreciate the value of a transversal analysis. Put simply, therefore, we need to focus our frustration on the appropriate target.

D. Outlining the Future for Effective (Data) Regulation

In the final section of Chapter 6, I argued that it is the mix of fears (personal and economic) and conceptual values (both of individuals and of those processing personal data) that create the environment in which data protection law frameworks are adopted. It is precisely the fact that personal data processing poses a threat to different group commitments that allows a consensus to be reached on what is clearly a contested issue.[2] Understanding our emotional responses as part of our evaluations and cultural perspectives explains why a mixture of fears and policy objectives has shaped data protection law. Arguably, data protection law then is always doomed to fail in that it aims to some extent to satisfy everyone and tries to promote objectives that are seemingly at odds. To put it simply, it is questionable whether we can truly protect the rights to privacy and/or data protection while at the same time legitimately achieving the benefits of intensive personal data processing.

For some scholars the instrumentalist critiques of the role of control are fatal for precisely this reason. I am more optimistic, however, because I believe that data protection law is not just about effective protections but is also concerned with expressing the importance of certain conceptual values and, hence, recognizing the potential for difference. The problem as I see it is that we are somewhat uncertain as to what conceptual values these laws are actually promoting and, perhaps even more problematically, we are unsure how these may or may not be ranked when there is a conflict. Lynskey, for instance,

[2] See Dan M Kahan, 'Emotion in Risk Regulation: Competing Theories' in Sabine Roeser (ed), *Emotions and Risky Technologies* (Springer Netherlands 2010).

suggests that individual control (or informational self-determination) could be the normative anchor in EU data protection law in the sense that it can be used as a conceptual value to interpret the application of the instrumental manifestations of control in the subjective rights provided for in the GDPR.[3] I find this suggestion compelling from the law and emotion perspective for the reasons identified. However, uncertainty remains, and this is significant as data protection law's values are likely to be in conflict. We may therefore need to understand the relationship between the different possible conceptual values and differences between jurisdictions when making comparisons. As I noted in Chapter 6, frustrations arise when scholars are speaking almost the language but with slightly different meanings attached to similar words. Legislators then have to account for these differences when adopting data protection law reforms.

Perhaps a limitation of this book, therefore, is that it has assessed the E-AI case study solely through the lens of the European Union's (EU) GDPR. There are clear challenges linked to the conflict between the fundamental rights-orientated approach to data protection law in the EU, for instance, and the more market-driven approach in other jurisdictions, such as the United States (US), Australia, etc. This is further exacerbated by the fact that conceptualizations of the cultural significance of the right to privacy (as the more globally accepted right compared to the right to data protection) and its value in terms of other rights and interests, in particular, vary considerably depending on the jurisdiction. This is significant even if inspiration in law reform may be taken from the EU.

Reference here can be made to the conflicting understandings of the importance of data protection law when comparing the US approach at the federal level or, for instance, the Singaporean focus on the private sector, but also in relation to how these differences may manifest themselves in the interpretation of the Singaporean Act or legislation such as the California Consumer Privacy Act at the state level in the US, which contain similar rights to the GDPR.[4] Effective regulation in a globalized digital economy presents important practical questions. However, the cross-jurisdictional push of legislative standards presents an interesting debate regarding the regulatory autonomy of states that wish to trade with the EU but also in terms of the subtle differences that may develop in regulatory and judicial interpretation.[5] There is a clear need to

[3] Orla Lynskey, *The Foundations of EU Data Protection Law* (OUP 2016) 177–96.

[4] See eg Franz-Stefan Gady, 'EU/U.S. Approaches to Data Privacy and the "Brussels Effect": A Comparative Analysis' [2014] Georgetown Journal of International Affairs; Washington 12.

[5] See Kristina Irion, Margot E Kaminski, and Svetlana Yakovleva, 'Privacy Peg, Trade Hole: Why We (Still) Shouldn't Put Data Privacy in Trade Law' (26 March 2023) <https://papers.ssrn.com/abstract=

explore these issues—they may be extremely significant in terms of the further development of data protection law in different jurisdictions.

Leaving aside these potential differences and their significance, it should be noted more generally that the law and emotion analysis has allowed for a clearer understanding of data protection law as one cog in a regulatory machine. Data protection law needs to move beyond siloed analyses, and boundaries may need to be better demarcated in data protection laws in order to conform to public expectations. I have identified specific areas where data protection law could be improved to avoid obvious problems, but many of the answers to the questions posed by developments in technology are not going to be answered by data protection law. Put simply, the focus on the processing of personal data rather than the substantive applications for which the data are used is a core feature of data protection law, not a limitation, even if it limits data protection law's capacity to respond to specific challenges. Data protection law should not be substituted but supplemented. More inter- and intra-disciplinary research is required to determine, interpret, and enforce the law and its intersections with other regulatory frameworks[6] but a whole range of regulatory frameworks already exist that allow for a transversal analysis.

For example, the need to align data and consumer protection is being increasingly recognized in order to further empower the data subject. More specifically, there is an increasing amount of discussion surrounding whether consumer protection can play two roles regarding its alignment with the data protection framework. First, as a supplement to data protection in order to protect data subjects in the context of data-gathering practices. And secondly, regarding the protection of consumers from potentially harmful commercial practices that rely on personalization. This reflects the desire for more holistic responses to the challenges posed by the emergence of new technologies, as individual autonomy in the mediated environment is affected in terms of both data protection and consumer protection safeguards. Such a desire can be illustrated by the perceived need to better cater for both the *ex ante* and *ex post* needs of consumers.

It seems easy to conclude, therefore, that there is a need to align the protections and provide a more transversal protection of data subjects. However, the

4402288> accessed 28 September 2023; Kristina Irion, Svetlana Yakovleva, and Marija Bartl, 'Trade and Privacy: Complicated Bedfellows? How to Achieve Data Protection-Proof Free Trade Agreements' (13 July 2016) <https://papers.ssrn.com/abstract=2877166> accessed 28 September 2023.

[6] Peggy Valcke, Inge Graef, and Damian Clifford, 'iFairness—Constructing Fairness in IT (and Other Areas of) Law through Intra- and Interdisciplinarity' (2018) 34 Computer Law & Security Review 707.

precise overlaps and subtle distinctions are far from clear and more research and collaboration between enforcement authorities are required. The potential for more holistic protection through the alignment of consumer and data protection law as an example is hardly a controversial claim, given that (1) there have been legislative proposals in this direction; (2) there is growing body of literature on this issue; and (3) various enforcement agencies have repeatedly called for such a development.[7] Although critics may question a reliance on consumer protection and national contract law doctrines, for example, as a supplement to data protection (as such an approach arguably reinforces the individualistic nature of the protections afforded, thereby distracting from the harms suffered and disparities in market power), such an approach recognizes the value of individual autonomy while also allowing for more paternalistic interventions.

As I have argued, together with a colleague, elsewhere, consumer law has the capacity to go beyond the monitoring of consent to exercising control over the substance of the bargains struck and thus to act as a response to calls for more paternalistic responses such as the targeted bans.[8] Recognizing control and providing data subject rights, therefore, do not mean that data protection law cannot be supplemented, constrained, or even limited to protect our collective interests in a paternalistic fashion in other intersecting areas of law. The coordination of data protection and consumer law is necessary and this is just one example; we can also look to labour law or public law, for example. Indeed, competition law analysis for instance is another important piece of the jigsaw with significant enforcement teeth.[9] The point is that more research is needed to further link these areas, and this is particularly significant in terms of enforcement. I believe there is much to be gained from a more transversal analysis to include intra-disciplinary insights that may be at play in conjunction with data protection law.

A more realistic understanding of data protection law's prescribed limits will allow us to understand its role, not as an all-encompassing solution to all of life's technological problems but rather (returning to its roots) as a specific

[7] European Data Protection Supervisor, 'Opinion on Coherent Enforcement of Fundamental Rights in the Age of Big Data' (European Data Protection Supervisor 2016) Opinion 8/2016.

[8] Damian Clifford and Jeannie Marie Paterson, 'Data Rights and Contract Law: Formation, Incorporation and Vitiating Factors' in Damian Clifford, Jeannie Marie Paterson, and Kwan Ho Lau (eds), *Data and Private Law* (Hart 2023).

[9] Inge Graef, *EU Competition Law, Data Protection and Online Platforms: Data as Essential Facility* (Kluwer Law International 2016); Inge Graef, Damian Clifford, and Peggy Valcke, 'Fairness and Enforcement: Bridging Competition, Data Protection, and Consumer Law' (2018) 8 International Data Privacy Law 200; Francisco Costa-Cabral and Orla Lynskey, 'Family Ties: The Intersection between Data Protection and Competition in EU Law' (2017) 54 Common Market Law Review 11.

framework designed to protect our personal data and protect us against the risks associated with its processing. This is not to say that data protection law is not effective or important. Nor does it mean that all of the answers are already provided in other areas of law. There is certainly a need for reform in specific areas. For instance, it is clear from the analysis in Chapters 3–5 that data protection fails to account for the full effects of technologies such as E-AI, and, as described, this need for a more transversal approach is also evident from the uncertain application of the GDPR in particular circumstances. But I also think that examples of technology such as E-AI may require the legislator to step in, as it may be that data protection is being applied merely as the best of an ill-fitting lot.[10] I believe therefore that there is a need for continuing research on data protection law's limits and intersections with other regulatory frameworks.

E. Conclusion

In conclusion, control rights in data protection law certainly need to be supplemented both within data protection law through accountability mechanisms and outside it through a more transversal analysis of law and policy. Control rights in data protection law are a necessary component of the protections provided but they are not sufficient in themselves. I believe that they are not, as some scholars suggest,[11] a block on future regulation, at least in the EU. Targeted interventions could improve the instrumental role of individual control and thus affirm rather than denigrate differing cultural identities and allow for the finding of common ground. We need to understand how we might appeal to different values in consensus building in the future development of more paternalistic protections in data protection law and the regulation of computational systems more broadly.

[10] Clearly, moves towards more specific legislation are already happening in the EU, where the legislator seems intent on introducing specific provisions banning the use of E-AI in certain contexts in the form of the AI Act (see Chapter 5). More specifically, in the final compromise version, applications of E-AI will be banned in the areas of the workplace and education.

[11] Ari Waldman, 'Privacy's Rights Trap' [2022] Northwestern University Law Review Online <https://scholarlycommons.law.northwestern.edu/nulr_online/327> accessed 4 October 2023.

Index

For the benefit of digital users, indexed terms that span two pages (e.g., 52–53) may, on occasion, appear on only one of those pages.

Tables are indicated by *t* following the page number